Going to Court

G000137486

Going to Court

Brian Fitzpatrick

Consultant Editors:
Christopher Menzies
and
Robert Hunter

OXFORD
UNIVERSITY PRESS

OXFORD

UNIVERSITY PRESS

Great Clarendon Street, Oxford OX2 6DP

Oxford University Press is a department of the University of Oxford.
It furthers the University's objective of excellence in research, scholarship,
and education by publishing worldwide in

Oxford New York

Auckland Cape Town Dar es Salaam Hong Kong Karachi
Kuala Lumpur Madrid Melbourne Mexico City Nairobi
New Delhi Shanghai Taipei Toronto

With offices in

Argentina Austria Brazil Chile Czech Republic France Greece
Guatemala Hungary Italy Japan Poland Portugal Singapore
South Korea Switzerland Thailand Turkey Ukraine Vietnam

Published in the United States
by Oxford University Press Inc., New York

© Brian Fitzpatrick, 2006

The moral rights of the authors have been asserted

Crown copyright material is reproduced under Class Licence
Number C01P0000148 with the permission of OPSI
and the Queen's Printer for Scotland

Cover photos: © ImageSource / Punchstock; StockDisc / Punchstock; Brand X Pictures /
Punchstock; ImageState / Punchstock; Up The Resolution (uptheres) / Alamy; Justin Kase / Alamy;
Stocksearch / Alamy; Stockbyte / Punchstock; DigitalVision / Punchstock; Dominic Harrison /
Alamy; Up The Resolution (uptheres) / Alamy; Photodisc / Punchstock

Database right Oxford University Press (maker)

First published 2006

All rights reserved. No part of this publication may be reproduced,
stored in a retrieval system, or transmitted, in any form or by any means,
without the prior permission in writing of Oxford University Press,
or as expressly permitted by law, or under terms agreed with the appropriate
reprographics rights organization. Enquiries concerning reproduction
outside the scope of the above should be sent to the Rights Department,
Oxford University Press, at the address above

You must not circulate this book in any other binding or cover
and you must impose the same condition on any acquirer

British Library Cataloguing in Publication Data

Data available

Library of Congress Cataloging in Publication Data

Fitzpatrick, Brian.
  Going to court / Brian Fitzpatrick ; consultant editors, Christopher Menzies, Rob Hunter.
    p. cm.
  Includes bibliographical references and index.
  ISBN-13: 978–0–19–928414–6 (alk. paper)
  ISBN-10: 0–19–928414–8 (alk. paper)
  1. Criminal procedure—Grant Britain. 2. Criminal Justice, Administration of—Great Britain.
  3. Courts—Great Britain. 4. Police—Great Britain—Handbooks, manuals, etc. I. Menzies, Christopher.
  II. Hunter, Rob. III. Title.
    KD8329.F58 2006
    345.41'05—dc22
                                        2005032145

ISBN 0–19–928414–8 978–0–19–928414–6

10 9 8 7 6 5 4 3 2 1

Typeset by Laserwords Private Limited, Chennai, India
Printed in Great Britain
on acid-free paper by
Antony Rowe Ltd., Chippenham, Wiltshire

Acknowledgements

Dr William Dollman, coroner for North London

Eric Jenkins, Coroner's Officer for the London Borough of Sutton

CPS at the Central Criminal Court

CPS at the Special Casework Section, Ludgate Hill

CPS at the Cooperage and Tolworth, South London

Barristers, junior and senior, too many to name

Treasury Counsel at the Old Bailey

Metropolitan Police officers far too many to name

The staff of the Old Bailey police room

Contents

List of Illustrations

1

Introduction

1.1 **Court and the Police Officer**

For various reasons many police officers do not relish attending court. Some complain that the process is disorganized and consumes an ever increasing amount of valuable time. Others object to fierce cross-examination by lawyers and criticism of their actions. If a defendant is acquitted, some feel disappointed by their own performance or the performance of the prosecutor. This book will help officers address these and other concerns.

One reason why knowledge of court procedure is so important is the recent advent of a variety of preventative orders. While the creation of the Crown Prosecution Service has relieved the police service of the responsibility to prosecute cases, anti-social behaviour orders (ASBOs), sex offender orders, and football banning orders may all be applied for directly by the police. The reality is that court based remedies now form a significantly greater part of modern policing than ever before.

The police officer's attitude towards going to court and towards the criminal justice system is frequently characterized by cynicism and pessimism. Police officers are influenced by the opinions of the rest of society. They read the same newspapers and watch the same news bulletins. Their attitudes and perceptions may also be influenced by difficult and sometimes distressing personal experience.

This book does not seek to persuade officers to abandon their cynicism. Neither is it an attempt to defend British justice or the participants in it. Instead, it is written in the belief that officers of every rank and role, regardless of their area of responsibility, will benefit from familiarity with the criminal justice process and court procedures. In short, the purpose is to improve officers' performance by increasing their understanding of the legal process. In this way, while cynicism may remain, it is hoped that pessimism about the criminal justice system may be eroded by greater success at court.

1.1.1 **Tension and tedium**

There are other reasons why police officers do not like going to court. Frustratingly, hours may be spent sitting in waiting rooms and corridors when they could be 'fighting crime' or 'doing what they are paid to do' and do best. Equally, it can be stressful. It is not an exaggeration to say that many officers, supremely confident and skilled in other challenging and often dangerous situations, enter a court building with feelings of trepidation and dread.

Why should a police officer feel uncomfortable attending court, often as an 'expert' witness or as an officer in the case? The answer is largely because he or she is unsure of the processes and protocols.

It is suggested that the main cause of this uncertainty is insufficient training associated with the ever-competing demands for scarce resources. By and large, an officer's understanding will be based only on hard learned experience and anecdotal advice from colleagues.

The creation of the Crown Prosecution Service (CPS) was intended not only to improve the quality and objectivity of prosecutions but also to relieve the police of a huge burden. With officers now witnesses and not prosecutors, the argument went, they would no longer have to spend as much time at court. This has simply not been the case: officers still attend court but in different roles. There are, of course, no longer specialist police prosecutors at the magistrates' court, but the requirement for officers to go to court for any number of other reasons has not diminished and has, in some cases, increased. Officers still have to give evidence at trials and if they are the officer in the case (OIC), will usually be expected to be present even where they may not give evidence. The problem is that without experience gained from presenting their own cases, it is easy for officers to feel detached from the workings of the criminal justice system.

1.1.2 Taking responsibility

Where the police are disappointed by the outcome of a case, there are a number of participants who may be blamed. The first and most common scapegoat is the CPS. As an easy target, they are often unfairly criticized by the public and the police, sometimes by both at the same time. The CPS is not an arm of the police service there simply to rubber stamp police decisions or to prosecute. Its independence is part of its 'raison d'être' and one of its strengths.

The next target will be the legal representatives of the defendant. Most commonly they will be accused of unscrupulously riding a publicly funded gravy train, upon which more cash will be heaped at every stop and contrived delay. However, the system of legal funding does not operate in this way. Alternatively, the defence lawyer will be suspected of concocting the client's defence. This is to misunderstand the nature of the lawyer/client relationship and professional responsibilities of the lawyer to the court.

Having convinced themselves that the defendant's legal representatives are unprincipled money-grabbers, officers may be tempted to turn their attention to the judiciary. A number of uncomplimentary and undeserved colloquialisms may accompany references to both the lay magistrate and the Crown Court judge.

The reality is that however officers feel about the other participants there are only two aspects of the proceedings over which they have control. The first is the collection of evidence. The second is their own performance at court. Both are essential parts of an officer's duty.

1.1.3 An important role

The police officer in court is a professional evidence gatherer and expert witness who will be assessed solely on the quality of the evidence they have gathered and the manner in which they present that evidence. Many police officers spend comparatively little time in court and ignorance of some procedures and principles is understandable. However, the barrister fighting for their client's liberty and the magistrate or judge presiding over the case will not make any allowance for this.

Going to court is a cornerstone of police work and the police officer should feel able to approach the task with the same confidence with which they approach other aspects of their work. No police officer would ever be let loose behind the wheel of a high-powered vehicle without a high level of training; no probationary constable could hope to make a decision to arrest without first knowing their powers. Why then are officers allowed to go to court with only the most basic training? It is asking much of an officer with such little training to explain to a frightened witness or nervous police probationer what they may not wholly understand themselves. Six to 12 months' work and considerable public resources can evaporate in the time it takes a magistrate or jury to reach a decision.

1.2 **Contents**

The mystique shrouding the English legal system is an illusion. The rules governing positional lights on vehicles, bald tyres or the evasion of liability by deception are actually more challenging than the 'complexities' of courtroom procedure and yet many police officers will be more familiar with them. This book is intended as a practical guide rather than a legal textbook. Accordingly, I do not, where it is possible to avoid it, quote chunks of legislation. Nothing would be more guaranteed to alienate the very people who may have most need of the information presented here. In any event, information technology now provides most police officers with all the resources they need to delve into case-law and legislation.

No book written about court procedure could ever hope to describe or predict all of the possibilities and eventualities that can and do occur at court. Going to court is nothing if not unpredictable and no two cases will ever be the same. One can only ever hope to describe what is most 'likely' to occur.

I have included sections on the magistrates', Crown and coroner's courts simply because these are the courts that police officers are most likely to go to. Officers may find themselves giving evidence at other courts or before a variety of commissions, tribunals and compensation boards but they are the exception and not the rule. Good practice in relation to the giving of evidence in the criminal courts, however, is relevant to any arena in which an officer is required to answer questions in public.

In addition to the sections which outline the procedure in particular courts, chapters 11 to 13 present practical guidance about attending court. The chapters consider how to prepare for court, explain the nature of the trial procedure, and provide advice on being a witness. This, it is hoped, will allow convenient reference by officers to the relevant section.

1.3 **Personal**

The idea to write this book first came to me whilst at Knightsbridge Crown Court which in 1997 was temporarily sitting at Borough in South East London. It was the first day of a rape trial in which I was officer in the case. I had just had a long consultation with the prosecuting barrister and had retired to consider his words in the sanctuary of a smoke filled police room. It slowly dawned on me that despite 10 years of investigative experience and 13 years in the police service, I didn't have a clue what he was talking about. I didn't even know if I had been castigated or not. There was no one to turn to. I didn't know how to explain the situation to the victim, her husband or their chaperone. I knew also that there was no one to blame but myself. I vowed that it would never happen again but it did. I realize now, given the unpredictability of any court case, that it is impossible to prepare for every eventuality but with a little knowledge and humility a police officer need never fear going to court.

2

The Legal Profession

2.1 **Introduction**

The language, the drama, and even the costume of criminal proceedings help to generate a sense of authority for the court. At the same time, the ritual of the courtroom has a tendency to create a sense of mystery about the participants. This is not to say that officers are in awe of lawyers. Even the celebrity status of barristers in the most high profile trials does not exempt them from criticism by police officers, victims or other agencies. Officers will talk endlessly, and frequently disparagingly, about particular solicitors or barristers (lawyers). Courtroom experiences are recalled like the huge fish that got away and it would seem that just about every police officer I have ever met has outwitted the most eminent Queen's Counsel (senior barrister) during a gruelling four-hour cross-examination.

It is useful to understand the role of other professionals in the legal system. Although members of the public are entitled to defend themselves and bring private prosecutions, such cases are rare. Therefore, to maximize their influence in the vast majority of cases, officers should arm themselves with knowledge of the other participants, specifically who they are, what they do, and their function in the proceedings.

Solicitors and barristers (for simplicity both are often referred to as lawyers) may be referred to as advocates when they appear before a court. The art of presenting a case in court is called 'advocacy'. Reference to an advocate throughout this book includes solicitors or barristers unless stated otherwise.

2.2 **Public Prosecutors**

2.2.1 **The Crown Prosecution Service (CPS)**

The Crown Prosecution Service, or CPS as it is most commonly known, suffers from almost as much adverse publicity as the police service itself. In many ways it has to cope with similar difficulties and obstacles for the CPS is maintained exclusively at tax payers' expense and may never enjoy the level of funding and support that some insist is required to provide the best and most efficient service. The CPS is often heavily criticized by those in the police service who are looking for a scapegoat for a rising tide of bureaucracy and crime. Problems with prosecution cases and in the courtroom itself are laid squarely at the door of the CPS. Many officers are nostalgic about pre-CPS days when the police investigated and prosecuted, when every constabulary had its own legal department and court officers. These were the days when, so legend has it, every officer knew how to prosecute his own case and all the villains 'went down'. This, of course, is nonsense. The truth is that the old systems, for there were many, were not better and were not perceived to be better by the public. It was for these reasons that the CPS was created, with a mandate to prosecute, objectively, realistically and, above all, fairly.

2.2.2 The creation of the CPS

The Royal Commission on Criminal Procedure 1981 identified the need for reform of a system where a prosecution was handled by the police or by solicitors acting on their behalf. The Commission examined the variability and inconsistency of the system wherein the 43 police forces in England and Wales operated their own procedures. The Commission concluded that an independent body must be established to conduct prosecutions. This body would be able to look dispassionately at the evidence gathered by the police and even in some cases at the decision to charge. It would be a body to which the police could turn for advice in the preparation of cases and their evidential requirements. It would be a body which would ultimately decide whether a prosecution would proceed and with what offences a defendant should be charged or indicted. Passage through Parliament of the Prosecution of Offences Act 1985 saw the creation of the CPS in 1986.

2.2.3 The purpose of the CPS

The CPS is the Government Department responsible for prosecuting those in England and Wales who have been charged or summoned with a criminal offence. As the principal prosecuting authority in England and Wales, it is responsible for:

- advising the police on cases for possible prosecution;
- reviewing cases submitted by the police;
- preparing cases for court;
- presentation of most cases at court.

2.2.4 The Code for Crown Prosecutors

The CPS are guided by The Code for Crown Prosecutors. This document provides structured guidance for the basis of a decision to prosecute. The most recent Code was published in November 2004 and copies of this are readily available but may be conveniently viewed at www.cps.gov.uk/victims/witnesses/codetest. It is refreshingly straightforward. All officers should be familiar with the 'Full Code' test, a two-part test that Crown prosecutors must apply to every prosecution before it either commences or continues.

2.2.5 **The evidential and the public interest tests**

This is the first stage in the decision to prosecute. Crown Prosecutors must be satisfied that there is enough evidence to provide a 'realistic prospect of conviction' against each defendant on each charge. They must consider whether the evidence can be used ('is admissable') and is reliable. They must also consider what the defence case may be and how that is likely to affect the prosecution case. A 'realistic prospect of conviction' is an objective test. It means that a jury or a bench of magistrates, properly directed in accordance with the law, will be more likely than not to convict the defendant of the charge alleged. If the case does not pass the evidential test, it must not go ahead, no matter how important or serious it may be.

If the case does pass the evidential test, Crown Prosecutors must then decide whether a prosecution is in the public interest. They must balance factors for and against prosecution carefully and fairly. One example of a factor that would weigh in favour of prosecution is if the offence was racially or religiously aggravated. In general, a prosecution will usually take place however, unless there are public interest factors tending against prosecution which clearly outweigh those tending in favour. Alternatively the CPS may conclude that minor matters may be more suitably dealt with by methods not requiring the offender to appear in court, for example, an official warning (for adults referred to as a 'caution'). The CPS will only begin or continue a prosecution if a case has passed and continues to satisfy both tests.

2.2.6 **The structure of the CPS**

In April 1999 the CPS was organized into 42 geographical areas. These areas correspond to the 43 police forces in England and Wales, with the London area covering both the Metropolitan and City of London police forces. The CPS employs 7,700 staff, including lawyers, caseworkers and administrators. In the year 2003 to 2004 they dealt with 1.3 million cases in the magistrates' courts and 115,000 cases in the Crown Court.

The national headquarters of the CPS is situated at High Holborn, a short distance away from the Old Bailey and St Paul's cathedral in the City of London. There is another regional headquarters in York. Each area has a Chief Crown Prosecutor who is responsible for prosecutions within their area. Each area is sub-divided into units or sections dealing with magistrates' or Crown Court work and each will include administrative support and other essential services as well as Senior Crown Prosecutors. Most CPS prosecutors are qualified lawyers but certain work in the magistrates' court is undertaken by Designated Case Workers (DCWs). DCWs are extensively trained and independently assessed before being allowed to prosecute cases. If a guilty plea is anticipated in a magistrates' court case that has been reviewed by a lawyer, then that case may be allocated to a DCW to prosecute.

In 1998 Sir Iain Glidewell undertook a review of the CPS. This review recommended that more resources be directed to the prosecution of Crown Court work and saw the establishment of 'trials units' servicing particular Crown Courts. A trials unit will deal only with the more serious offences transferred to Crown Court for trial or sentencing and will liaise directly with the police. The unit will typically consist of a Unit Head and Team Leader and will employ a number of caseworkers and lawyers each with their own workload. Barristers no longer have a monopoly over the prosecution of cases at the Crown Court but most prosecution work is still undertaken by barristers instructed by the CPS. The CPS now has a number of what are now known as Higher Court Advocates (HCAs), solicitors who have been trained to present prosecution cases at the Crown Court. The instruction of barristers by the CPS is dealt with later (see **2.4.2** below).

CPS lawyers and DCWs at the magistrates' court are given responsibility for particular courts, often in rotation. If there are four individual courts within a magistrates' court building, then there will be four CPS representatives dealing with the matters in those courts. The workload of a CPS lawyer or DCW varies from court area to court area and from day to day. A busy magistrates' court could see a lawyer prosecute as many as 60 cases in a single day. Such a volume of work provides a challenge to even the most experienced prosecutor. In coping with the volume of work at the magistrates' court the prosecutor is reliant on the quality of the case file that is prepared for them. Their task is not to be envied. Nevertheless, despite the intensity and volume of the work, magistrates' court conviction rates remain impressively high.

2.2.7 **The police and the CPS**

The relationship between the CPS and the police has often been uncomfortable and sometimes counterproductive. Though the CPS has now been in existence for nearly 20 years, many police officers still misunderstand its role and responsibilities. There is a perception that the CPS have usurped the police service's natural position in the justice system and that they do not and can never compete with the cunning of the criminal and his wily legal representative. However, as successive generations of police officers retire, attitudes have changed and the vast majority of currently serving police officers cannot imagine life without the CPS.

The well-informed police officer as a witness and as 'officer in the case' is a valuable asset to the CPS lawyer. The officer's observations about all aspects of a case are valued and frequently acted upon. For their part, officers should acknowledge that CPS advice as to how the case should be investigated and prepared is as important as its presentation at court.

2.2.8 **The Attorney General, Solicitor General and the Director of Public Prosecutions (DPP)**

The office of DPP has been in existence since 1879 and has always advised the police in criminal matters. The Prosecution of Offences Act 1985 designated the DPP as the national head of the CPS. The DPP is not a political appointment and candidates for the role must be a barrister or have at least 10 years' experience as a solicitor. The post is currently held by Ken Macdonald QC. The Attorney General, who has final responsibility for enforcing criminal law, superintends the DPP. The appointment of the Attorney General is political. The Attorney General is chosen by the Prime Minister from elected MPs and will have a legal background, normally as a Queen's Counsel (see **2.4.3** below). Whilst the 1985 Act places the decision to prosecute in the hands of the CPS and the DPP, there remain specific offences and occasions when the consent of the Attorney General (currently Lord Goldsmith QC) is required before prosecution can begin or proceed. The phrase 'requires the consent of the Attorney General' will be familiar to all police officers from examination studies and charging guides. The Solicitor General, another political appointment, assists the Attorney General.

2.3 **Solicitors**

No other professional can excite the police officer to such extremes of indignation as the criminal defence lawyer, the defence 'brief' who will fight for his client even against the most overwhelming evidence. The majority of practising solicitors in England and Wales do not work in the criminal justice system. The criminal justice system is said to be 'contentious' and there are other non-contentious ways for solicitors to make a living such as buying and selling property (conveyancing).

Solicitors who decide to work in the field of prosecution will usually join the CPS. However, most criminal law solicitors are engaged in defence work. In the past, a qualified solicitor would turn his hand to all types of work and some continue to take a wide range of work. However, the trend is increasingly for firms of solicitors to specialize in certain types of law. Most police officers will know the names of any number of criminal law defence specialists in their area. Whatever their area of expertise, solicitors receive similar education and training. Many officers will be familiar with the legal 'reps' that often represent arrested persons at police stations. They are not solicitors but are legally qualified.

Most solicitors have a degree in law. This is not essential but is the norm. Currently all qualifying graduates will then proceed to complete a one-year, full-time, practically based course assessed by examination and other written and skill-based assessments, including criminal litigation and advocacy. Having completed this course, the aspiring solicitor will work for up to two years as a trainee in a solicitor's office before they can become a 'solicitor'. During this two-year period the trainee was formerly known as an 'articled clerk' but is now a 'trainee solicitor'. What was previously referred to as a period of 'articles' is now referred to as a 'Training Contract'. Competition for training contracts is fierce despite the fact that trainee solicitors earn a small salary. During this period they may shadow barristers at Crown Court, sitting on the bench behind them, supporting and observing. They may even conduct simple matters of their own in the magistrates' court.

Whilst some solicitors practise alone, many form firms as partners. The senior solicitors ('partners') do not receive a salary but receive a share of the firm's profits. Not all solicitors working for a particular firm will be partners and many of them will be salaried and are often referred to as assistant solicitors. The offer of inclusion in a partnership is usually only made when the solicitor reaches a position of seniority within the firm.

A solicitor's clients will usually come to them by personal recommendation or through the duty solicitor scheme (see below at **2.3.1**). It is common for clients who are more 'familiar' with the criminal justice system to use the same solicitor or firm of solicitors time and time again. It is not unusual to see groups of friends and associates using the same firm. Certain firms will inevitably establish a good reputation locally and will figure prominently when arrested persons require the presence of a solicitor at the station or seek a telephone consultation. Such firms will usually be part of the duty solicitor scheme and their advice funded publicly. This scheme came into being in the 1980s to ensure that any arrested person at a police station requiring legal advice is able to receive that advice in compliance with s 58 of the Police and Criminal Evidence Act 1984 (an Act which police officers often refer to as PACE).

2.3.1 **The Criminal Defence Service**

Anyone who has been charged with a criminal offence and is to appear in the magistrates' court can apply to the magistrates for legal representation. If a defendant is to appear at the Crown Court either for trial, sentencing or appeal then they may apply for 'Advocacy Assistance' whereby a barrister will be instructed. There is no form of means testing whatsoever. The magistrates only have to establish that it is in the interests of justice that the defendant needs a lawyer to represent and protect their interests. If the magistrates decide that it is appropriate then a solicitor will be appointed from a firm contracted to the Legal Services Commission or from the Criminal Defence Service (CDS). Of course, the availability of legal advice does not remove a person's right either to defend themselves or to use a solicitor of their own choosing at their own expense.

The Criminal Defence Service (CDS) for England and Wales came into being in April 2001. It is a publicly funded body regulated by the Legal Services Commission and replaced the Legal Aid Scheme which had been in place for many years. In simple terms it was created to ensure that every person accused of a criminal offence or involved in criminal proceedings has access to legal advice, assistance and representation as the interests of justice require. Such advice at the police station is provided free of charge usually by the Duty Solicitor Scheme irrespective of an individual's ability to pay. Most assistance at court is also free and this includes most matters that proceed to trial.

Persons accused of a crime must have representation of a quality appropriate to the circumstances in which they find themselves. Representation available at police stations and at first appearances at a magistrates' court may be provided via the Public Defender Service (PDS) or Duty Solicitor scheme. The PDS directly employs criminal defence lawyers. They are, in practice, the same firms who had representation historically under the Legal Aid Scheme. These contracted firms now have an obligation to maintain standards and are paid a fixed hourly rate for their services.

There was considerable opposition to the creation of the CDS by solicitors and its effectiveness is yet to be evaluated. There are concerns that the Commission has and will continue to seek to cut costs to the detriment of the service and those it is designed to assist.

The Duty Solicitor scheme (part of the Criminal Defence Service), familiar to all police officers, is available to people at both police stations and magistrates' court. It remains largely unchanged though the Legal Services Commission now controls its management and administration. Free leaflets are available explaining the range of legal services available to those accused of committing criminal offences. Two of particular interest are 'Criminal Defence Services at the Police Station and in Court' and 'A Practical Guide to Criminal Defence Services'. Both can be viewed at www.legalservices.gov.uk/public/help/leaflets.asp. (For further details concerning the availability of representation by a duty solicitor see below at **3.2.9.**)

2.3.2 **The role of the solicitor**

The solicitor's role is to represent their client to the best of their ability from arrest through to the termination of a case at the Crown or magistrates' court (PACE Codes of Practice C NFG 6D). Solicitors at all times act upon the instructions of their client. The most common, dangerous and ill-informed criticism levelled at solicitors by police officers and the general public is that they collude with their clients in constructing and creating alibis and defences and lie for their clients. This is wholly unethical, would constitute a criminal offence and is extremely rare. Any solicitor found to have behaved in such a way, would, in addition to any criminal sanction, be disqualified from acting as a solicitor (referred to as being 'struck off') and be most unlikely ever to practice as a solicitor again.

A good criminal defence lawyer, however, will not represent their client in a state of subdued or timid silence. Officers often interpret active and efficient representation as aggressive, even unlawful, obstruction. It is not. The same solicitors may defend police officers against allegations of misconduct. Officers should consider the type of representation they would expect if accused of a criminal or disciplinary offence. The defendant may have confessed to their solicitor or there may be overwhelming evidence of their guilt. This does not mean that the defendant must plead guilty. They do not. The defendant is entitled to ask the prosecution to prove their case. This is referred to as 'putting the prosecution to proof'.

The solicitor will advise their client at the police station in person or on the telephone. They may be present at any interview in a police station. They will represent their client at a first appearance in the magistrates' court and thereafter at every subsequent appearance. If their client is in custody they may seek the grant of bail and argue for appropriate conditions to be attached. They will normally conduct trials in the magistrates' court, calling and cross-examining witnesses.

If the matter is transferred to the Crown Court solicitors will normally instruct a barrister but may represent their client at a hearing. Barristers no longer have exclusive rights of audience at the Crown Court and solicitors can and do represent their clients there during preliminary hearings. If a solicitor makes such an appearance he will wear a gown but not a wig. The solicitor is responsible for instructing a barrister and does so by way of a 'brief' which is a summary of the case and the client's instructions. A solicitor will deal personally with the client to the extent that the barrister defending may not actually meet his client until the day of the trial itself. The solicitor will prepare the case including the taking of witness statements and undertake any other research required.

2.3.3 The Law Society

Police officers will generally be familiar with the name of the Law Society because of the direct reference to it in Code C of the Police and Criminal Evidence Act 1985 Codes of Practice. It is there referred to as the body towards which a police officer can direct a complaint with regard to the conduct of a solicitor during an interview at a police station. Whilst the regulation of solicitors and legal representatives is one of its functions, the Law Society also controls training, admission to the profession and the right to practise. Solicitors must be insured against negligence through a scheme operated (or approved) by the Society. It is a professional association with a number of roles including the representation of its members' interests.

2.3.4 The police and solicitors

Whilst the advent of the CPS has reduced the amount of time police officers come into contact with defence solicitors, their attendance at court and at the police station remain part of the job. Police officers frequently bristle with suspicion in their dealings with defence solicitors. The defence 'brief' and the qualified representative are often viewed by the police officer as being the lowest part of the legal totem pole, poor relations to the learned barrister. The truth is that many solicitors are as skilled in the art of advocacy as many barristers. This is particularly so in the magistrates' court in which they appear far more often than barristers. The instruction of a barrister, for example, to argue for bail at a magistrates' court is not necessarily an acknowledgement of greater advocacy skills. There may be any number of reasons why a firm of solicitors will make such a decision, simple expediency being one of the most common.

The high street firm of solicitors specializing in publicly funded work acquires a good reputation for sound reasons. They represent their client in a professional fashion, with determination and tenacity.

2.4 **Barristers**

Barristers have been around since the 13th century. There are about 10,000 practising in England and Wales. For many years the vast majority were drawn from the public schools and had been educated at Oxford or Cambridge. This monopoly, as in many other professions, has been eroded in recent decades.

All barristers undergo the same training process. They must pass the Bar Vocational Course after completing either a law degree or a one-year conversion course. On satisfactorily completing this course the student is 'called to the bar'. At this stage the barrister may refer to themselves as a barrister but is not fully qualified to appear in court. To complete their training, barristers must undergo a 12-month 'pupillage' at an established firm of barristers, referred to as a 'chambers'. In simple terms, pupillage is an apprenticeship during which the pupil will learn his profession from an experienced barrister from the same chambers. However, after the first six months of their pupillage, a pupil is entitled to appear in court and, if their chosen area of practice is crime, they will often appear on more straightforward matters such as bail applications. Until recent changes that introduced minimum pay for pupillage, a pupil received no pay for the first six months of their pupillage and would need support from other means, perhaps the patronage of a wealthy family.

Once the year's pupillage is completed the barrister must apply for a place in chambers, referred to as a tenancy. Gaining a place in chambers is all-important to a young barrister, as without membership they cannot practise. There are more pupils than places available and the process of securing a tenancy may reasonably be described as Darwinian.

A chambers is a group of barristers who share common offices and facilities and whose work is organized and arranged by an administrative team called the clerks. The senior clerk at chambers is a powerful and important person. Barristers are not allowed to negotiate their own fees and the clerk will do it for them (although the vast majority of criminal work involves fees that are fixed by the Lord Chancellor's department). The clerks will also allocate the work given to them by solicitors. Experienced barristers are entitled to practise independently though very few do so.

Although the clerks will carry out administrative tasks on behalf of barristers, another of their primary functions is to 'market' the chambers and secure good quality and highly paid work. Barristers, despite being part of a chambers, are self-employed and do not operate as partnerships.

Every barrister must belong to one of the four Inns of Court. They register with a particular Inn as a student. The Inns of Court are Gray's Inn, Lincoln's Inn, Inner Temple and Middle Temple. They are to be found between the West End and the City of London, bordered by the Holborn area to the north and the River Thames to the south. An anarchic practice remains whereby aspiring barristers must eat a certain number of dinners at their Inn before they can qualify.

2.4.1 The Bar Council

The Bar Council was created in 1987 and is the governing body of the bar. Its functions are similar in many ways to those of the Law Society and it represents barristers in much the same way as that body represents solicitors. It is responsible for disciplining barristers and acts as a trade union.

2.4.2 The role of the barrister

In a famous Court of Appeal ruling Lord Denning describes the barrister's professional obligation to act as follows, 'A barrister cannot pick or choose his clients. He is bound to accept a brief for any man who comes before the courts. No matter how great a rascal the man may be. No matter how given to complaining. No matter how undeserving or unpopular his cause, the barrister must defend him to the end.' Lord Denning here articulates what is known as the 'cab-rank rule'. This is the principle whereby barristers must take cases which are properly paid and appropriate to their experience whatever their personal feelings or misgivings about the client or the circumstances. In practice prominent and sought after barristers will pick certain cases for professional and financial reasons.

In criminal cases work is referred to barristers by defence solicitors or the CPS. The solicitor will contact chambers with a view to booking a barrister and may express a preference for a particular person. The clerks will attempt to meet the solicitor's request and do their best to allocate work according to ability, expertise and experience. Frequently, however, an important factor is simply who is available.

When a solicitor books a barrister for a case, the barrister is said to be 'briefed' or 'instructed' on behalf of a party. For example, the CPS might say 'we have instructed Mr Smith of counsel on behalf of the Crown'. Somewhat confusingly, the expression 'instructions' also refers to a document that solicitors will send to counsel which includes a written summary of the case and any requests for advice or action by the barrister. The entirety of the documents that the solicitor sends to the barrister are referred to as a brief.

A barrister may not meet with a client until the morning of a hearing at court or even a trial. However, it is usually good practice when defending a case to meet a client in conference, at least prior to trial. It is unusual for the solicitor to visit the barrister. A solicitor (or a representative of their firm) would do so if a conference were arranged. However, it is not uncommon for a barrister to attend conferences at a solicitor's offices.

In prosecution cases it is the CPS who instruct a barrister. A CPS branch office will tend to use certain sets of chambers and will choose from within those sets. At present the choice will be made by a senior caseworker within a trials unit. Again, in theory the work is distributed in accordance with the preference of the senior caseworker with cases being matched to experience, suitability and specialism.

2.4.3 Junior and senior barristers

All practising barristers are called 'junior counsel' or 'senior counsel', whatever their age or appearance. Senior counsel are also known as Queen's Counsel (QC). The vast majority of barristers are junior counsel. After around 15 to 20 years of practice a successful barrister may apply to become a QC. Queen's Counsel are only appointed after undergoing a selection process overseen by the Lord Chancellor. It would be unusual to encounter a QC who is under the age of 38. Only 10 per cent of barristers are QCs. They are also commonly referred to as 'silks' because they are entitled to wear a gown made of silk. If a barrister is said to have 'taken silk' it means simply that he has been appointed as a QC. Most barristers who apply to become Queen's Counsel will not be successful.

At the Central Criminal Court, the Old Bailey, there is a panel of experienced QCs who are known as Treasury Counsel. They are appointed to prosecute the most serious cases at that court. There are, at present, 16 Treasury Counsel. The most serious cases, such as murder, will usually be prosecuted and defended by pairs of barristers. The senior barrister is referred to as leading counsel and will be a QC. The barrister who assists will be referred to as 'junior' counsel though they may actually be very experienced. The junior will make a note of proceedings and may deputize, where convenient, for leading counsel. It is common practice for leading counsel to allow their junior to deal with the less complex aspects of the case such as the reading of interviews, the examination or cross-examination of the less important witnesses, or the presentation of agreed evidence or facts.

The appointment of QCs has been subject to a great deal of criticism in recent years. The Lord Chancellor ultimately decides who will be appointed and the Lord Chancellor is, of course, politically appointed. This, therefore, leaves the system vulnerable to charges of 'cronyism' and political bias. There are usually only between 60 and 100 appointments a year. This inevitably creates a great deal of bitterness and rancour amongst those who fail the selection process.

Advocacy at the Crown Court was until relatively recently the exclusive preserve of barristers. This is no longer the case and solicitors can and do represent clients in the Crown Court. Many barristers opposed this change which was brought about by the Courts and Legal Services Act of 1990 but the first solicitor advocates took their place in the Crown Court in 1994. Although there are some solicitor advocates for the prosecution and defence, by and large, cases in the Crown Court are presented by barristers.

2.4.4 A change of barrister

One of the most common complaints made by police officers relates to the late appointment of a barrister to a case. A barrister is frequently given a case on the day before it is due at court. On some occasions they will be asked to deal with it on the morning of the appearance itself (although this is extremely rare if the case is listed for trial). It is also a source of dissatisfaction and disquiet to many police officers that more than one and sometimes many barristers are used to steer a case through its many appearances up to and including the trial.

The reality is that it is impossible to achieve certainty in a barrister's diary. Some cases are listed to take place at some point in a particular week when a court becomes available. Others that are scheduled for a particular date may be brought forward or delayed for any number of reasons. Even when a case does take place when expected, it is extremely difficult to know how long it will last. It may be resolved very quickly if, for example, a defendant pleads guilty on the first day of a trial, or witnesses fail to attend. It may begin but then be adjourned for legal reasons. Alternatively, the trial may take longer than expected perhaps because of the way evidence is given by witnesses or because of the time taken by the jury to reach and deliver their verdict.

The reality is that the barristers who are most in demand will inevitably be double-booked by their clerks in the knowledge that some of their cases will not take place when they are scheduled to do so. The idea is that if a trial finishes earlier than was predicted, the barrister will not be out of work. On the other hand, if a trial lasts longer than was expected, the brief, previously in the possession of a busy barrister, will then be passed or 'returned' to an available barrister. It is quite normal for a barrister to receive his brief in this way. Indeed, when booking barristers, solicitors will usually consider whether there is another barrister in the same chambers who would be acceptable if their first choice is not available.

One matter that officers should be reassured by is the ability of barristers to perform professionally in the most adverse, time restrained circumstances. In general, barristers are able to grasp the detail and requirements of their brief impressively quickly.

The ability to digest a brief at very short notice is a skill that barristers must possess. I have spoken to a prosecution counsel on the morning of a trial who has listened to the tape recording of the defendant's interview in their car on the way to the court. When the barrister received the brief is never as important as how well they deal with it.

2.4.5 The police and barristers

All too often, police officers find barristers remote and condescending. It is not unusual for the police officer to feel like a humble tradesman or artisan dealing with a particularly demanding customer. On the one hand, there are good reasons why a barrister must remain somewhat detached. The primary duty of prosecution counsel is to assist the court. It is not their function to secure a conviction at all costs. On the other hand, barristers should behave in a professional manner. If they fail to do so and are rude or overbearing then the officer should make their feelings known to the CPS. This is because in prosecution cases the police officer and the barrister are mutually dependent. The officer who is properly prepared and knowledgeable about the case is an asset. Equally, a sympathetic and well-briefed barrister is a friend and not a foe, and professional camaraderie will often develop during a case. The officer may even come to appreciate that in view of the pressure prosecution counsel is under, they deserve all the support the officer can provide.

2.5 Conclusion

In an era when an increasing demand on the judicial system is outstripped only by the pace of reform and public spending cuts, the judicial process is not an easy ride for any of the participants. Celebrated barristers will lose as many cases as they win. The demands made of solicitors are as high as the expectations of all involved in the criminal justice process.

The experience of the police officer at court is different from those in the legal profession whose lives and livelihoods are bound up with it. The strains exerted by both prosecution and defence in their roles can feel unbearable. The police officer who has prepared well for their day in court can feel pleased with a job well done and perhaps even a little smug that they, at least, may not be back at court for weeks or months. The legal profession can take no such consolation.

3

The Magistrates' Court

3.1 **The People's Court**

For many years the police officer's first courtroom experience came in the magistrates' court but this may no longer be the case. It is common for an officer's first appearance to be at the Crown Court, perhaps even giving evidence at a murder trial. Nevertheless the magistrates' court is where most criminal law cases are dealt with (approximately 95 per cent) and therefore the court in which most officers will find themselves sooner or later. This is particularly so with uniform and traffic patrol officers who will deal with the offences which are most likely to be heard in the magistrates' court. For example nearly all traffic matters, most of which are brought by way of summons, are dealt with in the absence of the defendant by the magistrates. The magistrates' court also incorporates the Youth Court and this deals with young offenders aged between 10 and 17. Officers do not only attend the magistrates' court in order to give evidence, but also to make applications for search warrants and other statutory orders. Most magistrates' courts are said to be 'open' (that is, they are open to the public) but exceptions do apply!

3.1.1 **Jurisdiction**

Magistrates' courts, frequently referred to as the people's or lower court, have been in existence for about 600 years. The term 'people's court' reflects the fact that to most people going to court means going to the magistrates' court. Their proceedings are regulated by a number of statutes and rules including the Magistrates Court Act 1980, the Criminal Justice Act 2003 and the Criminal Procedure Rules 2005. This is not an exhaustive list. This court currently has the power to impose a fine of up to £5,000 for each offence or to send an offender to prison for a maximum of six months. The current maximum term of imprisonment is 12 months for two or more either-way offences (see below at **3.1.3**). This will double once s 154 of the Criminal Justice Act 2003 (CJA 2003) comes into force. Some matters may only be dealt with by way of a fine as this is the only penalty permitted by the offence, for example, careless driving. The amount of the fine may also be capped. These limits are referred to as 'levels' of which there are five. Careless driving has a maximum fine capped at level three (currently £1,000) whilst level five has a current maximum of £5,000 (see below at **4.2.9**). A fine may be imposed as well as a term of imprisonment but this is unusual because the defendant is unlikely to have retained their employment.

The vast majority of all criminal cases are dealt with at this court. Most people will find themselves before the court as the result of committing a minor road traffic offence and will plead guilty by post avoiding the need to appear in person before the court. All offences which come before the magistrates' court are classified by law as either summary only, either-way or indictable only. This classification reflects the relative seriousness of the offence and governs the choice of court at which the matter must or may be heard.

3.1.2 **Summary only offences**

Summary only offences (for example, careless driving as discussed above) are those which are considered to be comparatively minor, and include many road traffic matters, drunkenness and some public order offences. Clearly there are a huge number of these and a full list of matters falling within the magistrates' summary jurisdiction can be found in the Stone's Justices Manual, the three volumes of which can usually be seen on the desk of any legal adviser. The third volume of this work contains a complete index for the three volumes. It is a very useful publication and will be used by the legal adviser to ensure compliance with court procedure and to advise the magistrates on other legal issues. Summary offences must usually proceed within six months of their commission. Part 37 of the Criminal Procedure Rules 2005 explains the general order of events where a defendant pleads not guilty to a summary offence and the matter proceeds to trial.

3.1.3 **Either-way offences**

These offences can be tried in both the magistrates' and the Crown Court. If a defendant is charged with such an offence he has the option to have the case transferred to the Crown Court for trial if he elects to stand trial before a judge and jury. The magistrates' court has the option to refuse jurisdiction (that is, to refuse to deal with the matter) where they do not consider that their powers of sentencing are sufficient following conviction. Additionally, the magistrates' court may send a convicted person to the Crown Court for sentencing if, on hearing the details of their previous convictions, etc they do not feel that they have sufficient powers to deal with the offender. In other words, after hearing all of the circumstances, they decide that the maximum punishment they can impose (see **3.1.1**) is insufficient. Commonly encountered 'either-way' offences are theft, burglary, deception, actual bodily harm, criminal damage (where the value of the damage exceeds £5,000), assault, and some sexual offences. If a person is convicted of two 'either-way' offences the maximum sentence is currently 12 months' imprisonment in the magistrates' court and or a fine capped at level five (see **3.1.1**) even though the statutory maximum exceed this. For example the maximum penalty for the offence of actual bodily harm is currently five years' imprisonment but this is limited to six months if the offender is sentenced in the magistrates' court.

3.1.4 **Indictable only**

'Indictable only' offences are those over which the magistrates' court has no jurisdiction. That is to say that the magistrates do not have the power to hear such matters. A defendant charged with such an offence will make his first appearance before the magistrate but must be sent (committed) to the Crown Court for trial as required currently by s 51 of the Crime and Disorder Act 1998. This process of committal is described in more detail at **4.5** below. The magistrate will still have the power to grant or refuse bail in such cases and can make an order with regard to public funding.

The law in relation to what is and what should be dealt with at the magistrates' or Crown Court has been subject to continuous comment and review for the last decade. Many proposals have been forwarded in an attempt to reduce the number of matters which fall into the 'either-way' category in an attempt to relieve the burden of the Crown Court system. Attempts to make offences of theft, where the amount concerned is relatively low, a summary only matter have been met with fierce argument about the inalienable right to jury trial in matters of dishonesty. It is likely the law will change over the years with regard to the jurisdiction of other offences.

3.2 The Magistrate, the Legal Adviser and Other 'Officers' of the Court

3.2.1 The magistrate

The Justice of the Peace and the District Judge (magistrates' court) sit in the magistrates' court. The former will usually sit as a bench of three and the latter on their own.

3.2.2 Justices of the Peace

The vast majority of magistrates are Justices of the Peace. They are commonly referred to as 'JPs' or lay magistrates as they are not legally qualified. There are at present about 30,000 JPs who do not receive a salary for performing this role though their travel expenses are reimbursed and they are compensated for loss of earnings. The role is unique to the criminal justice system in England and Wales. The selection and removal process for lay magistrates is governed by the Justices of the Peace Act 1997. The Crown appoints them on the advice of the Lord Chancellor. An appointed justice can only carry out their functions within a specified geographical or court catchment area, must live within 15 miles of the boundaries of that area, and must be aged between 18 and 70. Local advisory committees assess applicants and recommend prospective candidates to the Department for Constitutional Affairs (DCA), formerly the Lord Chancellor's Department. Serving or recently retired police officers or serving members of the Special Constabulary, their spouses or partners, cannot be considered for appointment as magistrates for obvious reasons (not least because they may know many of the defendants).

Whilst lay magistrates are not required to have any formal legal qualifications, they must undergo a prescribed training programme and be available to sit for a minimum number of days per year (currently 26 half days). Specialist training is required for justices who wish to 'chair' court proceedings, that is, assume leading responsibility at a hearing where there are two or more magistrates sitting and for magistrates who wish to sit at Youth Court proceedings.

Magistrates sitting at a magistrates' court are said to be sitting 'on the bench' and are referred to collectively as 'the bench'. Solicitors and police officers address the bench collectively as 'Your Worships'. The Chair of the bench (the senior magistrate) should be referred to as 'Sir' or 'Madam'. They do not wear any formal attire such as wigs or gowns. An appointed justice is given a seat on the bench of a particular petty sessions area and will normally only sit on the bench of the magistrates' court for that area. A bench of magistrates usually comprises a minimum of two lay magistrates as the law limits the powers of a single sitting justice. A single justice may be referred to as 'Your Worship', 'Sir' or 'Madam'.

The Lord Chancellor has the power to remove a magistrate. This is a rare and extreme sanction which is taken only in cases of the most serious misconduct or dereliction in their duties.

3.2.3 The District Judge (magistrates' court)

Often referred to as 'DJs', District Judges are fully paid qualified lawyers of at least seven years' standing. They were formerly known as stipendiary magistrates or 'stipes' and are sometimes referred to by their old title. They are appointed either by the Lord Chancellor or by Her Majesty at the Lord Chancellor's recommendation. The powers of a District Judge are identical to those of the magistrates but may be exercised fully when they sit alone. The District Judge will not wear formal attire and should be referred to as 'Sir' or 'Madam'.

3.2.4 The magistrate's legal adviser

The police officer at the magistrates' court will, or at least should, immediately be able to identify who the magistrates are simply by the prominence of their position behind the bench. It is perhaps more important for the officer to quickly identify their legal adviser (sometimes referred to as the magistrates' clerk or learned clerk). They usually sit directly in front of the magistrates' bench and control proceedings.

The legal adviser is legally qualified and will be in charge of their court. They are responsible for its efficient running including administrative matters and for providing legal advice to the magistrates. This is particularly so in respect of lay magistrates whose knowledge of the law will not be as extensive as that of the District Judge. They may also provide some assistance to those defendants appearing before the court who have not obtained legal advice. The legal adviser cannot defend an unrepresented defendant but they may advise them of

the availability of public funding (legal aid), the court's administrative requirements, how to proceed, and/or how to obtain further advice and assistance, for
example by consulting with the court Duty Solicitor (see **3.2.9**).

The role of the legal adviser does not include deciding whether people are
guilty or not guilty of the offences with which they are charged or summoned
nor does it include deciding upon what sentence to pass if the defendant is convicted of an offence. These are matters which the magistrates must decide and it
is important that the legal adviser does not give the impression that they can in
any way influence the outcome of matters being heard. They must not take part
in the decision-making and, strictly speaking, they may only give
legal advice to the magistrates. In practice, certainly in courts with lay justices,
a further role of the legal adviser is to make handwritten verbatim notes during a trial. This can be difficult as many witnesses and advocates deliver their
evidence and questions quickly. It will be appreciated by the legal adviser if witnesses are mindful that this written record is being prepared and regulate their
delivery accordingly. It is arguable that the legal adviser is the most important
person in the court.

Whilst the major part of the legal adviser's role is their work in court their
duties extend to include a great many administrative tasks. They will also check,
monitor and quality control any warrant, order or applications made by the
police before putting them before the court for consideration.

3.2.5 The court usher

Invaluable to every police officer and lawyer at the magistrates' court is the court
usher who will help to organize the order in which cases are heard. Ushers are
the first point of contact for those who attend the magistrates' court. They are
easily identifiable by the long black gowns they wear. They provide information
as to the listing of cases and physically call cases into court when instructed by
the magistrates or their legal adviser to do so. They keep a record of which witnesses have attended a hearing and hand to the court or witnesses documents
or exhibits.

It is always advisable for a police officer to make themselves known to the
usher at the earliest possible opportunity. If, for example, an officer is waiting
to make a warrant application and the next scheduled matter is not ready to
proceed the usher may be able to arrange to have the application dealt with
immediately. Whenever the magistrates enter or leave the court this will be preceded by the usher shouting, 'All stand.' The magistrates will bow and this is
returned by all those present in a professional capacity. Like all court personnel, they are not to be treated as personal assistants and should be addressed
with courtesy at all times. It is polite to refer to the court usher as 'gentleman or
lady usher'.

3.2.6 **Probation officers**

Probation officers from the probation service will be present throughout many magistrates' court sessions, particularly first appearances and will always attend those courts dedicated to sentencing. They are qualified to assist the court in determining the most appropriate sentence for the offender and are regularly asked to prepare detailed reports about offenders and their background, including any previous offending and financial circumstances. The most comprehensive form of report that the court can order is called a 'Pre-sentence Report' (referred to as a 'PSR'). These are discussed in detail at **4.1.1** below. The probation service also administers and supervises community sentences which are discussed at **4.2.7** below.

Probation officers are frequently positioned to one side of the court but facing the main body of the court as shown in the diagram at **3.2.11** below. Any assistance that the police officer can give to the probation services will be gratefully received and will expedite proceedings.

3.2.7 **The press**

The press are entitled to be present throughout most proceedings in the magistrates' court and reporters from the local press are always to be found moving from court to court. Reporting restrictions are in part regulated by statute and most recently by the Criminal Procedure Rules 2005 (Rule 16). Any breaches of restrictions may be punishable as contempt under the Contempt of Court Act 1981 which is sufficiently wide in scope to prohibit the unauthorized tape recording of court proceedings or photography in court, including pictures taken with mobile telephones.

It is not unusual for reporters to approach an individual police officer and they will often do so simply to clarify specific facts, perhaps the officer's name or the exact location of an offence. Police officers are bound by their force's own media policies and should be fully conversant with these before answering any questions regarding court proceedings. In general, it is perfectly acceptable to repeat information that has been given in open court but which was missed by the journalist such as the location of an offence, the age of the defendant or the officer's name. While it is good practice to assist the press where possible, the conduct of an entire interview involving questions about an officer's opinions and emotions is a different matter altogether. Such media interviews should not be conducted within the court building itself and the professional advice of a press or public relations officer should be sought beforehand.

Clearly, the place for any witness to give their evidence is at court and not before even if an earlier opportunity arises through an invitation from the press. Such interviews are not and never could be substitutes for the adduction of evidence into court or cross-examination. Witnesses must remember that a desire to be helpful may cause a trial to be abandoned because of a potentially prejudicial remark or statement. Where there is any doubt the advice of the prosecutor should be sought.

Police officers are far more likely to encounter the press and media when dealing with the more serious matters heard in the Crown Court. Handling the media and press responsibility will be expanded upon in the chapter dealing with the Crown Court (see **7.3** The Press).

3.2.8 **Custody staff**

Private security personnel from firms such as Group 4 Security Services and Securicor staff the cells at most courts. They transport all prisoners to and from court and are responsible for their detention and welfare at court. They have powers of restraint and can search people in their custody.

3.2.9 **The duty solicitor**

Defendants are entitled to be legally represented before the court (Article 6(3) of the European Convention on Human Rights 1950) and in many cases the Criminal Defence Service and Duty Solicitor Scheme will provide this legal assistance free of charge. There will be a duty solicitor present at the magistrates' court (usually a criminal lawyer from a local practice and often referred to as 'the duty') but his powers of representation are strictly limited. Legal advisers, ushers or even police officers may refer clients to the duty solicitor but they may also approach defendants directly and may subsequently act for them from their office in the usual way. The duty solicitor is invariably extremely busy but is a useful and invaluable first port of call for many defendants, especially those who have delayed taking legal advice because they have not, until they have arrived at the court, appreciated the seriousness of their position. Other defendants may well have attended court without vital paperwork and turn to the duty solicitor for assistance who may, of course, ask a police officer or the prosecutor for assistance. Typically this will include providing additional copies of documents so that they can advise the defendant properly. Such requests are not improper but such disclosure is most properly left to the prosecutor dealing with the case who may agree to the request. (For an explanation of the availability of free legal advice see above at **2.3.2**. Free leaflets explaining the type of free legal help available are published by the Legal Services Commission, as discussed earlier in this chapter.)

3.2.10 **The witness service**

The Witness Service was introduced into the magistrates' court in 2002 having previously been available only in the Crown Court (see **7.1.10**). It provides a range of support services to witnesses to ensure that they know when and where to attend court. They are a very important part of the criminal justice process.

3.2.11 **Layout of the court**

Below is a diagram representing the typical layout of a magistrates' court. It is important though to stress that the configuration of any two courts is rarely exactly the same. Much depends on when the court was built as alterations may well have been made to enhance security or access for those suffering from any disability.

A Typical Magistrates' Court

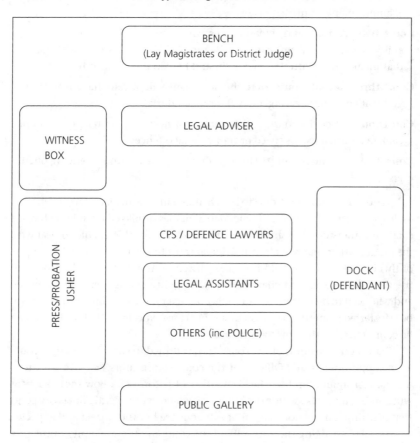

3.3 **Magistrates' Court Procedure**

3.3.1 **Court or courts**

The term magistrates' court may also refer to the building which houses a number of different court rooms, or courts. Almost all magistrates' court centres will have more than one court sitting at any one time and the different courts within the building will deal with different types of hearings. Typically, a magistrates' court with five separate courts will be divided into the following types of hearings:

Court one first appearances (Early First Hearing (EFH) courts—see below at **3.3.2**). Cases heard will include guilty pleas for immediate sentencing, for example, many drink drive cases.

Court two custody and remand cases which are not first hearings and not guilty pleas. Early Administrative Hearings (EAH) courts deal with matters that include those arrested overnight and held in police custody.

Court three a trials court. Here the defendant will already have pleaded not guilty at an earlier hearing and will now stand trial.

Court four specialist court, perhaps traffic or licensing matters, for example, camera detected excess speed or traffic signal offences.

Court five sentencing court. This court will only deal with sentencing offenders.

It is quite common for a case to be scheduled in a particular court (referred to as 'listed' because of the list of defendants' names displayed outside each court room) but transferred at short notice to another court that is able to deal with the matter rather than wait for the original court to become available. Examples of this include where a matter has been listed for trial but at the last moment the defendant decides to change his plea to guilty and is therefore convicted and will need to be sentenced. A trial is no longer necessary and the matter will be transferred to another court so that other cases expected to last for longer can be commenced in the now vacant court.

Whatever the business of the court, those entitled to enter should do so only at the appropriate time. Officers of the court (prosecutors, defence solicitors, ushers, etc) should dip their head slightly in the form of a bow (not as low as when receiving applause from an audience) whenever they enter or leave a court that is sitting. This is not a signal of subservience but the correct and expected way of acknowledging the authority of the court and the solemnity of the proceedings. Not to do so is discourteous and it has become the practice for police officers who are not witnesses to bow for this reason except when they have been called by the usher to give evidence. Police officers' caps or other headgear may not be worn in court and you should never eat, drink or chew in court! Finally, all radios and mobile phones should be turned off.

The vast majority of cases which come before the magistrates result in guilty pleas. Many cases come before the magistrates where the only issues that will be discussed are the defendant's suitability for public funding (legal aid), bail (release from custody pending trial or sentencing—see **4.4**) and jurisdictional matters (that is, whether the matter should be dealt with in the Crown Court or the magistrates' court). This is likely to happen in the most serious cases when the magistrates will not accept jurisdiction or when the matter is indictable only. Police officers do not routinely attend first hearings. In practice police officers should and do attend first appearances for complex or serious matters, particularly when bail is being objected to. This remains the case even where the police have submitted a remand file. Courts dealing with first appearances and what are now called 'early administrative hearings' and 'early first hearings' (see below at **3.3.5** and **3.3.6**) and are often referred to by lawyers as 'Narey courts' after Martin Narey's review of the criminal justice system.

3.3.2 **Guilty pleas to summary offences**

It is possible to plead guilty by post to many minor offences. For a large number of road traffic offences this is the way cases are normally disposed of. When writing to the court, the defendant may outline any matters (mitigation) which they would wish the magistrates to take into account before passing sentence. In the case of a speeding offence, this might affect the size of the fine the magistrates decide to impose.

If the defendant is present, the process will begin with the usher calling the defendant into the court from the public waiting area. The defendant will walk to the 'dock'. At this stage the legal adviser will usually take the opportunity to introduce both the prosecution representative (usually a lawyer, that is, a solicitor or a barrister) from the CPS and the defence lawyer to the bench. When appearing in court a lawyer may be referred to as an 'advocate' but this is an expression of purpose more than anything else. Frequently, they will respectfully acknowledge the magistrates by rising briefly from their seats and say 'Good afternoon (morning) madam'. By now the defendant has arrived at the 'dock' where they stand patiently (and often nervously) facing the court whilst the legal adviser confirms their identity and address. Having completed this, the legal adviser then reads aloud the allegations against the defendant before asking if they wish to plead guilty or not guilty.

Having pleaded guilty the offender (no longer a defendant) is usually asked to be seated whilst the prosecutor presents the facts of the case usually by quoting directly from form MG5. (See **11.1.3**.) This is one of the reasons why the skilful drafting of form MG5 by the police is so important. A well-prepared MG5 that precisely, accurately and concisely provides the facts relating to the offence is much appreciated by every prosecutor, especially if typed. Where the prosecutor has to struggle to read a handwritten version, this does not inspire confidence in the court. A very poorly drafted MG5 may well be returned to the drafts-man's supervisory officer for their consideration whereas one that is of a high standard may well prompt written appreciation from the prosecutor. Having provided the facts the prosecutor will provide copies of the offender's previous convictions (if any) and make applications for costs, compensation and, where weapons or drugs are involved, ask for the court to order these to be destroyed. Thereafter the prosecutor will sit down and the lawyer representing the offend-er will rise and often start by expressing gratitude to the prosecutor such as 'I am grateful to my friend' (if the prosecutor is a solicitor) or 'I am grateful to my learned friend' (if the prosecutor is a barrister) 'for the facts . . .' and continue by trying to persuade the court to deal with their client in the most lenient way possible by making a 'plea in mitigation'.

The magistrates may ask for any matter to be clarified and will confirm the disposable income of the offender. Following a brief discussion between them the 'chair' will usually pronounce sentence without the need to adjourn to con-sider matters further in terms similar to the following: 'Stand up please Mr. Jones. For driving without insurance you will pay a fine of £200 and your licence will be endorsed with six penalty points. You will also pay the prosecution costs of £60. Can that be paid today?' Further discussion may then follow about allow-ing time for the entire amount to be paid. Courts are pro-active in the recovery of fines and costs and most will now accept payment by credit card. This will usually conclude proceedings.

3.3.3 Guilty pleas to either-way offences

Turning now to the defendant who wishes to plead guilty to an either-way of-fence (see **3.1.3** above), the procedure is different for a number of reasons. Even though the defendant wishes to plead guilty the court must agree to sentence the offender. They will effectively assess if their sentencing powers are sufficient in all the circumstances. Following the usual introductions, courtesies and con-firmation of identity, etc the charges are read aloud to the accused. The legal adviser will then explain to the defendant that very shortly he will be asked to indicate his plea to the court but before doing so he is warned that even if he indicates that he would plead guilty, the magistrates, having heard all of the circumstances relating to the offence including any previous convictions, may consider that their sentencing powers are insufficient. If so, they will send the defendant to the Crown Court for sentencing. Having confirmed that the defendant clearly understands the position they will again be invited to indicate their plea. If the plea is 'guilty' then the defendant is convicted of the allegations to which he has pleaded guilty.

After the plea, the prosecutor will provide the facts to the court and matters continue in the same way as for a summary only offence although the plea in mitigation on behalf of the offender tends to be more detailed. The court now has a decision to make. They could sentence the offender now. If they do the case is said to have been dealt with summarily. Alternatively, they may adjourn the case for the probation service to provide a report (see **3.2.6** for detail as to the contents and structure of these reports) detailing the background of the offender. Where this course is taken it will normally be made clear to the accused on what grounds the court are adjourning (see **3.3.3**). If the magistrates announce that they are adjourning on an 'all options' basis then this indicates that a custodial sentence will be considered. The final option is for the court to send the offender to the Crown Court for sentencing. This decision may be made with or without the probation service reports but indicates that the court does not consider that the maximum punishment that it can impose is sufficient (see **3.1.1**). Where matters are adjourned, the issue of bail will need to be addressed.

3.3.4 **Sentence or adjournment**

Having heard from the prosecution and the defence lawyers the court will then consider what sentence to pass. They may 'retire' to consider the circumstances in their private room. This is called an 'adjournment' which is how any break in proceedings is referred to. The magistrates may seek the advice of their legal adviser with regard to the options which are open to them. The legal adviser may be required to join them in the course of an adjournment to give this advice. Any hearing that is for the time being concluded is also said to be adjourned.

The magistrates may adjourn proceedings to a future date so that 'presentence' reports can be prepared by the probation service. If the probation officer is not already present they will be called into the court and instructed accordingly. If the magistrates decide to proceed in this way then the case is adjourned and the defendant is remanded (officers are advised to note here that cases and hearings are adjourned and defendants are remanded). It is at this stage that the magistrate is obliged to consider the question of the defendant's suitability or otherwise for bail. Powers of sentencing and bail are considered in **Chapter 4**.

3.3.5 **Not guilty pleas: preliminaries**

A not guilty plea by the defendant makes it quite clear, at this stage, that they do not accept the allegations that have been made against them. The defendant is at liberty to change his mind at any point before trial but the later this is left the smaller the discount on sentence (see **9.1.5**). The procedure for guilty pleas is as discussed above.

There are a number of ways in which not guilty pleas are dealt with by the magistrates' court but where this plea is maintained there will be a trial for guilt or otherwise to be determined. The options may be summarized as follows:

- Summary only offence (see **3.1.2**), trial heard by the magistrates immediately, if found guilty, defendant sentenced.
- Summary only offence, date set for hearing, case adjourned, defendant remanded (promise to return at the appropriate time and venue).
- Either-way offence (see **3.1.3**), magistrate accepts jurisdiction, hearing date set, case adjourned, defendant remanded.
- Either-way offence, defendant elects trial, case proceeds to committal to the Crown Court (see **4.5 1**).
- Either-way offence, magistrate refuses jurisdiction, case proceeds to committal for trial at the Crown Court.

3.3.6 **Mode of trial proceedings**

If the offence is an either-way offence, the process of 'plea before venue' will take place and 'mode of trial proceedings' will follow. The latter is the process where an assessment is made of where the trial should take place, in the Crown Court or in the magistrates' court. After the initial procedure of confirming identity of the defendant, their address, reading aloud the allegations and completing the plea before venue procedure the prosecutor will be invited to make representations (their opinion) to the court with regard to the suitability or otherwise for the case to be heard by the magistrates' court. Where the prosecutor considers the magistrates' court suitable he may express this in a number of ways including, 'It is the Crown's view (Madam/Sir) that this matter is suitable for summary trial as it relates to simple theft of low value without any aggravating features (eg violence or similar previous convictions).' The defence lawyer will then rise and will either agree with the prosecutor or put forward reasons (referred to as representations) to try and persuade the court to send the matter for Crown Court trial.

In deciding whether the case should be heard in the Crown Court or in the magistrates' court, the bench will consider all of the circumstances. They are assisted in this determination by Part V of the Consolidated Criminal Practice Direction Mode of trial Guidelines. These provide general and specific advice as to what the magistrates should consider in order to determine if they can accept jurisdiction and are considered along with other statutory guidance. Examples include that theft should be tried summarily but possession of a Class A drug should be committed for trial. Following deliberation the court either agrees that the case is suitable for the magistrates' court (referred to as accepting jurisdiction) or declines jurisdiction. If the court accepts jurisdiction and the defendant agrees, a future trial date will be fixed for the magistrates' court to hear the case. On the other hand, the defendant may refuse to let the magistrates' court hear his case. If so he is said to elect trial at the Crown Court and the case is sent (committed) there for trial. Where the court refuses jurisdiction the defendant has no say in the matter: his case will be heard by the Crown Court. Finally, issues of bail and public funding will need to be considered along with the fixing of a trial date. When fixing the date for any trial or further hearing the court will consider the availability of all witnesses and will rely upon an accurately completed MG10 (see **11.1.6**).

In many simple and straightforward cases the procedure, referred to as 'Mode of trial' is almost unnoticeable as it is very quickly and efficiently dealt with by experienced legal advisers and lawyers.

The defendant may elect trial at the Crown Court because he may consider that a jury may be more easily convinced by his evidence and acquitted. However, the risk is that the sentence will be more severe as sentencing powers in the Crown Court are greater. They are limited only by the maximum permitted by the offence. For example, the maximum penalty for theft is seven years and whilst this could be imposed by the Crown Court, it could not be imposed at the magistrates' court where their sentencing powers are capped (see **3.1.1**).

3.3.7 **Equivocal pleas**

Defendants may occasionally qualify their plea by saying something like 'I'm guilty but it was a misunderstanding' or indicate that they may be guilty as a matter of law but not guilty morally. Such ambiguity is effectively stating 'guilty but not really' and is referred to as an 'equivocal' plea. It is most commonly encountered where the defendant is not legally represented. It is so vague that the court are unable to accept it and it is deemed to be a 'not guilty' plea. It may be recorded as such or the case may be adjourned in order that the defendant may obtain legal advice for matters to be clarified.

3.3.8 **Early administrative hearings (EAHs)**

In an attempt to speed up the judicial system early administrative hearings (EAHs) were introduced to the criminal justice system. The main purpose of these hearings is to allow a defendant to obtain public funding (legal aid) and advice and to resolve matters in relation to bail. It is desirable that a defendant charged with serious or imprisonable matters should be represented before being invited to plead guilty or not guilty or to elect to have their case heard by the magistrates or at the Crown Court before a jury. These type of hearings invariably deal with the more serious or complex cases coming before the magistrates and certainly those which are expected to be contested by the defendant. It is most likely that only a very basic case file will have been compiled by the police at this stage because of the short time span between the charging of the defendant and their appearance at court—usually no more than seven days. Where the defendant pleads not guilty then the police will be required to provide a more detailed file (this process is referred to as 'upgrading', see **11.1.4**). Public funding and bail will also be considered.

After appearance at an early administrative hearing it is likely that a defendant will be remanded to a date when either a 'pre-trial review' (PTR) or a 'mode of trial' hearing will take place. If it is to be a 'pre-trial review' this means, simply, that the defendant will be remanded to a date when a magistrate will give binding directions relating to the conduct of their trial at the magistrates' court. The magistrate will pay particular attention to such matters as the timetable of proceedings, the attendance of the parties, the service and disclosure of documents (including summaries of any legal arguments relied on by the parties) if those documents have not already been served, and which witnesses are to be called to give evidence at the forthcoming trial.

3.3.9 Early first hearings

This court will deal with those defendants who are appearing for the first time to plead guilty to matters that are simple and straightforward so that the magistrates can, having heard the facts from the prosecutor, proceed to sentencing. A typical example would include a guilty plea to a drink driving offence. It is now unusual for such defendants to be represented here because they are not disputing the facts or contesting the matter. The magistrates will ask the defendant if they wish to explain their behaviour or inform the magistrates of any relevant circumstances. They will be asked what their financial circumstances are before the court announces their sentence. Most who attend this court are surprised at the speed matters are able to be efficiently dealt with. It would be unusual for a police officer to attend this court unless for observation purposes.

3.3.10 Time limits

Case management within the Crown and magistrates' courts are regulated by the Criminal Procedure Rules 2005 (CPR) and the Consolidated Criminal Practice Direction. The overriding objectives of the CPR include 'discouraging delay' (Rule 3.2(2)(f)). Having fixed a trial date, a number of issues are likely to be resolved at hearings referred to as a 'pre-trial review' (or hearing). At these hearings it is often agreed what the issues for trial are and how many witnesses are being called by each side. Extensions may be granted by the court but they will need to be persuaded that any extension of time is essential and not unfair.

The major consideration for the police officer is what type of case file must be submitted and when. Detailed and helpful guidance can be obtained from the 'Manual of Guidance for the Preparation, Processing and Submission of Files' (referred to by police officers as the 'Manual of Guidance'). The most recent version of this 'manual' (renamed the Prosecution Team Manual of Guidance) may be viewed at <http://police.homeoffice.gov.uk/news-and-publications/publication/operational-policing/prosecution-manual-section3> and contains examples of all of the relevant forms along with comprehensive guidance on their completion.

Magistrates' Court Procedure

First Appearance Summary Only (less serious offence)
- Guilty plea
- Not guilty plea → Trial → Guilty / Not guilty
- REPORTS? (not always necessary)
- Sentence

Early Administrative Hearing (more serious offence)
- S.51 Transfer Indictable Only → Crown Court
- Either-Way Offence
  - Not guilty → Magistrates accept jurisdiction → Trial → Not guilty / Guilty → Reports? → Sentence
  - Guilty → Magistrates do not accept jurisdiction → Sentence at Crown Court
  - Guilty → Magistrates accept jurisdiction → Reports? → Sentence

3.3.11 Advance disclosure of evidence to the accused

This area must not be confused with the disclosure of evidence to a suspect before they are interviewed by the police. The suspect is not entitled to have anything disclosed to them but a failure by the police to disclose any evidence (as opposed to everything) may well result in the suspect's lawyer advising their 'client' to remain silent until sufficient disclosure is made so that proper legal advice may be provided. Where a lawyer advises their client to remain silent this should not be viewed with suspicion or regarded only as a tactic to delay matters. The lawyer has a professional responsibility to their client and a failure to meet the standards required may result in disciplinary action being taken by the Law Society against the lawyer and/or a claim for negligence by their client.

Where the defendant has been charged with a summary only offence (see **3.1.2**), so-called advanced information is available for them at the court where they are appearing. This will consist of a folder or envelope of some kind in which has been placed sufficient documentation for the accused to know of the case against him, a basic human right, so that he may take legal advice. Typically it will contain a copy of the charge and bail forms from the police station where the defendant was charged, copies of witness statements, pocket (report) book notes made by the arresting officer, and a copy of any audio taped interview that was held with the defendant. This package is often referred to as 'AI' and surprisingly is not always collected by defendants.

Where the defendant has been charged with an either-way offence (see **3.1.3**) the material that must be disclosed to them before the plea before venue or mode of trial procedures are commenced is clearly prescribed under the Criminal Procedure Rules 2005, Part 21.3. In practice the prosecution will usually have served copies of the evidence they intend to rely upon before any such hearing in compliance with this Rule. Once again this is prepared for the date of hearing and left for collection by the defendant.

The law governing the disclosure of prosecution evidence relating to *unused* material, that is, material that does not form part of the prosecution case, is regulated by the Criminal Procedures and Investigations Act 1996. This applies to all cases where the defendant is charged with an indictable only or either-way offence and any summary offence in respect of which he intends to plead not guilty. Its provisions, however, differentiate between cases which proceed to the Crown Court and those which are heard at the magistrates' court.

4

Magistrates' Court: Sentencing and Bail

4.1 **Introduction**

The range of sentences available to the magistrates is considerable. Imprisonment and the fine are two of the most well-known sentences but community sentences, conditional discharges, bind overs and curfew orders are all common ways of dealing with offenders. The court will try to determine which sentence or combination of sentences is most appropriate for the particular offender and the particular offence. In reaching their decision the magistrates must give due consideration to the relevant statutory provisions including the Criminal Justice Act 2003, and the guidance provided by the Magistrates' Association Sentencing Guidelines (MASG), decisions from the Court of Appeal, and the recommendations from the Sentencing Guidelines Council.

The court will structure its decision by asking itself the following questions:

- First, is a discharge or fine appropriate? (Approximately 71% of offenders are fined.)
- Secondly, is the offender's behaviour 'serious enough' for a community sentence? (Approximately 13% of offenders receive a community sentence.)
- Thirdly, is the offender's behaviour 'so serious' that only custody is appropriate? (Approximately 7% of offenders are sent to prison but two thirds of them for less than 12 months.)

Section 142 of the Criminal Justice Act 2003 lists the purposes of sentencing and requires consideration of a number of factors including the punishment and rehabilitation of offenders and the reduction of crime.

The sentence must reflect the seriousness of the offence for which it is imposed, how it was committed, and the personal circumstances of the offender. The seriousness of the offence depends not only on the charge itself but also what the offender did, how they did it, and the consequences of their behaviour. Although this may sound complicated, it is really a matter of common sense. For example, a case of dangerous driving would normally be more serious than a case of careless driving. Equally, a case of dangerous driving where a defendant deliberately drove at a person and caused injury would normally be more serious than one where there was no intention to cause injury and no one was hurt. Further assistance can be obtained from s 143 to s 147 of the Criminal Justice Act 2003.

4.1.1 **Magistrates' Association Sentencing Guidelines**

To assist them in their deliberations magistrates make use of the 'Magistrates' Association Sentencing Guidelines' (MASG) reproduced within Stone's Justices Manual. These Guidelines are not directions (but s 172 of the Criminal Justice Act 2003 requires every court to consider them) and cover the offences which the magistrate is most likely to encounter. They provide a structure by which magistrates can establish the seriousness of an offence, the most appropriate way of dealing with it, and the starting point (referred to as the 'entry point') for the offence. The format is as follows:

Consider the seriousness of the offence

The magistrate must first consider the question of seriousness with reference to the effect upon any victim caused by the behaviour of the offender. The court will also take account of the offender's intentions at the time they committed the offence and are likely to view an intention to commit it more seriously than where the offender has committed the offence recklessly. Where the offender has assaulted the victim causing them actual bodily harm (an example would be substantial bruising), their behaviour is likely to be considered to be more serious where the injury was caused by a frenzied and sustained attack than where it was caused by a single blow. Similarly, injury caused by a weapon would normally be regarded as more serious than injury caused by a fist. Features that make the offence more serious are said to be 'aggravating factors [indicated by a + sign in the MASG]' and those that make it less so are referred to as 'mitigating factors [indicated by a − sign in the MASG]'. These factors will help to persuade the court that they can or need to move away from the so-called 'entry point' and impose a lesser or more severe sentence.

Consider aggravating and mitigating factors

Examples of aggravating and mitigating factors are to be found in the Sentencing Guidelines but these short lists are not exhaustive. In relation to theft—the entry point for which is a community sentence (penalty)—aggravating factors may include the items stolen having a high value and/or evidence that the theft was pre-planned. The Guidelines, however, are not a substitute for the judgement of the court.

Without doubt, an aggravating factor would include the fact that the offence had been motivated by racism, sexism or prejudice on the grounds of religion, sexual orientation or disability. This is confirmed by ss 145 and 146 of the Criminal Justice Act 2003. Additionally, such racial or religious motivation has been further recognized by the creation of aggravated forms of some offences, for example, assault which may be charged as racially aggravated assault under s 29 of the Crime and Disorder Act 1998.

Where the offence was committed whilst the defendant was already on bail for another offence the court must treat that as an aggravating factor by virtue of s 143 of the Criminal Justice Act 2003. Previous convictions will usually constitute an aggravating factor (s 143 of the Criminal Justice Act 2003) along with any failure to respond to previous sentences.

Take a preliminary view of seriousness, then consider offender mitigation

When an assessment of the seriousness of the offence has been made the court must then consider mitigating factors. In relation to an offence of theft the MASG provides the following two examples, 'impulsive action' and 'low value' of the property stolen. If the court accepts the offender's mitigation then this must lead to some downward revision of the initial assessment of the seriousness of the offender's behaviour.

It may be that the court considers that an immediate custodial sentence remains the only option despite the strength of the pleas made on behalf of the offender. The effect of the plea may still influence the length of sentence passed even if it has not been sufficient to alter the type of sentence to be passed. A discount may also be applied to reduce the length or requirements of the sentence if the offender pleaded guilty. The earlier such a plea is made (entered) the greater the discount that can be expected. Section 144 of the Criminal Justice Act 2003 requires the court to consider not just when such a plea was entered but also the circumstances in which it was entered. The discount applied to a sentence is not the same as mitigation. Mitigation affects the type of sentence whereas discount applies to quantum.

Further guidance in this regard may be obtained from the Sentencing Guidelines Council from their publication, 'Reduction in Sentence for a Guilty Plea'. An offender who pleads guilty can expect a discount assessed on a sliding scale ranging from a maximum of one third reducing to one tenth.

Consider the sentence options

Despite any mitigation put forward on behalf of the offender and following deliberation by the magistrates, they may still consider that it is necessary for a detailed report, a Pre-sentence Report (PSR—this may also be referred to as a 'Magistrates' Court Report to reflect the new structure for these reports introduced in 2004/5) to be prepared by the probation service to enable the most appropriate sentence to be imposed (see **3.2.6** for further explanation of the role of the probation officer). It is usual for the report to take three weeks to be prepared. The court will then adjourn and the offender will usually be granted conditional bail on the basis that he attends any appointments arranged by the probation service for the purpose of compiling the report. Where the court is not considering a custodial sentence, it may request a specific-sentence report (commonly referred to as a 'stand-down' report because the offender stands down from the dock whilst it is prepared) which is a short and less detailed form of a PSR and usually requires an adjournment of a couple of hours.

The grounds for the adjournment are of particular significance and indicate the type of sentence the court is contemplating following any adjournment. If the 'Chair' of the bench announces that they are adjourning on a 'serious enough' basis this indicates that they are contemplating a community sentence whereas if they adjourn on a 'so serious' basis this indicates that they are considering a custodial penalty. Many benches will adjourn on an 'all options' basis which indicates that they are not ruling out any punishment available to them.

Eventually the offender will return and where a report has been ordered it will be considered by the court before passing sentence. Having read any reports, the court will give the offender or their lawyer an opportunity to address them as to the facts and circumstances concerning the offence and their personal circumstances including home-life, education and responsibilities. This is called making a plea in mitigation. This is a skilful process to try and secure the most lenient sentence for the offender by proposing a sentence that is appropriate both in type and duration taking account of all of the information provided within the PSR. During the speech the aspects of the offence that make it less serious will be emphasized and although there should not be an attempt to justify the behaviour of the offender, there may be reference to life circumstances such as bereavement, divorce or redundancy if it is suggested these have contributed to the commission of the offence. Having listened to the mitigation the magistrates may rise (technically adjourn) and retire to their private room to decide upon sentence.

Upon return the 'Chair' will announce the sentence in open court dealing with each offence, usually chronologically. When sentencing an offender the court is obliged to provide reasons for the sentence they have imposed in ordinary language, its effect and requirements, and the possible effect of a failure to comply (s 174 of the Criminal Justice Act 2003). Magistrates at different courts may use different forms of words when announcing sentence. Both prosecution and defence lawyers will make a careful note as to sentence especially where the terms 'concurrent' and 'consecutively' are used. The former means 'at the same time' whereas the latter means subsequent to any earlier penalty. Where the offender pleaded guilty this should be taken into account by the court when imposing their sentence and may result in a reduction of up to a third from the original sentence (see further **9.1.5**). Periods of mandatory disqualification and driving licence endorsement penalty points cannot be reduced for a guilty plea.

4.1.2 Compensation

Magistrates have a duty at this stage to consider the award of compensation and must give reasons if it is not awarded.

4.2 Sentencing Options

The range of sentencing options and their combinations open to the courts are vast (especially for the young offender in the Youth Court—see **Chapter six**). The most common of these are set out below.

4.2.1 **Imprisonment (adult): consecutive, concurrent or suspended**

This sentence is used only when there is no alternative, where matters are judged 'so serious' that only custody is appropriate (s 152(2) of the Criminal Justice Act 2003). It is confined to offenders over the age of 21 years. Those under 21 but aged 10 or over can receive a 'custodial sentence' but they will not serve it within an adult prison unless it includes a young offenders' facility (see below at **4.2.5**). The maximum aggregate term of imprisonment that can currently be imposed at the magistrates' court is 12 months (see below and also at **3.1.1**).

If the court deals with a defendant for two or more 'either-way' and similar or related offences then they may sentence that person to 12 months' imprisonment that is, two six-month sentences which follow one after the other. When sentences are passed in this way they are said to be 'consecutive'. If two or more sentences are passed which will be served at the same time then the sentences are said to be 'concurrent'.

Currently, in some pilot areas, an alternative to full-time custody is available, referred to as 'intermittent custody' (s 183 of the Criminal Justice Act 2003). In essence this enables the offender to serve their imprisonment at a time that permits them to keep their employment, complete an ongoing course of study, and/or care for their dependants. This alternative is intended for those offenders who pose a low risk to the public during their release period and who are sentenced to a term of imprisonment for less than 12 months.

The Criminal Justice Act 2003 will, in due course, replace all custodial sentences of less than 12 months with a new order, 'Custody Plus'. This will impose a period of imprisonment followed by supervised release during which period the offender will be required to comply with certain requirements, such as unpaid work, as listed within the Act.

A sentence of imprisonment of between 28 and 51 weeks (or 65 weeks for consecutively sentenced offences) may be 'suspended' for a period from between six months and two years. If suspended by the passing of a suspended sentence order it will not take effect unless the offender re-offends (whether imprisonable or not) during a defined period of time (the operational period) or fails to comply with a requirement during the supervision period of the sentence. In order to impose a suspended sentence of imprisonment, the court must be of the opinion that the threshold for imposing a custodial sentence has been met ('so serious' that there is no suitable alternative) but have decided not to activate the sentence immediately. Exceptional circumstances are no longer required before a custodial sentence may be suspended.

4.2.2 **Detention for young offenders**

Offenders aged between 12 and 17 will not be sent to an adult prison but may be subject to a Detention and Training Order (DTO) under s 100 of the Powers of Criminal Court (Sentencing) Act 2000 (PCC(S)A). Once again, before this form of sentence is imposed, the circumstances of the offending must meet the 'so serious' test (see above at **4.2.1**). If the offender is under the age of 15, they must be classified as a persistent young offender before a DTO may be imposed. The detention element of any DTO will be spent in appropriate and secure accommodation. This is completed before the training element of the order is commenced after the offender is released back into the community.

4.2.3 **Absolute discharge**

This is used when a person is found 'technically' guilty of an offence but the court feels that they should not be punished. An example could include where the offender has exceeded the speed limit but proves that through no fault of his own the vehicle's speedometer was providing an inaccurate reading.

4.2.4 **Conditional discharge**

This effectively places an offender on trust to be of good behaviour for the duration of the order. That is to say no punishment will be imposed for a specified period (up to a maximum of three years) unless the defendant commits a further offence. If the offender does commit another offence, they can be sentenced for the original and the new offence. This type of sentence is often referred to as a 'con dis' or 'CD'.

4.2.5 **Fines**

This is an order that the offender shall pay a sum of money as a financial penalty. It is the most commonly used penalty in the courts. Fines are suitable in cases which are not serious enough to merit a community or custodial sentence. The aim of the fining system is that its impact will be proportionate to the ability of the offender to pay it and the court is obliged therefore to enquire into the financial means of the offender before imposing the fine. Where the court is not satisfied with the means information they have received they may adjourn the case and make an order under s 162 of the Criminal Justice Act 2003 that a statement of means be provided. The maximum amount for a fine is capped at what are referred to as 'levels' and there are currently five of these:

- level 1, capped at £200
- level 2, capped at £500
- level 3, capped at £1,000
- level 4, capped at £2,500
- level 5, capped at £5,000

Technically, a fine is payable in full on the day of its imposition. Most courts are now able to accept payment by credit card. However, it is normal for the court to allow an offender to pay by instalments. To this end the offender or their legal representative may be asked to make the court 'an offer' as to how those instalments should be paid. The maximum fine that can be imposed by the magistrates' court, as we have seen, is £5,000 for each offence unless the offence specifies a maximum below this amount. Fines in the Crown Court are unlimited except by the offence maximum. A significant number of fines imposed by courts are never paid and courts are now very pro-active in their recovery of outstanding fines and costs and will issue a warrant for the arrest of any offender in default. These are normally referred to as non-payment of fines warrants.

4.2.6 Community sentences ('orders')

These are intended to provide an effective and proportionate sentence for an offender aged 16 or over whose offending is 'serious enough' (s 148 of the Criminal Justice Act 2003) that it requires more than a financial penalty but is not 'so serious' as to merit a custodial sentence. A community sentence has three main elements: restriction of liberty, reparation, and the reform of the offender. This type of sentence is tailor made to meet the precise circumstances of the offender and their offending and is currently regulated (for offenders aged 18 and over) by s 177 of the Criminal Justice Act 2003. Each order comprises specific 'requirements.' The most common of these is the requirement to perform unpaid work but the court may select one or more from a list of 12 'requirements' listed at s 177(1) (a) to (l) of the Act. In the main, these requirements reflect types of community orders which have been available for some time including curfews, supervision requirements (the requirement to attend appointments at such time and place as may be determined by the probation service) and alcohol or drug rehabilitation requirements (drug treatment and testing orders). There is also provision to make a prohibited activity requirement which forbids an offender from doing certain things. The activities might include attending football matches, contacting a certain person, or carrying a firearm.

Before imposing a community sentence, the sentencing court must normally obtain a pre-sentence or specific sentence report unless it considers it 'unnecessary' to do so. In practice, the court will nearly always obtain such a report. In pronouncing sentence the court should emphasize the need for the offender's co-operation and the consequences of breaching or failing to comply with the requirements of the order.

4.2.7 Penalties for breach of community sentence

Where the offender fails to comply with any of the 'requirements' of a community sentence order without reasonable excuse, they are said to be in breach of the order. In the first instance, they will be warned by the probation service that this is unacceptable. If they fail to comply for a second time within the next 12 months, this will result in their being summoned to re-appear before the court. At this stage the court has a number of options open to them including revocation of the order and re-sentencing for the original offence, and amending the terms of the order to make it more onerous. In many cases, the offender is in danger of being sent to prison. The court will take into account how much of the order has been completed and how quickly the breach occurred. It goes without saying that repeated and deliberate breaches will be viewed most seriously by the court. Further assistance can be gained from consulting Sch 8, paras 5 to 9 of the Criminal Justice Act 2003.

4.2.8 Anti social behaviour orders (ASBOs) and acceptable behaviour contracts (ABCs)

These are creations of the Crime and Disorder Act 1998 and are designed to prevent behaviour that causes or is likely to cause harassment, alarm or distress to others who are not resident with the offender. They may be effective against persistent excessive noise, drunken behaviour and graffiti. The ASBO is a civil and not a criminal order with a minimum duration of two years but may be imposed by the magistrates' court and applied for by the police. They will be considered further in **Chapter Seven**. Breach of an ASBO is a criminal offence, and under s 24 of PACE will carry a power to arrest where a constable considers the arrest is necessary as prescribed under ss 24(4) and 24(5) of PACE (as amended). The anti-social behaviour contract (ABC) is an informal and voluntary measure to stop anti-social behaviour and is often taken as an initial step before a full ASBO is considered. As it is an informal measure there is no penalty for breach of an ABC although this will provide useful evidence if it becomes necessary to apply for an ASBO.

4.2.9 Deferred sentence

The court may decide, with the consent of the defendant, to postpone sentencing in order to assess the defendant's behaviour over a specified period of time. This may be particularly relevant where the offender has received a job offer or has recently become a parent. Both events may alter the offender's behaviour because of the increased responsibility. Additionally, employment may mean that the offender can pay for the damage he caused. A sentence can only be 'deferred' for six months and usually only one deferment is possible. If the offender's conduct is satisfactory during the period of deferral (that is, they do not re-offend) then the court will take a more lenient approach when the offender returns. Where the offender re-offends during the deferral period then this will not help his cause, especially as there will now be two offences for sentencing!

4.2.10 **The 'bind over'**

The 'bind over' requires a person charged with a criminal offence to enter into an agreement, or recognizance, with the court to be of 'good behaviour'. This involves the forfeiture of a sum of money should the defendant breach his 'bind over' by offending during the 'bind over' period. No further penalty can be imposed. A 'bind over' is for a specific period of time, usually 12 months, and is often an appropriate penalty in cases of 'breach of the peace' or offences involving disorderly or aggressive behaviour in public or towards a specific person. The main difference between this and a conditional discharge is that a bind-over is not a sentence in its own right and so the subject of it is not convicted of a criminal offence. It is quite often used to prevent further disputes between neighbours or partners.

4.3 **Ancillary Orders**

These orders are not penalties in their own right but are ancillary, or additional, to the sentences described above. Examples are given below.

4.3.1 **Football banning orders**

These are granted following application by the police via the Football (Disorder) Act 2000. As implied by the title of the Act, they are only concerned with football matches and not sporting events in general. Their purpose is to prevent violent disorder by prohibiting a person from attending specified domestic and international football matches. The penalty for failing to comply with such an order is a term of imprisonment capped at six months and or a fine capped at level 5 (£5,000, see **4.2.9**).

4.3.2 **Compensation**

Compensation is an amount of money which an offender is ordered to pay to a victim who has suffered as a consequence of the offender's behaviour. The magistrates are under a duty to consider compensation in every case involving death, personal injury, loss or damage whether or not an application has been made.

If an offender is to be fined then the order of priorities is compensation, fine and then prosecution costs. Compensating the victim is viewed as being more important than remunerating the state. If an offender is to be imprisoned then a compensation order is unlikely (for obvious reasons the offender may lose their job). If a community sentence is to be imposed, then the magistrate should consider carefully the effect on the offender of making a compensation order. The inclusion of a compensation claim form with case papers submitted to the CPS should always be considered by the police officer who prepares the file (Form MG19—see **Chapter 11**).

4.3.3 **Forfeiture, destruction and restitution**

Where a person is convicted of an offence they may be deprived of their rights of ownership in any item of property which the offender intended to use for the commission of an offence. This is referred to as the forfeiture of property. If the item is 'forfeited' in this way then the court may order it to be destroyed. In cases involving drugs and weapons this is nearly always the outcome. Additionally, the court, in theft cases, may order that property stolen should be returned to its rightful owner. This is known as 'restitution'.

4.4 **Bail at the Magistrates' Court**

4.4.1 **General**

A magistrates' court may remand a person on conditional or unconditional bail (that is, bail with or without conditions) or, providing there is a reason to refuse bail, remand them into custody. Obviously, the former enables a defendant to retain their liberty whilst the latter does not. Where bail is granted requiring the defendant to return to the court at a future date, this amounts to a promise by the defendant to surrender to the custody of the court when and where directed.

The legislation governing the court's powers to grant or refuse bail is to be found in the Bail Act 1976 (as amended) although careful note must also be taken of the provisions of Article 5 of the European Convention of Human Rights (right to liberty). Section 4(1) of the Act creates a presumption that a defendant will be granted bail unless there is good reason to justify continued detention. Furthermore, conditional bail should be imposed instead of detention where a bail condition could adequately address the risk that would otherwise justify detention.

There are 'exceptions' to this presumption in favour of bail where a defendant who has previously been convicted or charged with murder, rape, attempted murder, attempted rape or manslaughter is again before the court charged with any one of the above offences (the full list can be found in s 25(2) of the Criminal Justice and Public Order Act 1994, in subsections a–m). This does not mean that the defendant must be charged with exactly the same offence again, any combination is capable of displacing the presumption in favour of bail. In this situation, the court may not grant bail to a defendant unless it is satisfied that there are exceptional circumstances which justify it.

4.4.2 **Reasons for the refusal of bail**

Section 2(1) of the Bail Act permits the presumption to the right to bail where the defendant is charged with an imprisonable offence to be displaced where the court is satisfied that there are substantial grounds for believing that one or more of the following criteria apply (referred to as 'statutory objections to bail'):

(1) the defendant will fail to surrender to custody OR

(2) will commit an offence whilst on bail OR

(3) will interfere with witnesses or otherwise obstruct the course of justice.

If bail is to be refused, the magistrates must have reached the view that there are 'substantial grounds' for believing that one or more of the circumstances described above is likely to occur. This is a higher threshold than mere possibility and should be supported by evidence. However, the strict rules of evidence that apply at a trial do not apply to the evidence provided at a contested bail application. In the magistrates' court it falls to the prosecutor to persuade the court that bail should not be granted, based upon the file prepared by the police. The decision to make the application to the court belongs to the prosecutor and they are entitled to disagree with the views of the police.

If the magistrates agree that there are 'substantial grounds' for believing that one or more of the circumstances described above is likely to occur, then the Bail Act states only that they 'need not', not 'must not', grant bail. In practice, where the court are so satisfied they are unlikely to grant bail unless they can be assured that the imposition of conditions will deal with their remaining concerns.

There are further circumstances where a defendant need not be granted bail and these include where:

(1) custody is necessary for his own protection or 'welfare' in the case of a child or young person;

(2) the defendant is already serving a term of imprisonment;

(3) there is insufficient information to make the assessment;

(4) the defendant has been arrested for breaking his existing bail conditions or for absconding (that is, he failed to surrender to court as earlier promised when released on bail);

(5) detention is necessary for the completion of a report required by the court such as a pre-sentence report or a medical report and there is reason to think that the defendant would not co-operate with the preparation of the report otherwise.

4.4.3 **The decision to refuse bail**

The decision to refuse bail and remand the defendant into custody is never taken lightly by any court. It must be remembered that the defendant is yet to be convicted of the offence with which they have been charged. They remain innocent until proven guilty in accordance with Article 6(2) of the European

Convention on Human Rights 1950. Where they are subsequently acquitted, there is generally no right to compensation for the time spent on remand.

There are many reasons why the court may refuse bail but in reaching their decision they must consider, at least, the factors prescribed by the Bail Act 1976 at para 9, Sch 1. These are as follows:

- The nature and seriousness of the offence and the probable method of dealing with the offender for it. Where the offence is serious the accused may be tempted to abscond rather than run the risk of a severe sentence.
- The accused's antecedents, character and associations. If he is of good character, this may indicate he is more likely to obey the order of a court. On the other hand, the accused's previous record may aggravate the likely sentence if, for example, a conviction would place him in breach of a court order. If the accused has previously committed offences whilst on bail, this will not be looked on favourably by the court.
- The accused's community ties. If these are substantial—for example, by marriage or employment—they may make it less likely the accused will abscond.
- The accused's previous record of surrendering to the court. If he has never absconded before why should he now?
- The strength of the evidence against the defendant. The stronger the evidence, the more likely a conviction and the greater the motive not to surrender to the court. On the other hand, if the evidence appears weak there may be a risk of a considerable period in custody before an acquittal.

It should be noted that the first of these grounds, 'nature and seriousness of the offence' cannot be forwarded in isolation to support any of the statutory objections but must be supported by other sustainable grounds. It is not sufficient to impress upon the magistrates that the offence with which the defendant is charged carries a lengthy term of imprisonment on conviction.

Defendants have a right of appeal to the Crown Court against any decision to refuse bail provided that the magistrates have heard full argument. The prosecution, conversely, may appeal to the Crown Court against a magistrate's decision to grant bail to a defendant charged with an imprisonable offence. An appeal against the grant or refusal to grant bail must be heard swiftly, as the defendant will remain in custody until the appeal is heard. It is incumbent upon the CPS to anticipate such an eventuality and to be ready for it.

Police officers may not be aware that a defendant can only make a certain number of applications (two in the magistrates' court) for bail unless there has been a change in circumstances. In many serious cases, particularly when the defendant has been charged and held overnight in custody, their solicitor may well not have had the time to either take full instructions from their client or to make the necessary preparations for an application to succeed. In these circumstances the application may be delayed until the next appearance. However, if the defendant insists that the application is made regardless of its likely chances of success then the advocate has no choice but to make it.

There are a great many factors which influence the outcome of a bail application and a defence solicitor may need to obtain details of securities, sureties, probation reports, availability of bail hostel rooms or other suitable accommodation. They may wish to speak to the CPS about the suitability of certain proposed conditions such as curfews or reporting at police stations. If this happens then the enquiry ought to be made through the CPS but is frequently made to an officer if one is present (see **4.4.4** and **4.4.5** below which deal with conditional bail, sureties and securities).

Police officers are not called to object to bail as frequently as they once were but it is not unusual for the CPS to ask for an officer to be present at the remand hearing for a defendant charged with a more serious offence. Magistrates may ask an officer with intimate knowledge of the case against the defendant to go into the witness box. An officer so required will swear an oath or attest which is different to that which they use when giving evidence during a trial. It will take the following form:

> 'I swear by almighty god that I will answer truthfully any questions which the court may ask of me.'

Questions may then be put by the magistrate, the prosecutor or the defendant or their legal representative in examination of the defendant's suitability for bail. Further detail of the grounds supporting the objection will be requested. It is of the utmost importance that an officer put in this position fully understands the statutory objections to bail (see **4.4.1** above). The form MG7 which must be prepared as part of a remand court file gives guidance as to these statutory objections (see **11.1.3**).

4.4.4 **Conditional bail**

Section 3 of the Bail Act 1976 (as amended) permits the court to attach conditions to the bail of the defendant in order to secure his surrender to custody, or to prevent the offender committing offences whilst on bail, or to prevent the interference with witnesses or obstruction of justice. (These are the same as the statutory objections to bail that may allow the court to refuse bail.) Where conditions are attached bail is said to be 'conditional'. This means that, as well as being under a duty to surrender to the court, they must also abide by those conditions during their remand while the case is adjourned.

Conditions must only be imposed to address the concerns the court has regarding the granting of bail. There is an infinite variety of conditions but amongst the most common are a requirement not to contact, directly or indirectly, named prosecution witnesses or a requirement that the accused report to their local police station at a time and frequency that persuades the court that they are unlikely to abscond. Police officers present in court are commonly asked to assist with some of the practicalities that arise, for example, the opening times of police stations where it is proposed for the defendant to report.

Any conditions must be necessary and proportionate. An example of an unsatisfactory condition would be that a shop-lifter must not enter any food shops. This should be replaced with a condition not to enter a specific store or branch. Remember, the more vague the condition the more unlikely the court is to agree to it as it may become too difficult for the defendant to comply with, or the police to enforce.

There is no limit on either the number or the nature of the conditions that may be attached to a person's bail providing that they are both relevant and necessary. Here are further examples of the most common bail conditions:

- residence at a named address
- curfew between specified hours
- not to enter licensed premises
- not to travel to or go within a certain distance of a specific place or locality.

4.4.5 Sureties and securities

Another commonly used condition of bail is the provision of a 'surety'. A surety is a person who undertakes (promises) to ensure that the defendant surrenders to the court as required on pain of forfeiting a specified sum of money. The identity of the surety is proposed by the defendant and is often a family member or friend. The court sets the sum. If a surety is proposed it is the duty of the police to check that person's suitability and also their ability to meet the sum required should it be forfeited. The police should examine the character, antecedents and solvency of the potential surety. If an officer is at court and is so instructed by the magistrates or CPS then it is their and no other person's responsibility to check the surety. Where the court is re-assured that the surety is suitable, that is, they have the financial resources, are of a suitable character by their attendance at court and replies to the magistrates' questions they may be persuaded to grant bail.

Distinct from a surety is the provision of a 'security'. This involves the depositing of money or something of equivalent value by or on behalf of the defendant with the court as a guarantee that the defendant will surrender to the court as directed or forfeit the security if they fail to do so.

4.4.6 Failure to surrender to the court or comply with bail conditions

Where a defendant is released by the court on conditional bail and does not comply with any of the conditions imposed or fails to appear then they are liable to be arrested and brought back to court. The court may then consider remanding that person into custody. Section 7 of the Bail Act 1976 provides police officers with a power of arrest for breach of bail conditions and failure to appear. The same section also gives the magistrate the power to issue an arrest warrant if a defendant or offender fails to appear. The issue of a warrant in such circumstances is discretionary as is the decision to attach a power of arrest to it. Magistrates will allow a reasonable amount of time for a defendant to appear before the issue of a warrant. If the warrant is issued the court will make it clear that it is 'backed for bail' or 'not backed for bail'. The former means that if the defendant is arrested under the warrant they will be charged and bailed by the police to appear at court on a future date. The latter means that they will be charged and kept in custody to appear at the next available sitting of the court.

The court is likely to accept a timely and reasonable explanation for a defendant's absence, such as a letter from a doctor or hospital. However, if there is no explanation a 's 7' warrant is issued and addressed to 'all constables'. The warrant should first be registered with the court office and is not normally taken directly from the court to the police station. As police are rarely present at issue, there will be local procedures in place to ensure that it is eventually lodged at a police station. Such procedures differ from one force area to the other. The issue of whether a non-appearance warrant is 'circulated' on the police national computer (PNC) is a matter of local service policy.

If a defendant's circumstances change then they may apply to the magistrate at the next hearing to have their conditions varied or changed completely. Twenty-four hours' notice of the application will usually be given to the court to enable the CPS to prepare a response to the application. This may include consultation with the police or the officer in the case.

4.5 **Committal and Transfer Proceedings to the Crown Court**

4.5.1 **Committal or transfer to the crown court**

Cases are transferred or sent to the Crown Court for the following reasons:

- the defendant is charged with an 'either-way' offence and elects trial at the Crown Court or the magistrates refuse jurisdiction
- the defendant is charged with an 'indictable only' offence

Committal proceedings (*only* for those offences that are being transferred to the Crown Court) are held at the magistrates' court before magistrates (referred to as examining justices when performing this role) so that they may determine whether there is a case for the defendant to answer, (also referred to as a 'prima facie' case). This is when the elements of the offence are present and are capable of proof on the basis of the evidence first presented by the prosecution. This determination may be made in one of two ways, that is with or without consideration of the evidence, as discussed below.

4.5.2 **Committal proceedings, old and new**

There are two routes for committals and these are often referred to as the 'old style' and the 'new style' committals under s 6(1) and (2) of the Magistrates Court Act 1980, respectively. Part 10, paras 10.2–10.3 of the Criminal Procedure Rules 2005 should also be consulted. The selection is tactical and the most obvious difference between them is that a '6(1)' committal is said to be contested. The magistrates hear and examine the evidence against the defendant and the defence advocate may ask the court (referred to as making a submission) to rule that there is not a prima facie case to answer. With a '6(2)' committal the court does not hear the evidence and the defence advocate may not, at this stage, make any submission that there is no case to answer.

For the '6(1)' committal the magistrates act as a filter as they may refuse to send the case to the Crown Court if they are not satisfied that on the evidence presented by the prosecution, there is a case for the defendant to answer. It must be remembered that simply because the magistrates commit (send) the case to the Crown Court for trial, they are not declaring that the defendant is guilty as charged.

Where the magistrates decide that there is no case to answer, then the defendant must be discharged forthwith unless they are in custody for other matters. A discharge in these circumstances is not the same as an acquittal and proceedings can be brought against the accused (re-instated) at a later date usually by way of fresh committal proceedings.

The alternative to this route is currently a so-called '6(2)' committal (without hearing the evidence). Where this route is chosen it is accepted by both the prosecution and the defence that there is a prima facie case to be transferred to the Crown Court and the magistrates' role is entirely procedural. In this situation they may make orders to ensure that the correct documents are served. There are tactical reasons for selecting either the '6(1)' or the '6(2)' routes. In such matters a plea is not taken. The magistrate will still have the power to grant or refuse bail in such cases and can make an order with regard to public funding (formerly called Legal Aid).

The reader should note that once Sch 3 of the Criminal Justice Act 2003 comes into force, 'committal proceedings' will be abolished, requiring either-way offences that are to proceed in the Crown Court to be sent there directly thereby abolishing transfer committal proceedings. Although transfer committal proceedings are not trials, usually the defendant must be present and will be represented in the normal way.

4.5.3 **Sending 'indictable only' offences to the Crown Court**

The manner with which 'indictable only' offences are sent to the Crown Court is currently regulated by s 51 of the Crime and Disorder Act 1998:

51.—(1)   Where an adult appears or is brought before a magistrates' court ['the court'] charged with an offence triable only on indictment ['the indictable only offence'], the court shall send him forthwith to the Crown Court for trial

There is no consideration by the court as to whether there is a 'prima facie' case and the matter is transferred immediately to the Crown Court. The role of the court at the first appearance is confined to dealing with matters relating to public funding and bail.

If the defendant is in custody then their next appearance at the Crown Court will be within eight calendar days. If the defendant is on bail it must be within 28 days.

4.5.4 Transfer of specific cases of serious or complex fraud

For particularly serious or complex fraud cases the magistrates' court can be given a 'notice of transfer' certifying that the case should be transferred immediately to the Crown Court. The bodies giving such notice are those charged with the investigation of serious fraud and include the Director of Public Prosecutions, the Serious Fraud Office, the Inland Revenue and Customs and Excise.

4.5.5 Transfer of specific cases of sexual offences and offences of cruelty and violence involving children

The Director of Public Prosecutions can give notice of transfer of any such cases in the manner described above in order to protect the well-being and welfare of any child witnesses involved in the case.

The Youth Court

5.1 **Composition and Jurisdiction**

5.1.1 **The youth court: general**

The principle which underpins the youth justice system and which has operated throughout the last 70 years is one which places the welfare of the young person as a primary consideration. The manner in which proceedings are conducted in the youth court reflects this. The imposition of a custodial sentence is the very last resort and officers involved in cases against young offenders should not expect the sentence to reflect that which might have been imposed on an adult.

While a number of legal terms are used to identify defendants aged between 10 and 17, including 'child' and 'young person', all those under the age of 18 who have committed a crime may be described as young offenders. Young offenders, unless there is a special feature of their case, will be dealt with in the youth court. Formerly known as the juvenile court, the youth court is part of the magistrates' court, but in contrast to most other courts, it is not open to the general public. It is said to be closed. If victims wish to attend hearings, they require the consent (referred to as 'leave') of the court.

The principle of 'youth justice' is set out in s 37(1) of the Crime and Disorder Act 1998, which states, 'It shall be the principal aim of the youth justice system to prevent offending by children and young persons'. Section 38 of this Act places a duty on local authorities, probation services and police to work together to achieve this end and s 39 requires local authorities to form 'youth offending teams' which must include, social workers, probation officers, police officers, and members of the health and education authorities.

The bench at a youth court must include both male and female magistrates and has a minimum requirement of three. By virtue of s 48 of the Crime and Disorder Act 1998 a district judge (magistrates' court) may sit alone. Whilst this court is 'closed' those allowed to be present, in addition to the magistrates and other officers of the court, include the defendant and their legal representative, witnesses, police officers involved in the case, parents or guardians and any other person authorized by the court. A police officer who is not giving evidence but wishes to sit in and observe the court should ask the prosecutor who will seek the agreement of the court, the defence advocate and defendant. The press are admitted to the youth court but must not publish the name or photograph of any young person involved in proceedings unless authorized by the court. The press are not allowed to use the words 'conviction' and 'sentence' in their reporting of matters involving children and young persons.

The court can make an order which guarantees the anonymity of any child or young person involved in any court proceedings by virtue of s 39 of the Children and Young Persons Act 1933. This section prohibits the publication of any details that reveal the name and address or school of such children and is widely drawn to include any particulars that are intended to identify the individual. Obviously, this would include a picture of the child.

5.1.2 **Procedure**

The youth court procedures are noticeably different to the adult court. The atmosphere is characterized by an air of informality. The young defendant or offender is referred to in all proceedings by their first name.

There is no mode of trial procedure (see above at **3.3.4**) so a young offender or defendant cannot elect to have his matter dealt with at the Crown Court. However, the youth court can decline to deal with a number of very serious offences referred to as 'grave crimes' and send the matter to the Crown Court. Homicide cases (murder and manslaughter) and certain firearms offences where minimum sentences apply must be sent for trial in the Crown Court. Such matters will be transferred to the Crown Court currently by the procedure under s 6(1) or (2) of the Magistrates Court Act 1980 (MCA).

Having accepted jurisdiction for the case the charge will be read and explained in simple language to the defendant who will then be asked if he pleads guilty or not guilty. The procedures followed in a trial are, in principle, the same as those followed in the adult court. Special measures are available in the youth court so evidence may be given by television link and pre-recorded video.

Young persons convicted of criminal offences may be sentenced similarly to adult offenders for example, fine and absolute or conditional discharge. It is not just the type of offence that influences the sentence available but also the age of the offender.

5.1.3 **The Crime and Disorder Act 1998**

The 1998 Act introduced a raft of new measures that apply to young persons convicted of criminal offences. The most important options relate to parenting orders, drug treatment and testing orders, reparation orders, action plan orders and detention and training orders. Further details can be obtained from the Powers of the Criminal Courts (Sentencing) Act 2000 (PCC(S)A).

5.1.4 **Custodial sentence**

Where the young person has committed a very serious crime for which an adult offender could receive at least 14 years' imprisonment by the Crown Court then the offender may be sent to serve a sentence up to the statutory maximum at a prison where this incorporates a 'young offenders' facility.

5.1.5 **Detention and training orders (DTO)**

If the offence with which the young offender (under 18) is convicted would be punishable with imprisonment in the adult court, then the offender may be made the subject of a detention and training order. The order cannot be imposed upon a young person aged 15 and under unless they are considered to be a 'persistent' young offender (PYO) or on a person aged 12 and under unless it is seen to be the only measure adequate to protect the public from further offending by them. Section 100(3) of the PCC(S)A defines the order as subjecting the offender to a 'period of detention and training followed by a period of supervision'. This order is deemed to be a 'custodial sentence' and is only imposed in the most serious cases.

The period of supervision will begin halfway through the order when the offender is released from detention. The person responsible for supervision will be a probation officer, a social worker or other member of a youth offending team. Breach of an order will be dealt with by way of summons or arrest warrant.

5.1.6 **Community punishment orders (CPO)**

This is very similar to the adult version and requires unpaid work to be performed, and is expressed in terms of 'hours'. The minimum period for the offender aged between 16 and 17 years is 40 hours and the maximum is currently capped at 240 hours.

5.1.7 **Community rehabilitation orders (CRO)**

This specific sentence is only available for those offenders aged between 16 and 17 years. Its title is descriptive in that it requires the offender to be rehabilitated and is very similar to the supervision order as described below. A CRO can be combined with a CPO to form a 'community punishment and rehabilitation order (CPRO)'.

5.1.8 **Intensive supervision and surveillance programme (ISSP)**

This programme is without doubt directed at persistent offenders who are committing the more serious criminal offences. It is designed to be intensive and intrusive and to ensure that the offender is subject to supervision every day.

5.1.9 **Attendance centre orders (ATO)**

The title is rather self explanatory. This order requires the offender to attend a centre for a maximum of 36 hours. During this time they will engage in physical training and other educational activities.

5.1.10 **Supervision orders**

This is a basic order to which other requirements may be added. The requirements are called specified activities and the aim is to design a programme that is most able to address the offending behaviour of the offender.

5.1.11 **Action plan orders**

Section 69 of the PCC(S)A provides this sentencing option for those offenders under the age of 18 and requires the offender, for a period of three months, to comply with a series of conditions including, staying away from specified places, participation in certain activities and reparation. They will remain under the supervision of a responsible person such as a probation officer, social worker or member of a youth offending team.

5.1.12 **Reparation orders**

Reparation orders, defined by s 73 of the Powers of Criminal Courts (Sentencing) Act 2000 (PCC(S)A), allow the youth court to require the offender to make the 'reparation' specified in that order. Reparation is a means by which the offender will carry out a job of work or service to the benefit of a specific individual or to the community as a whole. It does not include financial compensation. It may, in many cases, be more appropriate than other community sentences or compensation.

5.1.13 **Parenting orders**

This order, as defined by s 8 of the Crime and Disorder Act 1998, requires the parents or carer of the young offender to meet the certain requirements. Its purpose is to improve and encourage the skills and abilities of the offender's parents and may be made against one or both of them or the young person's guardian. Requirements may include counselling and guidance sessions under the supervision of a social worker, probation officer or member of a youth offending team. It is a statutory requirement, by virtue of s 9 of the 1998 Act for the court to consider whether such an order is appropriate if the person convicted is 16 or under. If they consider it is not, the magistrates must state their reasons in open court. If the young person is 17 then the order is discretionary. Breach of the order renders the parent or guardian liable to prosecution. The order may not last in excess of 12 months.

5.1.14 **Drug treatment and testing requirements**

This is similar to the option that is available for adult offenders in the adult court. It is now available in the Youth Court as part of an Action Plan or

Supervision Order in some areas for those offenders aged 14 or over. (See also **4.1.9** above.)

5.1.15 **Criminal capacity**

By law, children under the age of 10 are incapable of criminal responsibility. Of course, a person under 10 may perform all of the physical elements (technically referred to as actus reus) that constitute a crime, such as smashing another's window or taking items from a store without paying for them. However, s 50 of the Children and Young Persons Act 1933 provides that those under 10 are incapable of forming the mental element required to commit a crime, referred to as the presumption of 'doli incapax'.

The mental element required for the commission of most crimes is often referred to as 'mens rea' which means nothing more than intention to commit the crime or recklessness as to whether it was committed. Those under 10 who 'commit' crime may be the subject of action by their local authority to stop their offending.

However, under s 34 of the Crime and Disorder Act 1998, those aged between 10 and 13 are no longer presumed to be 'doli incapax' and may be convicted of committing a crime without proof that they knew what they were doing was seriously wrong. Furthermore, the Sexual Offences Act 1993 abolished the presumption that a boy under the age of 14 was incapable of sexual intercourse and therefore rape.

6

Applications in the Magistrates' Court

6.1 **A Powerful Preventative and Investigative Tool**

The magistrates' court does not exist solely to hear criminal cases. There are many different applications which police officers can make to the court to assist them in the detection of crime and prevention of offending. The more common include applications for warrants to arrest a person (effectively, permission to arrest) or search warrants (permission to search premises), and applications for orders forbidding people from doing certain things, foremost among them the anti-social behaviour order, or 'ASBO'.

The police may apply for warrants of arrest in the magistrates' court, but since 1 January 2006 when s 110 of the Serious Organised Crime and Police Act 2005 (SOCAP)(amending s 24 of the Police and Criminal Evidence Act 1984 (PACE)) came into force, the powers of arrest that may be exercised by a constable without a warrant have increased to include any offence provided it is necessary to make the arrest because one or more of the reasons within s 24(5) of PACE are also satisfied (the labels of 'arrestable' offence and 'serious arrestable' offence are abolished by s 111 and Sch 7 of SOCAP 2005). The application for an arrest warrant or summons commences by way of information and complaint and different applications will require officers to satisfy a variety of different criteria. The officer must also be prepared to respond to any questions in respect of their application and must always be able to justify their request and proposed action on the grounds of proportionality, legality, accountability and necessity. This section outlines the most commonly used application procedures in the magistrates' court.

6.1.1 **Laying an information**

'Laying an information' is a familiar if not a slightly odd expression, which means that information, either verbal or written, is given to a magistrate with the intention of persuading them to issue a warrant or summons.

The actual 'laying' of an information in respect of an arrest warrant is a simple procedure and is often made by civilian staff from the 'prosecutions' department. The appropriate form can be obtained from the court office and will contain headings which indicate exactly what information is required. This will include the name of the informant, the details of the offence alleged and the law which has been broken. The form is then signed by the informant and must be checked by the court's legal adviser before presentation to the court. The person who writes and signs the information, the informant, must be the same person that lays it before the magistrate. The informant may then be shown into a court or the magistrate's private rooms. The application and information may be heard in an open court. The informant will be asked to swear a particular form of the oath. It is similar to the following:

> 'I swear by almighty God that this is my information and handwriting and the contents thereof are true to the best of my knowledge and belief.'

The magistrate will read the information and may ask questions about it. They may consult their legal adviser. If the application and information is in order then the magistrate will issue the warrant there and then and their legal adviser will sign it.

The legal adviser of a magistrates' court may issue a summons but not a warrant. This is the process by which defendants are brought before the court for motoring offences. The police supply the information and the legal adviser issues the summons. The issue of a summons on receipt of an information is discretionary and the magistrate or their legal adviser must consider the legality of the information and all the attendant circumstances. Information given for the issue of a summons need not be given on oath. Due to the sheer volume of summonses that are required it is most likely that this process is dealt with almost entirely by a particular department which may be referred to as the 'Criminal Justice Unit' or the 'Prosecutions Department'.

6.2 **Arrest Warrants**

6.2.1 **'First instance' warrants**

Section 1 of the Magistrates Court Act 1980 (as amended by the Courts Act 2003) gives magistrates the power to issue arrest warrants in any case where they also have power to issue a summons provided that the information is properly laid and the offence alleged is indictable or punishable with imprisonment. If there is doubt about the whereabouts of the accused or the suitability of their address for service of a summons, then the issue of a warrant will be the proper course of action notwithstanding the seriousness of the offence.

There are other occasions when the issue of a warrant is statutorily required before an arrest can be made. A few powers of arrest are conditional in that the suspect must be 'found committing' the offence before they can be arrested otherwise the power to arrest does not exist and if exercised would obviously be unlawful. Hence the need to obtain a warrant or summons after the event to compel the suspected offender to appear before the court.

It is vitally important to remember that arrest under a 'first instance' warrant, whether backed for bail or not, prevents the officer from interviewing the accused about the offence for which the warrant was issued. It does not, however, prevent the carrying out of identification procedures or other investigative options. For this reason alone the 'information and warrant' procedure does not represent the most efficient or desirable option. Warrants for arrest in the 'first instance' under s 1 of the Magistrates Court Act 1980 are rarely sought by the police as most offences incorporate a power of arrest, through various statutory provisions, as considered earlier at **6.1**.

6.2.2 **Extradition warrants**

The term 'extradition warrant' is somewhat misleading. The type of warrant required for extradition purposes will be a 'first instance' warrant as described above. Application for it will be made to the magistrates' court in exactly the same fashion. Before any application for a warrant is made in these circumstances the CPS must be consulted to determine if there is sufficient evidence (often referred to as a 'prima facie case'), and they will then assist with the laying of the information and application. Many countries who have extradition agreements with the United Kingdom may not require such a warrant but it invariably bolsters the application which will be heard in the foreign country.

A date is set at the magistrates' court and, acting under the guidance of the CPS, the officer is required to warn a number of witnesses whose evidence taken together constitutes a prima facie case. They may then be called to make a 'deposition', in other words, give oral evidence under oath as to the truth of the statement they have made previously to the police. The officer in the case may be required to give evidence about the nature and extent of the investigation itself. The magistrate will consider the evidence before them and either issue or refuse the warrant. The warrant and statements of evidence that accompany it must then be approved by the Home Office before this 'package' of evidence is sealed and sent through diplomatic channels to the other country's jurisdiction.

Extradition procedures are becoming increasingly common and officers investigating serious offences are more likely now than ever before to become involved in them. It is important to note that once extradited the suspect cannot be interviewed and must be charged with the offence specified on the warrant and brought immediately before the court.

6.3 **Search Warrants**

6.3.1 **General**

The application for a warrant to search premises is probably the most common application that police officers will make in the magistrates' court. Reference to ss 8 to 16 of the Police and Criminal Evidence Act 1984 (PACE) as amended (by the Serious Organised Crime and Police Act 2005) should be made along with Code B of the PACE Codes of Practice (as amended and effective from 1 January 2006). The Code confirms many police powers but also provides invaluable guidance as to how those powers must be implemented. Some police forces issue the Codes of Practice on a personal basis. Where this is not the case, copies will be available in every police station. Every police officer must be fully conversant with the provisions of these codes and their supporting Annexes and notes for guidance. Every defence lawyer will be.

It must be remembered that the request to search premises, often a person's home, is an application for a licence to trespass and will often be viewed by the occupants as an alarming invasion of their privacy. The power to enter, if granted under s 8 of PACE (as amended by ss 113 and 114 of SOCAP), may permit entry to one or more sets of premises (a specific premises warrant, as you must specify the premises) or any premises occupied or controlled by the specified person (an 'all premises warrant' ie, all premises occupied or under the control of the specified person) and on more than one occasion. Further guidance is provided within COP B 3.6'.

Warrants to search premises, following the amendment of s 8 of PACE by SOCAP 2005 (ss 113 and 114), may now be granted for indictable offences (this includes either-way offences). Furthermore, it is worth emphasizing that some statutes, for example, the Misuse of Drugs Act 1971, incorporate the power for a court to issue a search warrant and prescribe the criteria necessary for doing so. Whatever the origin of the warrant, it must be used (referred to as executed) in accordance with PACE and the Codes of Practice.

Before issuing a warrant, the magistrate must receive an information and hear from the officer named in that application. The procedure is the same as that followed for 'laying' an information. Warrant informations differ depending on the particular magistrates' court where the application is made. Most police stations stock copies of the necessary forms and copies of the warrants themselves. It is now common for them to be stored on computer programmes that can be readily accessed by any officer. An information and warrant may sometimes be incorporated in the same booklet.

6.3.2 Preparing the application

Pre-application procedures vary according to the police force but it is a requirement of PACE Codes of Practice that the authority for a search warrant application must be given by an officer of at least Inspector rank (Code of Practice B, para 3.4) who should first check the application and sign an approved form stating that he has done so. In urgent cases the most senior officer available can authorize an application. Having been given the authority to proceed with the application, the officer should then complete the information.

*Please see Appendix 1 for template application forms and specimen warrant

The officer will have to fill out a copy of the application. There will be two copies usually on self-carbonating paper. This must be done carefully. The application will require the following details:

- the date on which the application is made;
- the name and number of the officer making the application;
- the Act and section under which the application is made;
- the full address of the premises or set of premises to be searched; and
- the nature of the objects or materials sought.

A full address may require the postcode and will certainly require a flat or apartment number or a full recognizable description of a location in the case of a building such as a garage. A magistrate is likely to refuse an application if the details supplied are incorrect or imprecise.

Before making a warrant application officers should consider the jurisdiction of the court at which they intend to make it. A magistrate in Shrewsbury, for example, might want to know why they are being asked to consider an application for a warrant to search an address in Swansea. There may be times when this is both practical and expeditious but where it is possible any warrant application should be made to a court which has jurisdiction for the area in which the warrant is to be executed.

Once the application has been prepared it is advisable to contact the court office and forewarn the court of the intention to make the application and to arrange a convenient time.

6.3.3 Making the application

The warrant and information will be checked by the court's legal adviser and it is therefore vitally important to speak to them. If an officer arrives at a court unannounced they may be in for a long wait, particularly at a busy magistrates' court at a busy time. The legal adviser will check that the application is properly completed. If the officer making the application is not the officer named in the information then the application falls at the first hurdle. They will wish to see a copy of the written authority from the Inspector. They will then arrange for the application to be made.

*Please see Appendix 1

The application for the warrant may be made in open or closed court. There are usually very good reasons why search warrant applications should not be heard in open court but it is not impossible for a magistrate and their legal adviser to overlook this. The reason for not so doing should be politely pointed out to the court and the public will be excluded or, more likely, the application will be heard in the magistrate's rooms. Most magistrates will understand the need for discretion when asking questions about the information in an open court. This is an important issue and every possible effort must be made to maintain the confidentiality of the source of information and in particular information from covert human sources (informants). The timing of any application must also be carefully considered as it might indirectly identify by elimination the only person who was able to give the information to the police.

A poorly prepared application will further irritate a magistrate who may already view the suddenness of an unannounced application as unnecessarily disruptive of the court schedule. It is important to remember that whilst the power to search you are asking for is available it is not a foregone conclusion that it will be granted. The warrant will not be granted unless the court is satisfied that it is essential. Nevertheless, the great majority of magistrates will be favourably disposed towards a police officer making a search warrant application and will not look to find fault. They will be fully aware that their legal adviser has verified the legality, necessity and proportionality of the application and will proceed. The officer swears an oath using the form of words:

> 'I swear by almighty God that this is my information and handwriting and the contents thereof are true to the best of my knowledge and belief.'

If the officer is to affirm then they will use the following:

> 'I do solemnly and sincerely declare that this is my information and handwriting and the contents thereof are true to the best of my knowledge and belief.'

The officer will then introduce themselves and wait. The magistrate reads the information and may then ask the officer questions. The officer is bound by s 15(4) of PACE to answer these questions. The nature and number of questions which magistrates ask varies enormously. It is increasingly common for magistrates to enquire as to the likelihood of children being on the premises to be searched, the extent of the search and whether force will be used to gain entry. The fact that the premises may have been searched in the recent past is of relevance and may even be listed in the information. If a police informant provides the grounds for the application then that may become the focus of the magistrate's interest and they are likely to inquire about the informant's previous reliability. Human rights issues such as proportionality and necessity might be raised. Satisfied that the application is lawful, well grounded and proportionate, the magistrate will sign and issue the warrant.

6.3.4 **Common search warrant applications**

Whilst there is legislation empowering magistrates to issue search warrants for all kinds of materials, the warrants most frequently applied for relate to stolen property, drugs, firearms and evidence.

Stolen property: Theft Act 1968, s 26

The power to grant a search warrant for stolen property is given to the magistrate by s 26 of the Theft Act 1968. This is the Act and section which must be written on the warrant. The warrant grants a power of seizure to the constable.

Drugs: Misuse of Drugs Act 1971, s 23(3)

The power to grant a search warrant for controlled drugs or related documents is given to the magistrate by s 23(3) of the Misuse of Drugs Act 1971. The warrant is addressed to a constable and allows the search not only of the premises but of any persons on the premises.

Firearms: Firearms Act 1968, s 46(1)

The power to grant a search warrant for firearms is given to the magistrate by s 46(1) of the Firearms Act 1968. This also allows the search of any persons found on the premises.

Evidence: Police and Criminal Evidence Act 1984, s 8

The power to grant a search warrant for evidence is given to the magistrate by s 8 of the Police and Criminal evidence Act 1984. This section relates to evidence and not intelligence and the offence referred to must be an indictable offence.

*Please see Appendix 1

Miscellaneous

Other powers under which search warrant applications can be made include:

- false instruments and materials for manufacturing the same: Forgery and Counterfeiting Act 1981, s 7
- counterfeit currency and materials for manufacturing the same: Forgery and Counterfeiting Act 1981, s 24
- articles for causing criminal damage: Criminal Damage Act 1971, s 6
- obscene articles: Obscene Publications Act 1959, s 3

Officers are reminded that irrespective of the origin of the search warrant, its use (execution) is regulated by ss 16 and 17 of the Police and Criminal Evidence Act 1984 (PACE) as amended by SOCAP 2005.

6.4 **Warrants of Further Detention**

6.4.1 **General**

A warrant to detain an arrested person beyond 36 hours without charge for any indictable offence must be applied for at the magistrates' court. The detained person must be present and they are entitled to and are likely to be represented. It is called a warrant of further detention and is provided for by s 43 of PACE. As the arrested person is still in police detention the CPS will play no part in the warrant application procedure. Similarly the transfer of the prisoner to and from the court and the prisoner's security at the court remain the responsibility of the police. An application for a warrant of detention for a young person can be made at the magistrates' court but the young person will not be required to sit in the dock. The maximum extension period for detention without charge that can be granted by this warrant is an additional 60 hours. This means that with the extensions beyond 24 hours that can be granted by a superintendent or above, a suspect may be detained for a maximum of 96 hours (excluding terrorism) without charge from when he arrived at the police station. After that period has expired he must be charged or released.

6.4.2 The application

The application is made by a police officer in the same way as any other warrant application. An information is laid before the magistrate. The officer swears an oath or affirms and is then subject to examination by the magistrate and cross-examination by the accused's legal representative.

The information will contain the following:

- the date and time
- the person to whom the information applies
- the offence for which they are under arrest
- the time when they arrived at the police station
- the name of the officer making the application and their station

The information must also outline the grounds upon which the arrest was made and the nature of the enquiries and investigation that have so far been carried out. Most importantly it must contain the details of what further enquiries are proposed and why the suspect's continued detention is necessary whilst those enquiries are being carried out. A copy of the information must be given to the detained person before the application is heard and that person is, of course, entitled to be legally represented at the hearing.

Police officers are constantly reminded, with good reason, to ensure that applications for warrants of further detention are timely and necessary. If an application is made and refused then no further application can be made unless it is based on new evidence not available before the first application. Section 43 of PACE allows for an application to be made at any time before the expiry of the first 36 hours of detention and also within the following six hours if it has not hitherto been practical for the court to sit. If the application is made in this additional six-hour period and the magistrate feels that it should have been made during the initial 36 hours then the application will, or should, be refused. So long as the application proceedings *begin* before the expiry of the 36 hours then it does not matter that the warrant is issued once that time has expired.

Section 44 of PACE allows for further applications to be made in respect of the same investigation. A further application should be made before the expiry of the previous extension and is made in exactly the same fashion.

Code C of the Codes of Practice, at para 15D, provide that applications for warrants of further detention should be made between 10am and 9pm, and where possible during normal court hours. Where this will be impossible the court's legal adviser should be notified where possible during normal hours of the prospect of an out of hours application and the need to arrange a special sitting of the court. Such a sitting may even be arranged over a weekend or bank holiday period. In general, it may be difficult to arrange court sittings outside of 'normal court hours' that is, 10am to 4pm and an investigating officer is well advised to avoid this eventuality if they are able to do so.

6.4.3 Grounds

Applications for warrants of further detention, whilst frequently made, are not everyday occurrences. Section 43 of PACE provides the police with a powerful tool in the investigation of the most serious offences and it is important that overuse or ill-considered applications do not undermine future essential applications. Close consideration must be given to the further enquiries which need to be carried out and the questions 'what' and 'why' must be answered in the information and examination. The information should first be shown to the court's legal adviser who will check it in the same way as an information is checked in relation to a search warrant.

The application should never be taken for granted simply because the offence being investigated is murder, rape or any other serious matter. The magistrate is not there to 'rubber stamp' a police request and may ask searching questions of the officer. Key issues which the officer must consider are as follows:

• what enquiries have so far been carried out
• whether they have been diligent and expeditious
• what enquiries are proposed
• why it is necessary to keep the prisoner in custody whilst they are carried out
• exactly what length of further detention is required and why

It is good practice for the officer making the application to address all of these issues in the information and to keep a copy for their own use when answering questions in the witness box. It has become increasingly common for officers to refer to 'time lines', a document prepared by the police that will detail precisely what has happened to the person detained since their arrest. Much of the information will be taken directly from the custody record and will include the reasons for any delays that have occurred.

It is common for a defendant not to resist the application entirely but to object to the length of further detention being applied for. The information and application must therefore be definite and precise with regard to this.

PACE and the Codes of Practice do not prescribe what particular rank an officer must be to make the application (it states that '... on application by a constable...'). It is simple common sense that the credibility of the application will be enhanced if an officer of senior standing, perhaps Inspector or above, makes it. If an officer with a sufficiently comprehensive grasp of the details of the case is not available at that rank then it should be made by an officer of lower rank who does have that knowledge. In the most serious cases it should be the senior investigating officer (SIO) or his deputy. Such applications are usually regulated by internal Force guidelines/policies which should be complied with.

If the warrant is granted it will be signed then and there by the magistrate and a copy should be taken by the officer and handed to the custody officer on the prisoner's return to the station.

6.4.4 Remands into police custody

Once a defendant has been charged with a particular offence he cannot be questioned further about that matter except under specific circumstances specified in the Codes of Practice (Code C, para 16.5). However, if that person is suspected of other offences then the police, through the CPS, can request that the magistrate remand that person back to the police station and into police custody for the sole purpose of enquiring into those other offences. The period of remand must not exceed three clear days or 24 hours if the person is under the age of 17. The obligation to review the need to continue to detain the individual must be reviewed in accordance with s 40 of PACE.

The grounds upon which the request is made must be specific. It may be that during the initial investigation the suspect has intimated that they have committed other offences. It may be that the facts of the offence with which they are charged are so similar to other offences previously undetected that there are reasonable grounds to suspect that person of having committed them. Whatever the grounds, the magistrate can only remand a person for a maximum of three days. If this type of remand is sought then the officer in the case must liaise as soon as possible with the CPS and be prepared to attend court if required.

Lawyers and police officers often refer to this type of remand as a 'three day lay down'. Its most common use is in respect of defendants charged with burglary or other theft offences who are suspected of having committed others.

6.5 Other Applications

6.5.1 Preventative measures

Recent legislation under a variety of Acts has given the police and local authorities a number of new and powerful options to deal with offenders and offending. Further guidance can also be obtained from Part 50 of the Criminal Procedure Rules 2005, 'Supplemental Orders Made on Conviction'.

6.5.2 Anti-social behaviour order (ASBO)

Further to **5.1.12** these were created by the Crime and Disorder Act 1998 and are designed to prevent behaviour by those aged 10 or over, that causes or is likely to cause harassment, alarm or distress to others not resident with the offender. Examples include excessive noise, drunken behaviour and graffiti. The ASBO is a civil and not a criminal order but may be imposed by the magistrates' court and applied for by the police.

The title of an ASBO succinctly describes the purpose for which it was created. In keeping with the rest of the 1998 Act, the responsibility for an application for an ASBO lies between the local authority and the Chief Officer of police for that area. Either may make the application but they have a statutory requirement to consult with each other beforehand. The application is made to a magistrate by way of complaint as opposed to an information and must be made to the court in whose catchment area the anti-social behaviour has been committed or is likely to be committed. There are two ways in which an ASBO can be applied for. The first is post conviction, the second purely by way of complaint. The first method is by far the most common and also the most simple.

6.5.3 **Post conviction ASBO**

Whilst any relevant authority may apply for an ASBO after the statutory consultation has taken place, those which will require police attendance are likely to be the applications instigated by the police themselves. The application for a post conviction ASBO should be timed where possible to coincide with the conviction itself. The CPS will make the application and will therefore need to be informed and consulted at the earliest possible stage. It would be sensible, where appropriate, to include form MG13, 'application for order on conviction', with the initial case file submitted to the CPS (see **11.1.6** below for MG forms). On hearing that an application is to be made the respondent's solicitor will almost certainly require time to consider the evidence that relates to it. Accordingly, a further file of evidence substantiating the grounds for the application and the conditions requested will need to be prepared before the ASBO hearing.

The case will be presented by the CPS but an officer may well be called to give evidence to substantiate the application and the grounds for it. This evidence will be given under oath and will be subject to cross-examination in the normal way. The civil rather than the criminal rules of evidence are applied which means that hearsay evidence will be admitted. Evidence about matters for which the respondent has not been convicted can be adduced. The standard of proof is said to be 'on the balance of probabilities' but in practice is treated as being indistinguishable from the criminal standard of 'beyond reasonable doubt'. Breach of the order is a criminal offence for which there is a power of arrest. A magistrate will not make the order lightly and must be satisfied that it is proportionate, comprehensible and necessary to protect the public.

6.5.4 **ASBO by complaint**

An application for an ASBO by complaint, sometimes referred to as a 'stand alone' ASBO, is a great deal more difficult and time consuming. The principles however remain the same. The evidence gathering will have been carried out before the final hearing, and the officer who attends should be familiar with the subject. A file will be prepared by the applicant in accordance with the Manual of Guidance (see **11.1.3** below) and submitted to the CPS. The application is made in the magistrates' court but a barrister may be instructed by the CPS to present the case. The application, like all matters dealt with in the magistrates' court by way of complaint, should be made within six months of the matter leading to the complaint. If there is evidence of anti-social behaviour within the last six months then evidence of that misbehaviour can also be introduced. There is likely to be a great deal more evidence and therefore a greater possibility that police officers and representatives from the local authority will be called to give evidence. The procedure will be the same as for the post conviction application.

The magistrate has the power to summons the respondent (the subject of the ASBO) to the hearing. If they fail to appear then a warrant for their arrest may be issued. If made an ASBO will run for a period of at least two years (Crime and Disorder Act 1998, s 1(7)). Any appeal against the making of the order must be made to the Crown Court.

6.5.5 **ASBOs: general**

Very few pieces of recent legislation have caused as much political and media controversy as that which created the ASBO. The orders were first available in April 1999. Between then and 2002 only 466 orders were made. By late 2004, just over 3,000 had been made by magistrates.

There are quite dramatic regional variations in the number of applications being made and a contributory factor in this is undoubtedly local social and political issues and different Force policies. It is difficult to give definitive guidelines and advice. But useful assistance can be obtained from the case of *R v Parkin* which can be found at *R v P (Shane Tony)* [2004] EWCA Crim 287. Police forces have recognized the difficult and time-consuming nature of the process and are increasingly employing officers to specialize in the gathering and presentation of ASBO evidence.

Guidance with regard to procedure and protocols is provided by the Magistrates' Courts (Sex Offender and Anti-Social Behaviour Orders) Rules 1998 which also reproduces copies of the forms to be used for the complaint, application and the order itself. ASBOs are circulated on a person's PNC record.

In April 2004 the Home Office announced the creation of a team of specialist prosecutors whose responsibility is to pursue anti-social behaviour matters through the courts. In principle they are a central contact point for all the agencies dealing with the problem. The specialist prosecutors are based in the following 12 CPS areas: Manchester, South Yorkshire, Merseyside, West Midlands, London (Borough of Camden), Avon and Somerset, South Wales, Lancashire, West Mercia, Sussex, Kent, and Northumbria. The new posts are funded by the Home Office.

6.5.6 Sexual Offences Act 2003

The Sexual Offences Act 2003 was introduced in May 2004. Part 2 of the Act provides for four new civil orders. Although the four new orders are intended for different purposes, the application procedures are the same. The four new orders are:

Notification orders (s 97)

An order which makes persons who have offended abroad and been charged or cautioned subject to the sex offender notification provisions as if they had offended in the United Kingdom. Notification requirements were originally provided for by the Sex Offenders Act 1997.

Sexual offences prevention orders (SOPOs, s 104)

This order can be made on application to a magistrate by the chief officer of police or by a court on conviction to protect the public from serious sexual harm by the offender. The order prohibits its subject for a period of at least five years from doing anything listed within the order (s 107 of the Sexual Offences Act 2003).

Foreign travel orders (s 114)

An order that enables the court to prevent those convicted of sexual offences against children aged under 16 from travelling overseas where there is evidence that they intend to cause serious sexual harm to children in a country other than the United Kingdom.

Risk of sexual harm orders (RSHOs, s 123)

An order that aims to restrict the activities of those aged 18 or over engaging or involving children in specified sexual activity (s 123(3), so-called 'grooming' for sexual activities) that lasts for at least two years. The order requires evidence of this prohibited activity on at least two other occasions.

6.5.7 **Application procedures**

The procedures are very similar to those which regulate ASBO applications. The applications may be heard by any magistrates' court and it is not necessary for them to be heard by a district judge.

The application is by way of complaint to the magistrates' court, with the exception of the SOPO made on conviction, and must be made within six months of the matter which forms the basis of the application. They are civil orders and therefore the civil rules of evidence apply and hearsay evidence will be admissible. The police should first consult their force legal department for advice before making the application, as there is no obligation on the CPS to be involved at this stage. The police officer responsible for the application may wish to seek the advice of the CPS with regard to the wording of any proposed prohibitions or restrictions, as this will be important in trying to prove a criminal breach of any of the orders made under this Act.

The court must be notified well in advance of the application for scheduling purposes and also to identify a date for the summons. The police summons the respondent to the court. The individual may be completely unfamiliar with the procedure and it might be advisable to reinforce the service of the summons with a personal visit to explain the gravity of the situation and the absolute requirement to respond to the summons.

Notwithstanding the civil nature of the proceedings the standard of proof required will be treated as equivalent to the criminal standard. This is very similar to the proceedings for an ASBO. The previous convictions and cautions of an offender must be capable of proof. This applies also to offences committed outside the UK and extracts or certificates of conviction may be required. Statements and documentation must be prepared and witnesses warned. Although there is no statutory obligation for the police to consult, much of the evidence could, in some cases, be provided by witnesses from the local authority or other community bodies. The application must be prepared and presented by the police officer as if it were a not guilty hearing or trial. The respondent is likely to be legally represented, as public funding will be available (see **2.3.2** above).

Any person summonsed in respect of any of the four orders must be a convicted sex offender. Any court proceedings involving a convicted sex offender present the police with the possibility of public disorder. The very fact that the police are seeking an order serves to highlight that they believe that the person presents a real and continuing risk to the public. There is therefore always the possibility of public disorder at such a hearing. The police and the court, usually with the agreement of the individual, should seek at the start of proceedings an order under s 11 of the Contempt of Court Act 1981 prohibiting the press or media from publishing or broadcasting the name and address of the respondent. (see **9.3.2** for contempt of court generally).

The magistrate listens to the details of the complaint made by the officer and will have read the details of the application. The magistrate will then inform the individual what the substance of the complaint is. If the complaint is contested then the officer and any other witnesses may be called to the witness box to give evidence under oath. They will be liable to cross-examination. The respondent or their representative may then make representations. If the order is made it should be served on the offender and a copy taken by the police officer. Where appropriate the 'notice of requirement to register' should also be served. The officer taking possession of the order should ensure that copies are given to any other interested parties such as the local authority.

6.5.8 **Adjournment or non-appearance**

If an offender fails to answer a summons the magistrate may issue a warrant for their arrest. This may or may not be backed for bail (backed for bail is a phrase used to indicate that bail is available in the circumstances otherwise the arrested person must be taken straight before the court and the warrant is said to be not backed for bail). The object of the imposition of any of these orders is the protection of the public and there should not be any unnecessary delay in proceedings. Adjournments should therefore be granted sparingly and only when it is in the interests of justice. The court may proceed in the respondent's absence but it is not desirable where prohibitions, restrictions or notification requirements are to be imposed and their breach renders the defendant liable to arrest, criminal charge, conviction and imprisonment.

6.5.9 **Variation, discharge and appeal**

The police, by way of complaint to the magistrates, or the offender may apply to have the order either varied or discharged. The procedures remain the same although the offender may not be required to attend such a hearing. Appeal against the making of an order is to the Crown Court. Public funding may be available to the defendant at variation, discharge and appeal hearings (see **2.3.2** above).

6.5.10 **Sex offender orders: general**

Mercifully the application procedures in relation to the four new orders are similar. The legislation itself is both novel and complex and a full examination of the law and the legal requirements of each order is beyond the scope of this book. Monitoring sex offenders and implementing the provisions of the Act requires a certain degree of specialism on the part of the officers dealing with it. This has been acknowledged by police forces across the UK and officers or teams of officers are often dedicated to the task in the same way that specialists deal with ASBOs. Undoubtedly different forces will tackle the problem in different ways but the procedures put in place under the Crime and Disorder Act 1998 and the Sex Offenders Act 1997 (notification requirements) should enable smooth implementation of the new provisions.

6.5.11 Football banning orders

Football banning orders are provided for by s 14A and 14B of the Football Spectators Act 1989 and were inserted by the provisions of the Football Disorder Act 2000. They can be applied for, like the ASBO, on conviction or on a complaint to the court. The orders are civil and preventative and not designed to punish past misdemeanours but to prevent violence and disorder at, or in connection with, regulated football matches. In principle a civil standard of proof is required but, as with sex offender and anti-social behaviour orders, in practice the criminal standard will apply.

6.5.12 Banning order on conviction (s 14A)

The Act requires that the magistrates must make a banning order if the person before them is convicted of a football related offence and they are satisfied that making the order would help to prevent violence or disorder at or in connection with any regulated football matches. However, the police still have an important role to play.

The person must be served written notice by the police that such an application will be made. The best time to do this would be when the person is charged. The officer must then inform the CPS that such a notice has been served. They must then prepare any evidence that will be necessary to satisfy the court that the granting of the order is necessary. This evidence will be additional to the evidence relating to the offence with which they have been charged. Section 14 states that it is immaterial whether the evidence heard in pursuance of the application would have been admissible in the proceedings in which the offender was convicted. Hearsay evidence can therefore be adduced in support of the application. The police officer best placed to deal with the application may be called by the CPS to give this crucial evidence. The evidence will be given under oath from the witness box and will be subject to cross-examination.

6.5.13 Banning order on complaint (s 14B)

This order has wider application as there is no requirement for the subject to have been convicted of a relevant offence. It must be established that the individual has at any time caused or contributed to any violence or disorder and the court satisfied on reasonable grounds that the granting of this application will prevent violence or disorder at or in connection with any regulated football matches.

The police may consult with the CPS beforehand but there is no obligation on the CPS to be involved in the process. The police officer responsible must gather the required evidence in the normal way and then serve notice on the person against whom the order is sought. A date will be set and the officer will take the oath and give their evidence. The respondent is likely to be represented but may choose to carry out the cross-examination themselves. The respondent is entitled to give evidence and call witnesses. If the magistrate is satisfied that the matter is proved 'on the balance of probabilities' then they must grant the banning order.

6.5.14 Football banning orders: general

If a banning order made under s 14A is in addition to a sentence of imprisonment then the maximum period is 10 years and the minimum six years. Other orders made under s 14A would be for a maximum of five and a minimum of three years. Orders made under s 14B will be for a maximum of three and a minimum of two years. Appeal against a banning order made on complaint is to the Crown Court only.

By late 2004 there had been more than 2,500 banning orders made. The vast majority of these have been made on conviction. Police forces have set up specialist teams to deal with football matters and it is likely that these officers will deal with banning order applications made on conviction. Banning order by complaint is a more difficult issue and is overseen by the National Crime Intelligence Service (NCIS) based in London. Applications made against people prevented from leaving the country are likely to be dealt with by NCIS.

During the five-day 'control period' which precedes an overseas match or tournament the police may intercept and prevent known troublemakers from travelling. If they do this then that person must face banning order proceedings within 24 hours. The notice of intention to make an application must therefore be served upon them immediately and the matter will proceed by the complaint procedure described above.

6.5.15 Closure orders

Provided for by s 1 of the Anti-Social Behaviour Act 2003, this power has been created in order to allow police forces, working in consultation with local authorities, to tackle 'crack houses' and other premises which cause disorder or serious nuisance to the local community through association with Class A drugs. Like the other orders dealt with in this section it is a civil order.

Once a closure notice has been properly served (on the authority of an officer not below the rank of Superintendent) the hearing must take place at the magistrates' court within 48 hours of its service. The police must satisfy the court that the making of the order is necessary to prevent the occurrence of disorder or serious nuisance. The court will wish to know if and what other measures have been used first to deal with the problem before they are willing to grant the closure order.

Although the closure notice must be authorized by an officer not below the rank of Superintendent the application to that officer and to the court may be made by any rank of police officer. The officer dealing with the matter should obtain evidence in the normal way including statements from all witnesses. They must ensure that any private or local authority witnesses are warned and will receive support and assistance on the day of the hearing. That officer must agree with the court a date, time and place for the hearing, prior to the service of the closure notice as these details need to be written on the notice itself.

The court must be satisfied on the civil standard of proof that is, on the balance of probabilities, that at the premises subject to the closure notice there is:

- the unlawful use, production or supply of a Class A controlled drug; *and*
- serious nuisance and disorder to the public; *and*
- that closure is necessary to prevent the reoccurrence of such disorder or serious nuisance for the duration of the order.

The officer in the case will give evidence under oath. Private and local authority witnesses may be called. Evidence, which may include hearsay evidence, will be heard in relation to the use and presence of drugs on the premises. The magistrates will not adjourn proceedings for forensic tests to be carried out but may do so for not more than 14 days for any relevant party to contest the application by showing why the order should not be made. During this adjournment period, closure may nevertheless be ordered.

In principle the court has three options: refusal of the application, closure, or adjournment. In practice the magistrates have the ability to vary the length of the order and this gives them the flexibility to be able to make a short order which may lessen the need to adjourn the case and may deal with the problem in the interim period. When an application for a closure notice is made then the magistrates should try to avoid an adjournment as this defeats the object of the power, which is speedy resolution of an anti-social problem. If the order is made then it will be served on the respondent and a copy given to the police.

The maximum length of an order is three months with the possibility of further extensions to a total of no more than six months. Appeal against refusal can be made by a police officer to the Crown Court but must be made within 21 days. Likewise an appeal by the person served with the order must be made to the Crown Court within the same period. Should an appeal be made against the making of the order, then the police officer most able to deal with the matter should attend and be ready to give evidence about all of the issues associated with the order. The magistrates may discharge the order at any stage before the three months expires should they feel there is evidence to support the view that it is no longer necessary.

6.6 Summonsing a Witness to the Magistrates' Court

Generally there are two powers under which a magistrate can summons a reluctant witnesses to court. The first is provided by s 97 of the Magistrates' Court Act 1980 and the second by the Crime and Disorder Act 1998 (para 4(1) depositions).

6.6.1 Summons before committal proceedings

Section 97 provides that where a magistrate is satisfied that any person in England and Wales is likely to be able to provide material evidence for summary proceedings but will not voluntarily attend as a witness or will not voluntarily produce the evidence, the justice shall issue a summons requiring them to attend before the court to give or provide that evidence if it is in the interests of justice to do so.

This section is simple and self-explanatory. The application must be made and the matter heard before any committal proceedings take place. A deposition was previously referred to in respect of extradition and committal proceedings as oral evidence given under oath as to the truth of a statement previously made. Here, the deposition is simply the sworn statement of a witness under oath.

If the service of summons is deemed impracticable then a warrant for arrest may be issued in either case. This is likely to be backed for bail. If a person so summonsed fails to appear then a warrant of arrest can be issued. If a person so summonsed refuses to give evidence or produce an exhibit then they are liable to fine not exceeding level 4 (currently, £2,500) or imprisonment (not exceeding one month).

6.6.2 Procedure

Consultation should take place with the CPS before an application is made to a magistrate to issue a warrant under this section. The application will thereafter be made by laying an information before the magistrate in the normal way. The application procedure for a summons under this legislation and the summons under the Crime and Disorder Act are similar and described below.

6.6.3 Summons after s 51 transfer of an indictable offence

Schedule 3, para 4 of the Crime and Disorder Act 1998 defines the power of a justice to take a 'deposition' (sworn statement) after an indictable only offence has been transferred under s 51 of the Crime and Disorder Act 1998. It states:

4(1)   Sub-paragraph (2) applies where a justice of the peace for a commission area is satisfied that:

(a)   a person in England and Wales ("the witness") is likely, on behalf of the prosecutor, to be able to make a written statement containing material evidence, or produce a document or other exhibit likely to be material evidence, for the purpose of proceedings for an offence for which another person has been sent for trial under section 51 by a magistrates court for that area; and

(b) the witness will not voluntarily make the statement or produce the document or other exhibit.

4(2)   In such a case the justice must issue a summons addressed to the witness requiring him to attend before a justice at the time and place specified therein, and to have his evidence taken as a deposition or to produce the document or other exhibit.

6.6.4 **Procedure**

The circumstances in which this power can be exercised are limited and specific. Another person must have been transferred under s 51 to the Crown Court (see **4.5.3** above) and the evidence which the person to be summonsed may give must be in relation to that matter. The deposition procedure must be used before the service of the prosecution case. This will usually be some two weeks before the plea and case management hearing (see **8.1.1** below) and perhaps seven to eight weeks after a preliminary hearing at the Crown Court. The opportunity to use this power is therefore limited by strict time constraints.

The power will therefore only be used by officers investigating the most serious 'indictable only' offences. The CPS must be consulted about the proportionality, legality and strategic advisability of taking this course of action before it is embarked upon.

Police will initiate the procedure by way of an information and follow the same procedure as for a warrant application. If it appears to the officer making the application and the magistrate hearing it that the service of a summons is likely to be impracticable for whatever reason then a warrant of arrest may be issued. This will be backed for bail.

The officer making the application must contact the court's legal adviser and agree a date and time for the proposed hearing. This must be done in order that the summons or warrant will have the appropriate date on it. The information must be prepared by the officer and checked by the legal adviser. The officer will then be asked to enter the witness box and take the appropriate oath (see **6.3.3** above).

Exercise of this power must be as a last resort. The officer must have substantial grounds for believing that the witness is likely to be able to give 'material' evidence. The proportionality of the application will be in direct relation to the importance of the evidence which it is believed the witness may give. If the request is being made for an arrest warrant then the officer must be able to state why service of a summons is impracticable. The magistrate will examine the information and the officer must be prepared to answer any questions. If the summons is issued then it must be served in such a way as to be capable of proof that it was in fact served before an arrest warrant was issued.

6.6.5 **The hearing**

The CPS will represent the police at the hearing. It may be that they will instruct a barrister. The witness summonsed in this way is also likely to be legally represented. They will appear in court and hear the information laid in support of the application. They will then be required to go in to the witness box and take the oath. The advocate for the prosecution will then ask questions of the witness. Their answers, their deposition, will be written long hand by the clerk of the court. When the magistrate is satisfied that the witness has given all the evidence they are capable of doing they will require the witness to sign the deposition. The original copy of this deposition will be kept by the court and a copy given to the prosecution and the witness.

6.6.6 **Witness summons procedure: general**

Whenever possible, it is, of course, better to allow a witness to make a statement of their own volition, but there are circumstances when it is appropriate to make an application under this legislation. This may be so particularly with a witness who does not want to be seen to be too co-operative with the police but is nevertheless a key witness. Alternatively, it may be valuable in the case of a person arrested but not charged with an offence who has given an account under caution in a taped interview but later refuses to assist the police by making a statement.

The witness who is summonsed in this way is unlikely to be co-operative or reliable and their attendance at a future trial cannot be relied upon notwithstanding the existence of the deposition. Like many apparently draconian powers it ought to be used sparingly and only when all other means of obtaining the evidence have been exhausted.

6.7 **Conclusion**

The magistrates' court is the great clearing house of the criminal justice system. Approximately 180,000 cases will be received but only 19,000 of them will proceed to the Crown Court by way of committal. But cases in the magistrates' court are not limited to those that occur after a crime is committed. The functions of the court are numerous and the variety of proceedings much greater than at the Crown Court. As is clear from the above, many investigations are progressed by searches or detention authorized by the magistrates' court. In recent years, the significance of this court in the criminal justice system has increased still further with the grant of powers to make a number of preventative orders. These are important new powers that present challenges and opportunities to the police service.

7

The Crown Court

7.1 **The People Decide**

Like the proverbial iceberg the great bulk of the work of the criminal justice system is unseen and largely unappreciated by the majority of the public. What lies above the waterline however is imposing, impressive and sometimes dramatic. The splendour of the Crown Court, with its pomp and ceremony, is what commonly defines the justice system for the public. With few exceptions, the cases which capture the public's imagination—the most horrific murders, the million pound frauds, or the trials of political or sporting celebrities—are heard in the Crown Court.

There are many differences between the functions and procedures of the magistrates' and Crown Court but the most obvious and important is that trial proceedings at the Crown Court take place before a jury of 12 citizens. But it is not only the deliberations of the jury that are the subject of speculation, for the idiosyncrasies of the presiding judge are scrutinized mercilessly. Similarly, it is the court where the performance and professionalism of the police officer is most thoroughly tested and where ignorance or poor preparation are likely to have the most damaging repercussions for both justice and the police service.

In the past, the journey of the young police officer through the court system would begin with evidence or presentation of the most simple cases in the magistrates' court. This is no longer the case. The first appearance may often be at the Crown Court where the officer may not only be giving evidence but acting as 'officer in the case' (OIC). In this role, they will be expected to co-ordinate and support witnesses, deal with seemingly endless defence requests for disclosure, assist prosecution counsel, and, if that were not enough, impress a jury. However, the experience of going to Crown Court need not be a trial for the defendant *and* the police officer.

7.1.1 **Origins and administration**

In principle, the Crown Court is a unified court which sits at a number of different locations. In practice, each Crown Court belongs to a 'circuit' of which there are six in England and Wales. The circuits are:

- Northern
- North-Eastern
- Wales and Chester
- Midlands and Oxford
- Western
- South-Eastern

Certain towns within the circuits are designated as Crown Court 'centres' and house the buildings themselves. Crown Court centres are further categorized as either first, second or third tier centres. The first tier centres try both civil and criminal cases and are largely based in the major urban centres of England

and Wales. Second and third tier centres deal only with criminal cases and are differentiated only by the judges who preside there. When the Crown Court sits in the City of London it is called the Central Criminal Court and is to be found on a street called 'Old Bailey'. It is nearly always referred to as 'the Bailey'.

In deciding where a trial should be heard, consideration is given to the gravity and complexity of the case. Offences are categorized accordingly from class one to four. Murder, not surprisingly, falls into class one. The offence categorization is important as it determines what kind of judge may hear the case.

7.1.2 Jurisdiction

The Crown Court is the only court that may deal with the most serious criminal cases. These cases involve offences that are classified as triable only on indictment (see **8.1.1** below for indictment). However, the Crown Court may also try cases which are classified as 'either-way' offences. This means that the offences can be tried in either the Crown Court or the magistrates' court. The Crown Court will hear either-way offences when the defendant has 'elected' (chosen) trial before the Crown Court instead of the magistrates' court. Other types of case heard at the Crown Court include those where the defendant has been sent there by the magistrates' court for sentence and those where the defendant appeals to the Crown Court against decisions regarding bail, sentence or conviction at the magistrates' court.

The manner in which a case is transferred from the magistrates' court is described in the previous chapter (see **4.5** above for committal and transfer proceedings).

Typical Crown Court Layout

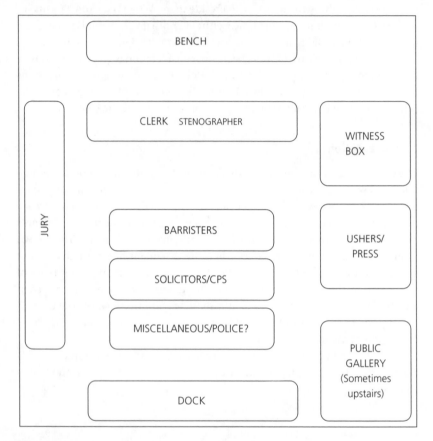

7.1.3 **The judges, their clerks and others**

There are four classes of judiciary that sit in judgment in the Crown Court. They are: the High Court judge, the circuit judge, the recorder and the justice of the peace.

High court judges

High Court judges must have what is known as a High Court qualification or must have sat as a circuit judge for at least two years. High Court judges are sometimes called 'puisne' judges. There are in total only 98 High Court judges and they are empowered to hear any case, both civil and criminal. High Court judges are addressed in open court as 'My Lord' or 'My Lady' or 'your Lordship' or 'your Ladyship'.

Circuit judges

Circuit judges are in principal appointed by the Queen on the recommendation of the Lord Chancellor and must have a 10-year Crown Court or 10-year County Court qualification or must have been a Recorder. The circuit judge is a full-time appointment. Before their appointment the Lord Chancellor must be satisfied that they are in good health. The circuit judge retires at the age of 70 and can be removed from office only by the Lord Chancellor. The circuit judge is addressed in open court as 'Your Honour'. An exception to this is when they sit at the Central Criminal Court or as honorary Recorder of Liverpool or Manchester in which case they are addressed as 'My Lord' or 'My lady'.

Recorders

Unlike circuit judges the appointment of recorder is a part-time appointment. They are appointed by the Queen on the recommendation of the Lord Chancellor. Their appointments are for specified periods only. They will not be appointed beyond the age of 75. Like the circuit judge the recorder must have a 10-year Crown Court or 10-year County Court qualification. Many barristers are qualified to sit as recorders and it is not unusual to encounter a prosecution or defence counsel whom one has previously seen sitting as a judge. The recorder is addressed in open court as 'Your Honour' except when sitting as previously described for circuit judges in which case they too are addressed as 'My Lord' or 'My Lady'.

7.1.4 Justices of the peace

A justice of the peace may only hear cases in the Crown Court with one of the afore-mentioned judges. The maximum number of justices who may sit at any one time is four. If the matter being heard at the Crown Court is in relation to appeal against sentence or conviction in the magistrates' court then between two and four justices must sit with the judge.

In addition to all of the above the Lord Chancellor may appoint further suitably qualified persons as judges. A circuit judge so appointed is called a 'deputy' and a recorder so appointed is called an 'assistant'. Such deputies and assistants will have all the powers of the circuit judge and recorder. When a judge sits in open court the court is said to be 'in session' and when the judge sits in a closed court or their private rooms they are said to be 'in chambers'. Somewhat confusingly, the judge's private rooms are also referred to as 'chambers' as, incidentally, are barristers' firms.

7.1.5 The clerk of the court

The role of the clerk in the Crown Court is not as influential as that of the justices' clerk in the magistrates' court. The role is more administrative and they will assist the judge in their management of the court time and in fixing dates for hearings and trial. They maintain contact with the court list office usually by telephone. They can also contact, by the same means, the judge in their chambers to give them notice, for example, that the court session is ready to begin. The clerk will sit on a bench in front of and below the judge and will be assisted by a stenographer or shorthand typist who makes a full record of proceedings which are also tape-recorded.

7.1.6 **Ushers and security**

Ushers and court and dock security personnel fulfil the same role as that which they perform in the magistrates' court. The usher however, as we shall see, has a much more vocal part to play and effectively acts as a chaperone for the jury. Private security firms now provide court security.

7.1.7 **The list office**

One of the most difficult aspects of Crown Court work is the efficient listing of cases for hearing and trial. This is the responsibility of the list office. Their job is made particularly difficult by the uncertain nature of all the proceedings in the court. It is almost impossible to predict with any certainty when matters will begin or end. Even the most straightforward of hearings can become troublesome and prolonged. Trials may take longer than predicted but a high proportion of trials result in far shorter hearings than the original estimate. It is to the list office that the court clerk will turn during proceedings in order to fix a trial date. If a date for a future hearing or trial is not set during proceedings then the interested parties, defence and prosecution barristers, and the CPS will have to liaise with the list office. Often unfairly maligned, list offices operate under intense pressure of work and in many cases are bound to disappoint one or other of the parties concerned. The police officer who does not submit current 'dates to avoid' in a case (Form MG10) will receive little sympathy from the court when it transpires the trial is fixed for a date that is inconvenient to them.

7.1.8 **The court office**

The court office is the administrative centre and manages general enquiries and customer service issues. It deals with any request to examine archives. It administers the issue of witness summonses and warrants and should be the first port of call for officers wishing to make applications in the Crown Court for warrants and orders (see **8.5** for Applications in the Crown Court).

7.1.9 **The witness service**

The witness service is run by the independent charity, Victim Support and helps witnesses, victims and their families before, during and after the hearing. The service gives support to defence and prosecution witnesses. Trained volunteers in every Crown Court centre and magistrates' court in England and Wales give free and confidential support and practical information about court procedures.

The creation of the witness service at courts has been of immense practical assistance to police officers dealing with cases. They provide a reception point and a private waiting room for witnesses. The witnesses' waiting room is intended to prevent the discomfort and anxiety that witnesses formerly experienced whilst waiting in the foyers and lobbies of the court building, frequently in the presence of the defendant, the defendant's family and their friends.

The officer in the case should first visit the witness service and confirm which civilian witnesses are expected to attend the day's proceedings. It is helpful for the witness service to know as much as possible about a witness before they meet them. If a witness is particularly fearful, nervous or demanding, forewarning and preparation will help the witness service to assist the witness. The witness service does not deal with the issue of expenses for prosecution witnesses; this is a matter for the CPS.

The Government programme 'No witness, no justice' launched in 2003 recommends a great many improvements and changes to the way in which witnesses are treated by the criminal justice system (see **14.2** below). The implementation of recommendations as a result of this programme will undoubtedly mean significant and welcome changes to the care and welfare of both prosecution and defence witnesses at court.

7.2 **Practical Matters**

From the moment a police officer is warned to attend court to the moment he steps over the threshold of the courtroom itself, there are a number of matters which they must consider and address (see also **Chapter 11**, Preparing for court).

7.2.1 **Court warning**

Police officers warned to attend court are given varying degrees of notice. A trial date may be set many months in advance but an appeal—for example, against bail refused at the magistrates' court—could be heard at very short notice indeed. Even when a trial date is set well in advance, unless it requires a specific technical facility only available at a particular court, the court number will not be set. It is normal for the time and court to be allocated by the list office on the day before the proceedings. Court warnings are then issued to the police in the late afternoon.

Court warnings will detail the time, the court number, and the name of the officer in the case who is required to be warned. The name of the officer in the case on court warnings is generally taken from the first set of case papers submitted. Even though the officer in the case may subsequently change, if the list office is not informed of that change then they will continue to issue warnings in the name of the first named officer. This is an issue which the officer in the case should deal with at the earliest possible opportunity. A simple phone call to the list office of CPS should suffice. Having received a court warning it is then the responsibility of the police to warn those witnesses, both police and private, who are required on the following day.

The warning will sometimes qualify the start time of a case and the nature of the proceedings by use of a number of phrases which may include the following: 'for trial', 'for mention', 'plea and case management', 'application to break fixture', 'bail application' or 'preliminary hearing'. These hearings are explained in Crown Court procedure below although it should be noted that they are not exhaustive.

Cases may be listed as 'floaters'. This means simply that there is no definite starting time for the case and that it will commence as soon as a courtroom becomes available. A case may be a 'floater' in a particular court or may be a 'floater' which may be heard in whichever courtroom becomes available. Alternatively, a case may be listed to start at a time described as 'not before' a certain hour. Of all the combinations of warning that the officer will receive, the one that describes a case as 'not before' is the one which is most likely to match reality.

As any interested party enters the Crown Court building, they will find the daily court lists displayed in a prominent position. These lists are typed and prepared each day and will confirm the details of what cases are scheduled in which courts at which time.

7.2.2 The police room

It is normal for there to be a specific 'police room' at the Crown Court (as well as at the magistrates' court). This is and ought to be the first port of call for the officer attending the Crown Court. It is still common practice for the officer to have to 'book on' at the police room and in many forces this will be a regulatory requirement. This is particularly important where the officer is 'officer in the case'. By booking on the officer announces to any interested party that they are in the building and ready to deal with their case. The police room is frequently where barristers and the CPS first look for an officer. It is also the place where the officer can have ready access to such facilities as a telephone, fax, photocopier, microfiche reader or desk space.

7.2.3 **The Crown Prosecution Service in the Crown Court**

The CPS has offices in all Crown Court centres. It is the responsibility of the CPS to prepare cases for court hearings and they will invariably have access to better facilities than the police room can offer. Each case is allocated to a designated caseworker (DCW) who will be able to assist with the majority of queries that an officer may have. At the very least they will be able to tell you the name of the prosecuting counsel and provide a physical description of them which, usually, will go further than 'they will be wearing a wig'. Caseworkers will normally be dealing with more than one case at the same time and will move from one court to another. The CPS prepares witness expense claim forms and will usually present them to the witnesses either before or after they have given evidence. It may be more appropriate in many cases for the officer to do this and also to explain how to make the claim. Expense claim forms are provided with a 'notes of guidance' leaflet but will appear complex to an often flustered and nervous witness who may have just left the witness box. It is wise for an officer to familiarize themselves with the contents of this form. Protocol dictates that officers should approach the CPS with any requests or enquiries before approaching prosecuting counsel. In practice, in cases of any length, a relationship between prosecution counsel and the officer in the case will usually render this unnecessary. However, it remains the position that defence counsel and solicitors should not be approached without the knowledge and blessing of the prosecution. There will always be at a Crown Court centre, a CPS prosecutor of sufficient experience and standing to deal with any matters that arise.

7.2.4 **Paging**

All crown court buildings will have a tannoy or 'paging' system. Use of the system will save the officer a lot of time and energy. Rather than roaming the corridors, foyer and courts of the building in an increasingly desperate search for witnesses, colleagues or counsel, it is wise to first contact the switchboard and have a message relayed by the tannoy system. A simple 'Could prosecution counsel in the case of Jones and others please come to court nine' should suffice. In many cases the officer will know the name of counsel dealing with their case. If so then they should page them by name, for example, 'Could Mr Golding of counsel please come to the police room'. Such common sense is often overlooked by the inexperienced officer who thinks that use of the paging system is only for those who are much more important than they are. Only the loftiest of prosecution counsel will begrudge being dragged from their coffee to meet requests and enquiries. Conversely, it is incumbent upon the officer to listen carefully to any announcements in relation to themselves, their case or the court in which they are appearing.

7.2.5 **Conference**

Crown Courts provide private facilities for officers, barristers, solicitors and any other interested parties to hold conferences. Officers should take witnesses and others to these rooms, and not to the police or CPS offices, to talk and discuss, especially sensitive, matters which arise. Some courts will allow these rooms to be booked in advance.

7.2.6 **Attendance of witnesses**

A simple letter of warning and verbal communication should be sufficient for the vast majority of witnesses but there are occasions when a witness will be reluctant or determined not to attend a trial. In these circumstances a judge may issue a summons for the attendance of that witness. The judge must be first satisfied that the witness's evidence is important to the conduct of the trial and that the witness is unlikely to attend voluntarily. The notice will specify the time and place at which the witness must attend. In the case of the reluctant or unwilling witness the judge will need to be satisfied also that they were actually warned to attend in the first place. If this is the case then the officer may be called to explain what steps have been taken to warn the witness.

If the judge concludes that the witness has been properly warned, the summons has been properly served, and the witness has failed to attend without 'just excuse' then they may issue a warrant for the arrest of that witness. The witness can then be remanded into custody or on bail until they have given their evidence. This procedure is rarely used and the officer in the case and their prosecuting counsel may well consider that their case may be better served by not calling such a reluctant witness. There are very few reasons that a witness can put forward as 'just excuse'. It would seem that sheer impossibility of attendance is the only justification.

Neither the police nor the witness service has the ability to pay witnesses their expenses for attendance at criminal trials. In fact, there are no provisions for the payment of travelling or subsistence expenses to witnesses. This presents a particularly difficult problem for the officer who has to deal with reluctant and frequently penniless witnesses. An officer tempted out of sympathy and generosity to subsidize a witness at court by buying them cigarettes or refreshments cannot properly claim back these expenses and may even be accused by the defence of trying to influence the witness. There is provision, however, for the CPS to provide travel warrants and hotel accommodation for witnesses and officers who find themselves in this position are well advised to seek the early assistance of the CPS.

7.2.7 **The layout of the court**

The layout of the Crown Court is similar to that of the magistrates' court. The most noticeable difference is, of course, the presence of the jury box. The position of the jury in relation to the rest of the court is not established by any law or regulation but by convention is most often to be found directly opposite the witness box in order that the jury can best hear and see the witnesses giving evidence. A notable exception to this is the number one court at the Old Bailey where the jury is seated to the right of and below the witness box. Prosecution and defence barristers and their teams will occupy the benches immediately before the clerk's bench and directly below the judge. The defendant will stand or sit according to whatever stage proceedings have reached in what is always referred to as 'the dock'. At the Crown Court this is always situated directly opposite the judge's bench itself. Ushers will occupy a table to the side with further areas reserved for, or habitually occupied by, the press and the probation services.

7.3 **The Press**

Some aspects of dealing with the press were discussed in Chapter 5 in the context of the magistrates' court. In the Crown Court, the general principles of cooperation and common sense remain the same. The police officer must adhere to the guidelines laid down by their own press office and would be well advised to seek their advice and attendance at high profile trials. Officers should be aware that there are strict limitations on the reporting of proceedings which are still 'active' and, generally speaking, should not comment upon active proceedings.

At the close of a case the press may request a copy of a picture of the convicted person for publication. A picture should only be released if it is in the public interest and may assist in the prevention or detection of other offences. In truth, the publication of pictures of convicted persons can rarely be justified, particularly if they are to begin a long custodial sentence during which their appearance will undoubtedly change. The publication of such photographs might also jeopardize future prosecutions if identification were in issue.

The Contempt of Court Act 1981 provides that a person, which would include a publisher as well as a journalist, could be guilty of contempt by publishing an article where:

- the publication creates a substantial (that is, not minimal) risk of serious prejudice or impediment to particular proceedings; and
- proceedings are active.

Criminal proceedings become active from the moment a summons or warrant is issued for a person's arrest or if a person has been either arrested or charged. The proceedings cease to be active when the defendant is acquitted or sentenced, the proceedings are discontinued or when enquiries by the police come to an end.

Journalists are able to report the progress of active proceedings but must do so fairly and accurately so as not to prejudice the proceedings. They must be particularly careful about reporting proceedings which are held 'in chambers' or 'in camera', that is, in the absence of the jury and the public. Journalists may be held in contempt of court by revealing matters which might be inadmissible in evidence but which could influence jurors, by publishing material that was the subject of an order restricting disclosure, by making payments to witnesses on terms which may encourage perjured evidence, or by putting pressure on litigants to abandon their case.

Crown Court Proceedings

As with proceedings in the magistrates' court, a great deal of Crown Court time is taken up with matters other than the hearing of trials. This is not surprising: the vast majority of cases that reach the Crown Court are the subject of a guilty plea and do not require the full panoply of the jury trial. However, even in a straightforward case where the defendant pleads guilty at an early stage, it is likely that more than one hearing will be required.

The most important of the pre-trial proceedings is the plea and case management hearing during which the defendant will enter their plea and, if it is not guilty, the judge will set a timetable for trial. However, there is a range of other hearings that may occur; the more common being listings for mention, for pre-trial issues, for public interest immunity applications, or for applications to vacate the trial date. Each of these hearings is designed to ensure that the trial, when it finally takes place, runs as smoothly as possible.

8.1 **The Indictment**

At the heart of trial in the Crown Court is the indictment. The 'indictment' is simply the document that records the charges that are brought against the defendant in the Crown Court. However, it is so fundamental that Crown Court trial is formally referred to as 'trial on indictment' (trial in the magistrates court is referred to as 'summary trial—see **Chapter 4**).

The indictment is made up of one or more charges (referred to as counts) which are each read to the defendant before they enter their plea. Often the indictment will resemble the charge sheet used by the police although the offence or offences with which the police charge a defendant need not be the same as those included in the indictment. There may also be changes from the charges which were committed or transferred from the magistrates' court. It is not unusual for the indictment which the defendant faces to differ greatly from the charges they originally faced. It is useful for the police officer, for the sake of completion and future reference, to obtain a copy of the indictment and to attach it to their own case papers. Obviously, this is particularly important where the indictment has changed from the offences that were initially charged by the police.

There may be a number of counts in the same indictment and some may be alternatives to each other. Common examples of alternative counts are offences of assault occasioning actual bodily harm (commonly referred to as ABH) with the lesser offence of common assault (which requires no evidence of injury); theft together with handling; and possession of drugs with intent to supply together with the lesser offence of simple possession for personal use.

Every indictment follows the same format. It will have its own reference or serial number which is given to it by the court. The counts within it will be divided into a Statement of Offence which specifies the name of the offence and its statutory basis (for example, assault occasioning actual bodily harm, contrary to s 47 of the Offences against the Person Act 1861), and a Particulars of Offence which is a brief summary of the allegation (for example, John Smith, on 1 January 2006, assaulted Steve Brown thereby occasioning him actual bodily harm). An indictment must be signed by an officer of the Crown Court and until it has been, is described as a 'bill of indictment' rather than an indictment.

When a bill of indictment is prepared it is said to be 'settled' or 'drafted'. Counsel (another term for a barrister) for the prosecution may draft the indictment and will often be asked to do so in more complex cases, but the task is usually carried out by a CPS lawyer. Ultimate responsibility for the indictment always rests with counsel for the Crown. The prosecution must not 'overload' or unnecessarily complicate an indictment by including too many counts nor should counts be included with the aim of encouraging the defendant to plead guilty to a proportion of them. The Code for Crown prosecutors prescribes that charges should be selected which reflect the seriousness of the offending, provide the court with adequate powers of sentence, and allow the case to be presented in a clear and simple way. In appropriate cases, specimen counts can be used as examples of a greater number of offences. For example, in a case of benefit fraud lasting for several years, the court might be informed of the total loss to public funds without requiring the defendant to admit an offence for every time they visited the benefit office.

8.2 Pre-trial Proceedings

8.2.1 The plea and case management hearing (PCMH)

The purpose of the plea and case management hearing (often referred to as the PCMH) is similar to the 'early administrative hearing' at the magistrates' court. The hearing may conveniently be divided into two parts. The first stage is to take pleas from the defendant. Then, if any of the pleas are not guilty and are unacceptable to the Crown, the second stage is to manage the case by setting a timetable for trial. This is done by the judge who will make a range of orders (often by agreement) designed to promote the efficient conduct of the trial. One of the more important matters that is resolved is the question of which witnesses will be required to give live evidence at the trial (see further **12.3.1**).

'Arraignment' is the grand name given to the procedure whereby the counts on the indictment are put to the defendant and they enter a plea of guilty or not guilty. The clerk of the court will ask the defendant to stand while they read the indictment. If the indictment contains a number of counts then each count will be put to the defendant individually and they will plead guilty or not guilty to each in turn. Having read the statement and particulars of each count, the clerk will say to the defendant, 'Do you plead guilty or not guilty?' The defendant is expected only to answer simply 'guilty' or 'not guilty'.

After this has occurred, the defendant will be asked to sit down and the judge will turn expectantly to the prosecution counsel. The judge will usually know the names of the barristers and may even know them personally. The judge will address the prosecution counsel by their surname preceded by Mr, Miss or Mrs.

Prosecution counsel will stand and introduce themselves and their defence counterpart with that peculiar deference which characterizes all of counsel's dealings with the judge at the Crown Court. They will say something like, 'May it please Your Honour, I represent the Crown in this matter and my learned friend, Mr Hopkins represents the defendant'. What follows is then, of course, determined by whether the defendant pleads guilty or not guilty.

8.2.2 **The guilty plea**

Should the defendant plead guilty to the indictment at arraignment then the jury will not be required. The court and the prosecution may have advance notice of a defendant's intention to plead guilty (or may reasonably anticipate a guilty plea from the answers given in interview) and will be prepared to respond appropriately. The judge may proceed directly to sentencing but is more likely to adjourn the case in order that 'pre-sentence' (commonly referred to as PSR) or other reports can be prepared. The sentencing procedure is described fully in **Chapter 9.**

8.2.3 **The not guilty plea**

The plea of not guilty puts the onus of proof squarely on the prosecution's shoulders and nothing thereafter can be taken for granted. Potentially the whole of the prosecution case is at issue and the defence team has a duty to do their best to protect their client from conviction within the limits of professional conduct.

If the plea is not guilty then the defence and prosecution must inform the court about all those matters upon which they have reached agreement or seek a ruling from the judge. In order to expedite this process of information, the defence and prosecution counsel will hand to the judge a questionnaire which they have completed. The questionnaire addresses such issues as exhibits, the order of witnesses, alibi evidence, vulnerable witnesses, the estimated length of trial and convenient dates for trial.

8.2.4 **Case management**

The judge will normally begin giving directions by setting a date for the trial. Although an early date may be convenient for the parties in court, there may be other reasons why it cannot take place. It may be that the list office cannot find a suitable slot for the estimated duration of the trial. If such a situation arises then the list office may set the date administratively and both parties will be informed in correspondence. Although there are nominal targets which proscribe that the trial should take place no longer than eight weeks after arraignment, this limit is rarely met and there is often a long passage of time between the plea and the trial.

If the date is set at the PCMH it is the responsibility of the CPS to liaise with the appropriate court preparation office at a police station. Where there is no such support office, as is quite often the case with major enquiries, then it is the responsibility of the officer present to make written notification of the date and the witnesses that are to be warned. Confirmation should arrive from the CPS in due course.

In advance of the PCMH hearing, the CPS will have served a file of evidence on the defence either before or at committal proceedings in the magistrates' court or following transfer under s 51 of the Crime and Disorder Act 1998. This may or may not be the whole of the prosecution case but will incorporate all the statements available at that time and transcripts of the defendant's tape-recorded interviews. This evidence should be served on the defence sufficiently early to allow them a reasonable amount of time to consider it and advise the defendant. Having received the evidence from the CPS the defence will not only be in a position to advise the defendant as to their plea but also to assess which witnesses they require to give live evidence at the trial.

The question of which witnesses are required to give live evidence is of some importance to officers. First, it is still normal for the police to undertake the task of informing the prosecution witnesses when they are needed. Secondly, police officers themselves may be required to give evidence either because they were eye witnesses to the commission of the alleged offence or because they were involved in the investigative process.

It goes without saying that the witnesses who are called to give live evidence will normally be the most important. They will include the witnesses whose evidence the defence challenge. However, it is not unusual for witnesses to be required even though there is no dispute as to their evidence. This often occurs with the officer in the case (OIC) who may be required even though there is no challenge to their evidence. A full explanation of why officers may be required to give evidence themselves is provided in Chapter 12 (see **12.3.1**).

As well as deciding which witnesses will be required, the judge may also consider procedural matters. Common examples include 'special measures' made under the Youth Justice and Criminal Evidence Act 1999 which may allow evidence in chief to be given by pre-recorded video evidence and cross examination to be given by live television link for young and vulnerable witnesses.

8.2.5 **Attendance of officers at PCMHs**

The police officer will not normally attend at the PCMH but when they do they should approach it in the same way as they approach the bail application. The officer in the case has an important role to play and should not expect to be a passive observer. All parties will wish to know what stage the investigation has reached and what, if any, more evidence can be expected and what enquiries are still being conducted. Counsel for the prosecution is the mouthpiece for the Crown in court and will, in all probability, ask the appropriate questions of the officer before the hearing begins. The questions will invariably include the interrogatives 'what?' and 'when?' Ultimately, an officer who does not allow sufficient time to liaise with prosecution counsel before a PCMH faces the possibility of being asked to enter the witness box to answer the judge's queries directly. Explaining to a judge in open court why certain evidence is not yet available is extremely rare but can be one of the least rewarding tasks that a police officer is required to carry out. It is particularly galling for the officer when the delay being scrutinized is no fault of their own or the service. To lay blame directly at the door of another agency, however, such as the Forensic Science Service is perhaps not the most prudent way of dealing with the situation, although if this is the reality there may be no alternative. Best by far is for the officer to be in a position to supply a date of delivery for the outstanding evidence.

The officer who attends a PCMH without accurate witness availability dates for the prosecution witnesses (see **11.1.6** and Form MG10) will not impress the judge or their own counsel unless there is good reason for the failure, such as the non-cooperation of a civilian or professional witness.

8.2.6 **For mention**

Cases will frequently be listed 'for mention'. This simple phrase covers a multitude of possibilities. The prosecution or defence may, for example, ask for the case to be listed because they have not received certain evidence promised at the PCMH. The defence may wish to seek a ruling by the judge on editing requests. There may be 'disclosure' or other timetable issues to discuss. The defendant will not be present at such hearings but will be represented. It is very unusual for the attendance of a police officer (including the officer in the case) to be required although officers should not hesitate to consult the CPS prosecutor dealing with the case beforehand if there is any doubt.

The case may also be listed for 'mention and fix' which will normally refer to a brief hearing where the trial date is set in open court.

8.2.7 **Application to break the fixture**

An application to break the fixture (also referred to as an application to vacate or an 'app to vac') may be made by both defence or prosecution. It is simply a request by either party to change the date of the trial set by the judge at the PCMH or other preliminary hearing. The reasons for such an application are endless but must be reasonable and supported by circumstances. The judge will always need to be convinced that there is good reason to delay the trial because of the inevitable administrative inconvenience and the tribulation it may cause witnesses. Should an application to break the fixture be successful then a new date for the trial will not necessarily be set there and then as there may be no up-to-date availability for witnesses. If this occurs, the case will normally be adjourned for a short period 'for mention and fix'.

8.2.8 **Preparatory hearings**

Preparatory hearings may be held in cases which are likely to be long or very complicated. The decision to hold such a hearing will usually be made by the judge at the PCMH. The judge who presides at a preparatory hearing will be the judge who hears the trial. The hearing will take place before a jury is sworn. Preparatory hearings are largely confined to complex fraud cases and are designed to help the jury to identify and understand the important issues and to assist the judge in their management of the trial.

8.2.9 **Public interest immunity (PII)**

There are two types of public interest immunity (PII) hearings. The first relates to material that is in the hands of the prosecution but which they do not wish to disclose. The second relates to material that is in the possession of other agencies such as social services. In both cases, the court has the power to decide whether or not this material ought to be disclosed to the defence. It is likely that officers will only be required to deal with the first type of PII hearing.

The vast majority of material generated by a police investigation will be disclosable and should not present a problem. Some of the material may be categorized as 'sensitive' by the police or the CPS but may then be edited and disclosed. The editing, in particular, of names, addresses and telephone numbers will not normally, or reasonably, be objected to by the defence. There are occasions, however, where the police and the CPS agree that material is so sensitive and confidential that it should not be disclosed and an application will be made for a ruling that the material should not be disclosed. Non-disclosure applications can be made at both the magistrates' court and the Crown Court.

The only times when a judge will rule that certain material should not be disclosed to the defence is when it is not deemed to be in the 'public interest'. The judge alone can make this decision. Material falling into this category may relate to the following:

- Police internal communications
- National security
- The identity of informants and undercover police officers
- Observation points
- Surveillance
- Investigative techniques

The application for a ruling under public interest immunity (PII) is made in chambers and is normally but not exclusively 'ex parte', which is to say that the defendant will not be present or represented. If the application is made and the defendant is represented it is said to be 'inter partes'. The defence in most cases must be informed that the application is taking place even if it is to be 'ex parte'. A case will be made by the prosecution and examined by the judge. It is normal for a police officer to be called and to provide evidence on oath in answer to the judge's questions.

Internal police policy usually dictates that an officer of at least Inspector or Chief Inspector rank supervises sensitive matters, particularly in relation to the use of surveillance and informants. It is therefore most appropriate that the officer with responsibility for these matters and first hand knowledge of the issues to be addressed should attend these hearings. In such cases force policy should be consulted.

It must be stressed that only a court, whether magistrates' or Crown, can make the final decision with regard to PII. The mere fact that the prosecution are to make a non-disclosure application may alert the defence to the possibilities of what it may be based on. This fact alone may discourage the prosecution from making the application. If this situation arises and the prosecution feel that they cannot make the application with confidence then the case will almost certainly be abandoned and no evidence offered. The CPS will not be able to deal properly with a PII non-disclosure hearing unless they have been properly briefed and early case conference is particularly advisable where these issues are likely to arise.

The 'ex parte' hearing of PII non-disclosure applications has raised serious concerns for defence lawyers and civil rights campaigners who believe that it may be a breach of Article 6 of the Human Rights Act of 1998, the 'right to a fair trial'.

8.2.10 Abuse of process

This is a term which often baffles both police officers and members of the public. On application by the defence, a judge, and indeed a magistrate, has an inherent power to terminate ('stay') proceedings if there has been an 'abuse of process'. The 'process' in this context refers to the judicial process. Circumstances justifying the exercise of the power will occur rarely and it is for the defendant to establish that the pursuit of the particular proceedings would be seriously unjust. This is quite different from the suggestion that the prosecution is unwise or the evidence is weak. In many cases, the application will be refused on the ground that the trial process itself will be equipped to deal with the complaint.

It has been suggested that the two categories of abuse of process are, first, where the defendant would not receive a fair trial and, secondly, where it would be unfair for the defendant to be tried. The categories may overlap as they did in the case of Gell where the defendants were charged with a fraud arising from dealings in duty suspended alcohol. After conviction, a failure to disclose that various informants had acted with the encouragement of Customs and Excise came to light. It also appeared that a prosecution witness had lied in the course of giving evidence. The appeals were allowed on the basis that the defence had been prevented from making an effective application to stay the proceedings as an abuse of process as a result of that non-disclosure. Had there been full disclosure, the application might have been successful.

In this context it is important that police internal procedures, for example in relation to the continuity of exhibits and the preservation of evidence, are followed. If an important exhibit is lost or destroyed prematurely and its loss puts the defendant at a significant disadvantage then the prosecution might be 'stayed' (stopped) under this type of abuse.

An unsatisfactory delay in bringing a prosecution could give rise to an abuse of process if it was very lengthy as it would prejudice a defendant by affecting their recollection of events and opportunity to gather witness evidence.

The second category of abuse concerns manipulation or misuse of the process of the court by the prosecution. In this regard a useful test is that there should be either an element of bad faith or at least some serious fault. As an example, the prosecution of a person who, in exchange for their co-operation received an undertaking from the police that they would not be charged with an offence, is capable of amounting to an abuse of process. However, breach of a promise not to prosecute does not necessarily give rise to an abuse. An example of an abuse of process in the magistrates' court was when the prosecution, after the magistrates had retired to consider their sentence, asked the bench to return to court and invited them to substitute a different charge which carried the possibility of a custodial sentence because they realized that the old charge was punishable only by way of a fine.

There is a wide variety of circumstances that might constitute an abuse of process, none of which is easily explained to victims and witnesses. It is a step, however, which the judge or magistrate will not take lightly.

8.3 Failure to Appear

Section 7(1) of the Bail Act 1976 allows a judge to issue a warrant for the arrest of a defendant who fails to surrender to his bail at the Crown Court. The warrant issued by a judge is called a 'bench warrant'. A warrant may be backed for bail or not backed for bail. A person arrested under a bench warrant which is not backed for bail must be held in custody until they are brought before the court at its next sitting. It is not unusual for a police officer to accompany the prisoner in order to answer any questions which the judge may ask about the circumstances of the arrest. It does not follow that a person so arrested will necessarily be remanded into custody by the judge.

8.4 **Trial by Jury**

8.4.1 **Introduction**

The right to trial by jury has existed in some form in England and Wales for a thousand years. It is often described as the 'cornerstone' of the English legal system and represents an opportunity for the community to participate meaningfully in the judicial system. Whilst consistently under the threat of reform or abolition, the jury remains at the heart of British justice and the envy of many other criminal justice systems.

During trial in the Crown Court, it is impossible to overlook the presence of the jury. The judge will address them at the start of the trial and will summarize the evidence for their benefit at the end. Counsel will deliver their opening and closing speeches directly to the jury. Throughout, they will be treated with the utmost courtesy by the judge and counsel. While their presence inevitably lengthens the trial process, almost all involved in the criminal justice system agree that their involvement is important.

8.4.2 **Who may sit on a jury?**

Until relatively recently police officers and other categories of person concerned with the administration of justice were ineligible for jury service. Several other large groups were also excused for service as of right. However, the Criminal Justice Act 2003 repealed such exclusionary rules and the position is now that potential jury members must merely be:

- aged 18 to 70, and
- on the electoral register, and
- ordinarily resident in the UK, Channel Islands or Isle of Man for at least five years since the age of 13, and
- not a 'mentally disordered' person [meaning, in essence, a person who suffers/suffered from severe mental illness or mental handicap], and
- not a person who is disqualified from jury service.

Disqualification refers to persons who are on bail, have served substantial terms of imprisonment, or have been sentenced to a custodial or a community sentence in the last 10 years.

Jurors are summoned to attend the Crown Court by officers of the Crown Court acting on behalf of the Lord Chancellor. The summons is in writing and may be sent by post or served (delivered) by hand. The summons sets out the grounds for ineligibility and disqualification and relies upon the honesty of the person receiving the summons. It is an offence to make false representations for the purposes of evading jury service or enabling another to do so.

8.4.3 **Selection of the jury**

Once the prospective jurors have been summoned, their names are put on to a list which is called a 'panel'. The panel or part of the panel is then brought into court in order that a jury of 12 may be selected from it. Both the defence and the prosecution have the right to inspect the panel but only the prosecution may object to particular jurors before they are selected. This process is referred to as requiring jurors to 'stand by for the Crown'. The Attorney General has issued guidelines as to the exercise of this power which emphasize that it should be used rarely. Accordingly, although it is lawful for inquiries to be made as to whether potential jurors have previous convictions, jurors are not routinely vetted. For this reason, it is not beyond the bounds of possibility to suppose that convicted people have sat on juries. However, they would have committed a criminal offence punishable with a fine of up to £5,000.

Once 20 or more members of the jury panel have been brought into the court by the usher, the clerk of the court will read 12 names randomly selected from the panel and those persons (jurors) enter the jury box. Once they are all present the clerk of the court will then address the defendant as follows:

> The names that you are about to hear called are the names of the jurors who are to try you. If therefore you wish to object to them or any of them, you must do so as they come to the book to be sworn, and before they are sworn, and your objection shall be heard.

Challenges to jurors by either the defence or the prosecution must be made before the juror has been sworn. A challenge is only permitted for certain reasons and is therefore referred to as 'challenge for cause'. The practice, commonplace in the American courts, of routinely objecting to potential jurors does not take place in the Crown Court. In the English courts, it is unusual for jurors to be challenged unless they are known to either party.

Providing there is no challenge, the clerk will then call on each of the 12 individually to swear the juror's oath which is as follows:

> 'I swear by almighty God that I will faithfully try the defendant and give a true verdict according to the evidence.'

Jurors will read the oath from a printed card and will hold in their right hand the book which is most appropriate for their religion. The juror may elect to affirm as opposed to swearing an oath. This procedure is commonly referred to as the 'swearing in' or the 'empanelling' of the jury. Having been sworn in the defendant is in the charge of the jury and the trial may begin.

8.4.4 **Discharge**

In most cases the jury that is sworn in will hear the entire case and return a verdict at the end of it. A judge, however, has the power to discharge up to three members or, alternatively, the entire jury if they decide that that is the correct course of action. A common ground for discharge of an individual juror is because they are sick and physically incapable of continuing. However, a juror may also be discharged if there is good reason to doubt that juror's objectivity and their ability to return a true and fair verdict. A judge will guard against this by warning the members of the jury not to speak to friends or family about the case when they go home in the evening or during breaks in the trial.

There are occasions when the entire jury will be discharged. This will occur when the jury fails to reach a verdict and is considered in **8.4.7** below. Other circumstances in which an entire jury may be discharged are as follows:

- Inadmissible evidence which is prejudicial to the accused is inadvertently given during the trial so that a fair trial cannot continue. An example of such a situation might be where the police officer giving evidence mistakenly refers to one or all of the defendant's previous convictions. This is a grave mistake which may well necessitate a re-trial (see also **13.4.5** for evidence of bad character in general).
- Where there are grave concerns that the conduct of one or more juror has placed the integrity of the whole jury into doubt and the matter cannot therefore be dealt with by the discharge of those jurors alone.
- Where inappropriate media coverage of the trial which is prejudicial to the defendant is likely to have been seen by members of the jury and is equally likely to affect their deliberations. A very high profile example of this was seen in the trial of two Leeds United footballers and others at Middlesbrough Crown Court in 2001 where an interview with the father of an assault victim whose son had given evidence at the trial was published by a national newspaper before the trial had finished. The judge ordered that the jury be discharged (see also **7.3** above for the press).

The discharge of a jury does not mean that the defendant is acquitted. In the ordinary course of events, a re-trial will be ordered and a new date set. The defendant may be remanded on bail or in custody until the time of the new trial.

8.4.5 **Intimidating witnesses and jurors**

The intimidation of witnesses and jurors in criminal cases is contrary to s 51 of the Criminal Justice and Public Order Act 1994. To constitute the offence, the intimidation must be intended to cause the investigation or the course of justice to be interfered with, and carried out in the knowledge that the person being intimidated is a witness or juror in any proceedings. This section also covers acts of intimidation towards or by third parties with the same intent. The maximum penalty is five years' imprisonment.

It is also possible for a trial judge to direct that while away from the court, the jurors should be afforded police protection. This may be in response from an application from the prosecution but the judge may exercise their discretion without hearing evidence.

8.4.6 **Summing up**

Having listened patiently to the closing speeches, ideally brief but rarely so, the judge will then sum up the case. In the summing up the judge will direct the jury in respect of the law, outline the issues of fact which the jury must decide and then summarize the evidence and arguments on both sides.

The judge's summing up is a crucial part of a Crown Court trial and the judge must strike a fair balance between the prosecution case and the defence case, being careful not to fall too heavily on one side or the other. Omissions and impartiality can provide grounds for an appeal and may give rise to criticism of the trial judge by the Court of Appeal.

Judges sum up in their own style but all will refresh their memory from their own note of the evidence which they will keep throughout the trial. As well as a summary of the evidence that often draws from this note, the summing up is structured to incorporate certain key directions on the law which normally include:

- An explanation of the role of judge and jury that indicates the judge is the sole arbiter of legal matters but that the jury decide what facts have been established or proved by the evidence.
- An explanation of the burden and standard of proof that indicates it is not for the defendant to prove innocence but for the prosecution to prove guilt and that the jury must be satisfied 'beyond reasonable doubt' that the accused committed the offence.
- An explanation of the charge including the elements that the prosecution must prove and any defences to it.
- A direction that if two or more accused are joined in the one indictment the jury must consider each case separately.
- An instruction to the jury to appoint a foreman and to retire and consider their verdict and to seek to reach a unanimous decision.

In common with closing speeches, the judge's summing up may have an important bearing on the verdict of the jury. The judge is obliged to place the defendant's defence before the jury but is not required to rehearse it without criticism. It goes without saying that greater emphasis will be given to parts of the evidence that the judge perceives to be the most important. However, it is now routine for the judge to direct that if the jury disagree with any of the comments they make, the comments should be ignored.

It is often the case that the police officer feels the judge placed too great an emphasis on the elements that support the defence case while at the same time the defence consider the reverse to be true. However, there is guidance from the Court of Appeal to the effect that no matter how distasteful the offence, however repulsive the defendant, however laughable his defence, they are entitled to have their defence fairly presented to the jury. Justice, it has been said, is not served by a one-sided account given to the jury shortly before retirement. On a more pragmatic level, many counsel will say that a summing up that is too favourable to the prosecution will often encourage a verdict for the defence.

When the summing up is complete the court usher will take an oath to keep the jury in a 'private and convenient' place and not to allow anybody else to speak to them. The usher will also not speak to the jury other than to ask them if they have reached a verdict. The usher now referred to, as the 'jury bailiff' will take the jury from the court in order that they can consider their verdict.

8.4.7 **The verdict**

Once the jury has retired the jury bailiff will keep them in a private room within the court building. Jury members should not talk to anyone about the case save for their fellow jurors. Prior to 1994, if a jury had not reached a verdict by the end of the day then they would have to stay overnight in a hotel. This is no longer the case but before leaving the court at the end of the day the judge will remind the jury of their responsibilities and tell them that they should not discuss the case even with members of their own families.

During their retirement the jury may wish to ask further questions of the judge. In this case they will write the question down and hand it to the jury bailiff who, in turn, will hand it to the judge. The judge will call both counsel back into the court and read the question to them. They will endeavour to agree on the best way of answering the question, the jury will be called in and the judge will address them. The jury or members of it may wish to examine items exhibited during the trial and the officer in the case must always be mindful of this and ensure in consultation with the jury bailiff that they are readily available for inspection.

The privacy of the jury room and the confidentiality of the jury's deliberations are sacrosanct. Section 8 of the Contempt of Court Act 1981 makes it an offence for a juror to disclose details of their deliberations. It is also an offence for another, such as a journalist, to try to obtain details of jury deliberations.

Once the jury has reached its verdict they will inform the jury bailiff who will then inform the clerk of the court. The judge is then notified and all parties are summoned, usually by the paging system, to the court. The jury will file back into the jury box and the foreman will stand. The clerk of the court will ask the foreman if the jury has reached a verdict upon which they are all agreed. If the answer is 'yes' the clerk will ask the foreman, 'To the first count in the indictment, do you find the defendant guilty or not guilty?'. The foreman will then announce the verdict. If there is only one count on the indictment then the process is finished at that point. If there is more than one count the procedure is repeated until all the counts have been dealt with.

The delivery of the verdict is beyond doubt the most gripping and dramatic moment of any trial and tension invariably runs high. It is not unusual for there to be an outburst of emotion whatever the verdict, usually from the public gallery but occasionally from the defendant. It is important that the police officer remains impassive and professional. An expression of dismay at a not guilty verdict does the officer or the service no credit. Equally a clear indication of delight at a guilty verdict does not meet the dignity or gravity of the situation. It is common for jurors to look first to the defendant and then to the officer in the case and any friends or family of a victim for a response to their verdict. The officer's demeanour should neither unsettle nor intimidate the jury whatever their inner disappointment or satisfaction. At the moment the verdict is delivered the officer in the case or their colleagues may be with a victim or perhaps the family of a deceased person. If this is the case then their attention will inevitably be focused upon their support of that person.

8.4.8 Unanimous and majority verdicts

In summing up the judge will always direct the jury to try to reach a unanimous decision. The judge may mention the possibility of a majority verdict but will tell the jury that for the time being they should attempt to reach a verdict upon which they are all agreed. A unanimous verdict is obviously the most desirable outcome and it is to that conclusion that the jury must first seek to arrive.

If, after a reasonable amount of time, a jury cannot reach a unanimous verdict then the judge will call them back into court and tell them that a majority verdict would now be acceptable. There is no set amount of time which must pass before such a 'majority direction' is given but the judge must allow the jury at least two hours and 10 minutes to reach a unanimous verdict. A deliberation of between three and five hours is the norm. The gravity and complexity of the offence will naturally have a bearing on the length of a jury's deliberations and the time allowed by the judge for a unanimous verdict. Having called the jury back in to court the judge will always ask them if there is still a possibility that they may yet reach a unanimous verdict. If the jury indicates that this is the case then the judge will allow them more time to consider. If the answer is no then the majority direction will be given.

Before 1967 a jury had to reach a unanimous verdict before there could be a conviction. Section 17 of the Criminal Justice Act 1967 now allows for a majority verdict. The permissible voting combinations depend on the number of people in the jury. As we have seen there must always be 12 jurors at the start of a trial but it is not uncommon for jurors to be discharged, usually for medical reasons, during the course of the trial. The number of jurors cannot drop below nine. If there are nine jurors only then their verdict must be unanimous. If there are 12 jurors and they are to reach a majority verdict it must be by 11 to 1 or 10 to 2. If the jury is reduced to less than 12 members then the majority verdict must be either 10 to 1 or 9 to 1. It cannot be by 9 to 2 and a jury reduced to 9 must be unanimous.

When the jury returns to the court with a majority verdict the foreman will stand and the clerk of the court will ask if they have reached a verdict upon which at least 10 or nine of them (depending on the size of the jury) are agreed.

If the verdict is guilty then the foreman will be asked what the majority was. Failure to determine the majority after a guilty verdict gives grounds for appeal.

Police officers habitually make an assessment of the jury's appearance and may conclude, quite irrationally, that it is either a 'good', 'bad', 'interested' or 'disinterested' jury. They may even have seen a juror fall asleep or display signs of exasperation or impatience during proceedings. They will frequently speculate for the duration of the jury's deliberations about what the significance of the length of the retirement might be. Victims, witnesses and relatives will ask questions about the meaning of what may seem to them to be a lengthy deliberation.

The wait for the verdict can be the most stressful part of the trial for many of the parties involved but the length of the jury's deliberations tells the officer nothing about what the eventual verdict will be. A rash or unfounded prediction about the outcome may not relieve the tension but will unreasonably raise expectations or cause unnecessary dejection and, if mistaken, ultimately damage the officer's credibility. A speedy and sudden recall to the court cannot be interpreted one way or the other just as a lengthy deliberation or majority direction indicates neither the likelihood of a guilty nor a not guilty verdict.

The only certainty is the uncertainty and the knowledge that almost as many contested trials result in not guilty verdicts as guilty. A jury's verdict can never be confidently predicted. Barristers will very rarely be drawn and do not tempt fate by predicting the outcome. The police officer would do well to use the time allowed by the deliberation more constructively.

8.4.9 The 'hung' jury

Where, after a reasonable amount of time and despite a majority direction, the jury cannot agree upon a verdict, they will be called back into the court and asked by the judge whether there is any possibility of their returning a verdict. If the foreman intimates that agreement is very unlikely then the judge will discharge them from their duty. In such cases the jury is said to be 'hung'. The defendant is not acquitted and in most cases there will be a re-trial. In the event of the second jury disagreeing it is common practice for the prosecution formally to offer no evidence. This may take place after the second jury being discharged and will not require a jury to formally acquit the defendant.

The 'hung' jury is an unsatisfactory outcome in many ways for both parties but preferable to an acquittal in the eyes of the prosecution and to a conviction in the eyes of the defence. For the police officer it means that they and their witnesses will have to go through the whole process again. It may be wise to forewarn victims and witnesses of the possibility of a 'hung' jury, as many will not be aware of it. The discharge of the jury in this way or the abortion of a trial for any other reason presents the officer in the case with the opportunity to address any difficulties that arose during the trial and to present as near perfect a case as is possible at the re-trial. Whilst they may dread a second trial, witnesses will at least have had the benefit of giving evidence once and will know what to expect.

8.5 **Applications in the Crown Court**

There are many applications which a police officer can make to the Crown Court judge, particularly in respect of fraud, drug trafficking, money laundering and terrorism. The legislation governing these applications is complex, extensive and beyond the scope of this work. In most cases, the application procedures are essentially the same as those followed for warrant applications in the magistrates' court. The two applications which are most commonly made are the applications for the PACE indictable offence production order and the PACE indictable offence production warrant.

8.5.1 **The PACE 'Production Order'**

An application for this order is governed by s 9(1) of the Police and Criminal Evidence Act 1984. A production order is an order issued by a circuit judge requiring a person, organization or business to produce specified material to the police within a specified period of time. The type of material being sought is defined by PACE as 'special procedure material' and the offence being investigated, also defined by PACE, must be 'indictable'. This is a power available not only to police investigations but also to investigations into indictable offences by the Department of Trade and Industry (DTI).

An application for a PACE production order must be authorized by a Superintendent or a suitably authorized Chief Inspector. Notice must be served on the party from whom the material is sought that the application is to be made. That person may not conceal, destroy, alter or dispose of the material without permission of a judge or written permission of a constable until the application is dismissed or abandoned, or until they have complied with the order. To do so constitutes contempt of court. The party has no right to be heard on the application but the judge may allow them to do so if they wish.

The officer making the application should first complete an information in exactly the same manner as they would for an application in the magistrates' court. They should contact the Crown Court office and speak to a clerk in order to arrange a time to make the application. The application will be made 'in chambers' and where the other party is represented is described as 'inter partes'. The officer will swear an oath in relation to their information and proceed to answer any questions that may be asked of them by the judge or other interested party.

If the judge decides to make the order they will specify the period of time within which the material must be supplied or the officer given access to it. The order will be signed by the judge and addressed to all the constables of a specific police force. The order should then be taken to the court office where it will be registered before it is taken from the building and served.

8.5.2 Search Warrant Issued by a Circuit Judge

Application for these warrants is governed by Sch 1, para 12 of the Police and Criminal Evidence Act 1984. It is granted where a s 9 production order has been served and not complied with or where the service of a production order would not be appropriate either because access to the material cannot be gained or advance notice would frustrate the purposes of the investigation. An application for a search warrant under this provision should be made on the authority of an officer of at least the rank of inspector, but where no such officer is on duty, the senior officer on duty may authorize an application.

The application procedure is exactly the same as for the production order except that the application is made 'ex parte', that is, without the other party being represented or notified. The warrant may name a person who may accompany the officers on the search. This may be particularly important where expert assistance is required particularly in relation to computing or financial matters. However, even when accompanied by others the police are responsible for the execution of the warrant.

8.5.3 General

As with applications in the magistrates' court, Code of Practice B applies to all of the above applications. The Code requires that an officer check the accuracy of their information, and where possible the motive behind the giving of the information. An application may not be made on the basis of anonymous information. The officer should ascertain as much information as possible about the premises, the likely occupier and the articles concerned. Finally, an officer must not state that the purposes of the search will be frustrated or prejudiced unless immediate access is granted unless they believe this to be true.

Crown Court: Guilty Pleas and Sentencing

9.1 The Plea of Guilty

9.1.1 Introduction

It might be thought that when a defendant pleads guilty all will be admitted and so the facts of the offence will not be in dispute. Indeed, the point has already been made that if a guilty plea is entered to all of the counts on the indictment, the jury will not be required. However, frequently a guilty plea does not resolve the case, either because there is a dispute about the facts of the offence, or because there are other counts on the indictment to which the defendant has pleaded not guilty.

A dispute about the facts of the offence may occur because when pleading guilty, it is common for defendants to accept that they committed an offence while at the same time denying some of the allegations made against them. There may be a need for a further hearing to decide whether the prosecution case or the defendant's account is accurate. The factual basis of sentence is obviously important; justice requires that the punishment fits the crime.

There are times when a plea to every count on the indictment will not be necessary to resolve the case. On occasion, the prosecution will be prepared to accept guilty pleas to a lesser offence than a count on the indictment. Alternatively, the Crown may be content with guilty pleas to certain counts but not others. Such arrangements are a regular occurrence in the Crown Court and may be reached for a wide range of reasons.

In light of the above, and for other reasons, it is unusual for the sentencing hearing to take place immediately after the plea of guilty. It is normal for the court to take the plea and then adjourn the proceedings, very often to allow 'pre-sentence' or other reports to be prepared. The case may also be postponed to await the outcome of other proceedings outstanding against the defendant with a view to sentencing for all matters on one occasion. Finally, if a defendant enters mixed pleas to an indictment and the prosecution will not accept those pleas, sentencing for the counts to which they have pleaded guilty should be postponed until after trial on the not guilty counts.

9.1.2 The basis of plea

Following a guilty plea, sentence will ordinarily be passed on the basis of the prosecution case, as contained within the witness statements. However, if the defendant denies some important fact or facts relating to the crime, the onus is on the defence to bring this to the attention of the prosecutor and the court. This should be done by recording the defendant's instructions in writing, and by handing this document (referred to as the 'basis of plea') to the prosecution and the court. Obviously, when this occurs, the dispute is not whether the offence was committed, but how it was committed, and the defendant remains convicted by their own admission.

Any written basis should be considered carefully by the prosecution. It is now common practice for the views of the police and the victim to be sought, although the final decision rests with the Crown Prosecution Service. Where the prosecution accepts the defendant's account of the disputed facts, the agreement (the basis of plea) should be written down and signed by both advocates. It should then be made available to the judge. Where the Crown has no evidence to contradict the defendant's account, the Crown should not normally agree the defendant's basis of plea unless supported by other material.

Whatever view is formed by the Crown on any proposed basis of plea, the judge is not bound by it. The judge is entitled to insist that any evidence relevant to the facts in dispute should be called, although they should have regard to the reason for any agreement reached between the advocates. Alternatively, if the judge regards the case advanced on the defendant's behalf as absurd, they may decline to hear evidence but should explain why the decision to reject the basis of plea has been reached.

The final consideration in relation to the basis of plea is that if the judge considers that the impact of the dispute on the sentencing decision is minimal, the judge should simply sentence on the defendant's account without hearing evidence on the disputed facts.

9.1.3 **The Newton hearing**

If the situation arises where the judge considers that a dispute between the basis of plea and the Crown's case is likely to affect the level of sentence, a hearing will take place that is referred to as a Newton hearing. This will normally happen on a different occasion to the time when the plea was entered so that witnesses can be brought to court. A jury will not be required.

An example of where the need for a Newton hearing might arise would be where a defendant was prepared to plead guilty to an assault on the basis that the injuries sustained by the victim were caused by his fist. The Crown's case, however, might be that the defendant struck the victim with a pool cue. As indicated above, if the judge came to the conclusion that the Crown's version of events was unlikely to have any bearing on the severity of the sentence, then a Newton hearing would be unnecessary and the judge would sentence on the basis of the defendant's account. However, if the Crown's version of the facts was likely to have a bearing on the sentence passed (as would probably be the case in this example) then the judge would hear evidence to resolve the dispute. The evidence is heard without a jury and the judge alone will make the decision. Witnesses are called, sworn, and give evidence just as if it were a trial.

9.1.4 **Plea bargaining**

In British courts, the phrase 'plea bargaining' is not favoured, because it is often interpreted to mean the imposition of a certain sentence in exchange for particular pleas by the defendant. In the past, the practice of a judge giving an indication of what sentence a defendant might receive if he entered a guilty plea was strongly discouraged by the Court of Appeal. It was thought that an indication might place undue pressure upon a defendant to plead guilty to a crime he did not commit. However, in a recent case (*R v Goodyear*, April 2005) the Court of Appeal endorsed indications of sentence in the Crown Court if a plea of guilty was to be tendered at the stage the indication was sought. Such indications should not be given unless sought by the defendant and the judge may refuse to give them or may reserve their position until they feel able to give an advance indication (for example, where reports on the defendant are awaited).

One type of bargain between the defence and prosecution is well established and common practice. In certain circumstances, the prosecution and defence will agree that, in the event of the defendant pleading guilty to parts of the indictment, the Crown will not pursue the other counts. The agreement can follow the defendant pleading guilty to a lesser offence than that on the indictment, or pleas to certain counts on the indictment and not others. The agreement can be reached without the prior knowledge and consent of the judge. However, the prosecution may wish to take account of the judge's view and if the prosecution seek the judge's views, they should abide by them.

A common example of the first type would be where an offence of 'wounding or causing grievous (serious) bodily harm with intent' contrary to s 18 of the Offences Against the Person Act 1861, is on the indictment but the Crown would be prepared to accept a plea to an offence of 'wounding' contrary to s 20 of the Offences Against the Person Act 1861. This type of plea bargain will even take place where a defendant is indicted for murder but there is an agreement that a plea to the offence of manslaughter would be acceptable.

The second type of bargain is where there are a number of counts on the indictment and the defendant will plead guilty to some but not others on the understanding that the others will not be proceeded with by the prosecution. In these cases it is usual for the prosecution to ask the judge that the matters denied by the defendant 'lie on the court file' not to be proceeded with without leave (permission) of the court or of the Court of Appeal. There are numerous examples of this type of arrangement which are not restricted to cases where all the counts on the indictment are similar.

Prosecution barristers will always consult with the CPS in respect of a proposed plea bargain and are restricted and guided by a code of conduct in relation to it. The CPS in turn is guided by their own Code for Prosecutors. Where the officer in the case or another police officer with sufficient knowledge of the case is in court, it is good practice for their views to be sought. The same applies to the views of any victim. However, the decision to accept the offer is not one for the officer or the victim and will ultimately be made by the CPS having been advised by prosecution counsel.

There are many cases where the plea bargain is the most appropriate course of action. In considering any proposed pleas, the CPS must have in mind the saving in expense and court time, the fact that witnesses will not have to attend trial, and the strength of the evidence. In many cases, the overriding concern will be whether the pursuit of all charges would make a material difference to the sentence. In all cases, it is worth remembering that the decision of the jury cannot be guaranteed regardless of the strength of the evidence.

There are occasions however where the plea bargain is viewed with a great deal of scepticism by the police officer and the public and it is believed that the bargain has been struck simply out of expediency and for the convenience of the barristers. Of course, ultimate responsibility for the decision rests with the CPS. Officers must learn to be realistic about the sentence that the accused is likely to receive and what the prospects of a conviction were. They should be prepared to listen to the explanation provided and attempt to be objective about whether the offences with which the defendant was charged by the police were in fact the most appropriate.

In many cases a plea bargain agreement will cause considerable distress to families of victims and the victims themselves, particularly in cases where an agreement to plead guilty to manslaughter rather than stand trial for murder is reached. The police officer dealing with the family, whether they are a trained family liaison officer (FLO) or not, will have to draw on all their reserves of experience, sympathy and diplomacy to allay any sense of grievance. An understanding by the officer of the Code for Prosecutors would be helpful. At the very least officers should be familiar with the two elements of the 'Full Code' test for prosecutors, that is, the evidential and prospect of conviction tests. These can be viewed at www.cps.gov.uk/victims_witnesses/codetest and are considered at 2.2.4–2.2.5 above.

9.1.5 Credit for plea

Where a defendant pleads guilty to an offence, the judge will give them 'credit' for the guilty plea so that their sentence will be more lenient than if they had pleaded not guilty. While a plea of guilty does not make the offence itself any less serious, the reasons for the reduction are obvious. It will encourage defendants who are inclined to take their chances with a trial to plead guilty and save court time and expense. It might be thought that if there were no credit for a guilty plea, very few defendants would admit what they had done.

In determining sentence, the court is obliged to take into account what stage in the proceedings the guilty plea was entered, and the circumstances in which it was given. The circumstances might include (amongst other things) the strength of the evidence and the extent to which the plea made it unnecessary for witnesses to give evidence. Credit will be given for a guilty plea whatever stage proceedings have reached and no matter how strong the evidence of guilt. However, the maximum reduction of a third will only be given for a plea entered at the first reasonable opportunity. The court will then operate a sliding scale by giving maximum reductions of a quarter where a trial date has been set and one tenth for a guilty plea entered at the 'door of court'.

There are exceptions to the above discounts. Certain minimum sentences, including seven years for a third class A drug trafficking offence and three years for a third domestic burglary, may only be reduced by up to 20 per cent by a guilty plea. There are also special rules for the offence of murder where a different sliding scale operates so that the maximum reduction is one sixth for a plea at the first reasonable opportunity and five percent for a late guilty plea. In a case where a defendant is prepared to plead guilty to manslaughter and is subsequently found not guilty of murder but guilty of manslaughter, the judge will take into account the fact that the defendant was willing to plead guilty to manslaughter.

9.1.6 Change of plea

A defendant may change their plea from not guilty to guilty at any stage of the proceedings even after a trial has commenced. In these circumstances, defence counsel will ask for the indictment to be put again to their client and the defendant will formally plead guilty. The jury is then requested by the judge to return a verdict of guilty. The judge may well withhold credit for this type of guilty plea.

A change of plea from guilty to not guilty is possible but will only be accepted by the court in certain circumstances. The order of a judge is required to allow a change of plea from guilty to not guilty and it is difficult to persuade a judge to allow such a change. If the judge accepts that the original plea was entered as a result of a genuine misunderstanding by the accused or as a result of improper pressure by their counsel then their change of plea will be accepted. The nature of Crown Court proceedings is such that there may be a long gap between the plea and the sentence. As a result some defendants may enter a guilty plea at the PCMH but then seek further legal advice before sentencing which may cause them to change their mind and apply to change their plea.

More common, however, is for defendants to enter not guilty pleas at the plea and case management hearing but admit their guilt at or near to trial. A 'cracked trial' is a case that is concluded on the day of trial, either because the defendant pleads guilty at that stage or because the Crown decides not to proceed with the case, perhaps because witnesses have not attended or refuse to give evidence. An 'ineffective' trial is when a hearing is cancelled on the day it was due to go ahead. Cracked and ineffective trials are a huge waste of public money and effort of all those involved but are inevitable given that criminal cases involve civilian witnesses and defendants (see also **14.2**, **'No Witness, No Justice'**).

9.2 **The Sentencing Hearing**

In a case where there has been a trial then the facts of the offence will normally be familiar to the judge and often they will not need to be reminded of them. However, where the defendant pleads guilty then prosecuting counsel will be required to summarize the facts of the offence. This is the prosecution's version of events and is based strictly upon the evidence which has been served upon the defence either at committal or prior to the PCMH. In some circumstances, the prosecution's summary of the facts may also be restricted by the basis of plea. Prosecution counsel will also apply for costs and compensation and any other orders such as destruction of drugs or weapons.

9.2.1 **Antecedents and reports**

After a summary of the facts, prosecution counsel will tell the court about the offender's antecedent history. The word antecedents is understood by police officers and refers to the offender's criminal convictions. Having heard from counsel for the prosecution, the judge will then read, if they have not already done so, any reports which have been prepared about the offender. The defence will also have copies of these reports but they are very rarely read out loud in court. The two main types of reports are 'pre-sentence reports' (previously known as social enquiry reports) and medical, such as psychiatric, reports. The authors of reports, particularly psychiatric reports, are sometimes called to give evidence at this stage of proceedings.

Counsel for the defence will then present a plea in mitigation. This involves setting out circumstances which present the offender in a more favourable light and arguments intended to lessen the judge's perception of the gravity of the offence. Counsel mitigating on behalf of their client treads a very fine line between irritating and convincing the judge. There will be many occasions when the police officer in attendance is tempted to gasp in astonishment at some of what is included in such pleas. They should bear in mind that however many times they have heard a plea of mitigation, the judge has heard many more and will very rarely give credit where it is not due.

9.3 **The Sentencing Decision**

9.3.1 **Introduction**

Whilst the sentences imposed in the Crown Court arouse considerable interest from the police, it is rare that an officer's knowledge of the sentencing procedure will reflect their curiosity. In practice, for the busy officer, there is simply not the time to study the convoluted rules that govern the law and practice of sentencing. Even if an officer became familiar with the current regime, the enthusiasm of governments for changing the rules would ensure their understanding was soon out of date.

In a book such as this, it is impossible to provide more than an introduction to the topic. However, the more severe sentences available in Crown Court but not available in the magistrates' court are explained, and there is a summary of the principles of sentencing. It is likely that this will be all that is required in everyday practice as a police officer.

9.3.2 **The sentencing framework**

Officers will probably be aware that the there have been significant changes to the law in recent years. The Criminal Justice Act 2003 (the CJA) governs sentencing for all offences committed after 4 April 2005. It introduces a new sentencing framework which includes, for the first time, a list of the purposes of sentencing. It provides that any court dealing with a defendant for an offence committed after 4 April 2005 must have regard to the following purposes:

- the punishment of offenders;
- the reduction of crime (including reduction by deterrence);
- the reform and rehabilitation of offenders;
- the protection of the public; and
- the making of reparation by offenders to persons affected by their offences.

There are exceptions as the above principles do not apply to defendants who are under 18 at the time of conviction, offences which carry minimum sentences or required sentences, or mental health disposals. Furthermore, the CJA does not specify any particular weight to be attached to each provision.

The CJA requires that in considering the seriousness of any offence, the court should consider the defendant's culpability in committing it and any harm that was caused, was intended to be caused or might foreseeably have been caused. Any previous convictions must—provided that the court considers it reasonable—be treated as an aggravating feature. Furthermore, if the offence was committed on bail, was racially or religiously aggravated, or was motivated by reference to disability or sexual orientation, these aspects of the offence must also be treated as making it more serious.

9.3.3 **Guidelines**

In addition to the statutory framework, for many of the more common types of offences, there are 'guideline cases'. Although the principles are not meant to be applied rigidly, the judgments of the Court of Appeal in such cases provide practical guidance which relate to particular types of offences, offenders and penalties. For example, the case of *R v Webbe* provides guidance in relation to the offence of handling stolen goods. Amongst other things, the guidance suggests that where the property handled is worth less than £1,000 and was acquired for the receiver's own use, the starting point should generally be a modest fine, unless any of one of nine identified aggravating features was present.

The other source of guidelines is the Sentencing Advisory Council. Established by the CJA, the Council consists of 12 members (eight judicial members and four non-judicial) that was set up to formulate and issue sentencing guidelines that are ready to be used by sentencers. The Council is assisted by the Sentencing Advisory Panel that provides advice on sentencing guidelines following consultation and research, if required. One of the more important documents issued by the Council to date is guidance on the reduction in sentence defendants can expect for a guilty plea.

9.3.4 **Powers of sentence**

The sentencing options available to the magistrates are available to the Crown Court judge and are described in the chapter on the magistrates' court. However, in the Crown Court there is no upper limit (other than that provided by statute) for terms of imprisonment or financial penalties. In certain circumstances, there are minimum sentences which must be passed by the court.

9.3.5 **Life imprisonment**

In all cases of murder, the sentence is fixed by law. An offender who is aged 21 years or over must be sentenced to life imprisonment. At the time of passing sentence the judge may make a recommendation as to the minimum term that the offender must spend in prison. It will not usually be less than 12 years. Offenders under the age of 21 convicted of murder must be sentenced to either 'custody for life' or 'detained during Her Majesty's pleasure'.

By virtue of s 109 of the Powers of Criminal Courts (Sentencing) Act 2000 any offender aged 18 and over who is convicted for a second time of a 'serious offence' committed after 30 September 1997 will receive a mandatory life sentence unless there are exceptional circumstances relating to either of the offences or to the offender. In order to qualify, at the time the second offence was committed, the defendant must have been 18 or over and already convicted of the first serious offence. The following are 'serious offences' for the purposes of this section:

- manslaughter
- attempted murder
- conspiracy, incitement or solicitation to murder
- wounding or causing grievous bodily harm with intent
- rape or attempted rape
- unlawful sexual intercourse with a girl under 13
- robbery with a firearm or imitation firearm
- offences contrary to ss 16, 17 or 18 of the Firearms Act 1968

9.3.6 **Mandatory minimum sentences**

Sections 110 and 111 of the Powers of Criminal Courts (Sentencing) Act 2000 require that a person convicted of a third class A drug trafficking offence or of a third domestic burglary committed after 30 September 1997 should be made the subject of a minimum sentence of imprisonment unless it would be unjust. The minimum periods of sentence are seven years for drug trafficking and three years for burglary. There are also minimum sentences in relation to certain firearms offences pursuant to the Firearms Act 1968 and the CJA 2003.

9.3.7 **Appeal against leniency of sentence**

There are occasions when the prosecution may wish to appeal against the sentence passed by the judge. Such an appeal is referred to as an 'Attorney General's Reference' and is possible where the sentence has been unduly lenient. A reference is only possible where the Court of Appeal gives leave, and where the offence is triable only in the Crown Court (that is, triable on indictment), or is triable either way and specified in an order made by the Home Secretary. To begin the process requires the support of the Attorney General who must give personal consideration to the matter bearing in mind the difference between a lenient and an 'unduly' lenient sentence. Where mandatory sentences, such as those considered above, have not been passed when they should have been, there will be grounds for a reference to be made to the Court of Appeal.

One of the duties of prosecution counsel is to consider whether the sentence could be described as unduly lenient. However, if an officer in the case feels strongly that a sentence was far more lenient than the normal standards of sentencing, he should consult the CPS. The CPS may then seek the Attorney General's permission to proceed. If it is granted, notice seeking leave to review the sentence from the Court of Appeal must be given within 28 days.

The Coroner's Court

10.1 **Introduction**

For the historian the ancient origin of the coroner's court may be the cause of considerable interest. For the police officer, its significance is its purpose. By way of a public hearing called an inquest this court determines, with regard to deaths reported to them, the identity of the deceased and how, when and where they died. The inquest is not a trial nor does it seek to apportion blame for the death of the deceased. It is a court of enquiry (see below at **10.3.1**).

The word 'inquest' is ominous in a way that 'trial' or 'hearing' is not. This may be associated with the subject matter but is most likely also related to the relative unfamiliarity of the coroner's court. The reality is that the experience of attending an inquest is often in stark contrast with the worst expectations. Police officers used to the adversarial cut and thrust of other proceedings will find the inquisitorial nature of the coroner's court a refreshing comparison.

In 2003, 210,700 deaths were referred to the coroner for investigation. Notwithstanding the number of referrals, a police officer may never attend the coroner's court throughout their entire service. Much will depend on the officer's role. Officers who are attached to traffic operations or scenes of crime departments are more likely to be required to attend. However, most officers will attend the scene of a 'sudden death' of an elderly person. Whilst there may be no suspicious circumstances, the appropriate paperwork will need to be completed for the coroner, and this may lead to the police officer who first attended the body being called to the inquest at the coroner's court.

10.2 **Composition and Jurisdiction**

10.2.1 **The coroner**

The office of coroner has existed for 800 years. The investigation of unexplained deaths has always been one of their functions and is now their primary duty. The Coroner's Act of 1988 defines the role and powers of the coroner and these are currently supported by the Coroners Rules 1984 (as amended most recently by the Coroners (Amendment) Rules 2005, which came into force on 1 June 2005). The Coroners Rules govern and inform, with commendable clarity, all of the coroner's responsibilities.

Originally appointed royally the coroner is now appointed by local authorities in accordance with s 1(1) of the Coroners Act 1988. Candidates must apply for a vacancy and thereafter submit themselves to be interviewed by local authority officials before a decision to appoint them is made. The approval of the Lord Chancellor is still required for some appointments to this role.

The boundaries of a coroner's jurisdiction are known as the 'coroner's district'. In accordance with s 2 of the Act, a coroner must be a barrister, solicitor or legally qualified medical practitioner of not less than five years standing in his profession. The Lord Chancellor may remove any coroner from office for inability or misbehaviour in the discharge of his duty.

10.2.2 **The coroner's role**

The primary role of the coroner is his duty to inquire, in other words to hold an inquest, into any violent, unnatural or sudden death of unknown cause or death in custody of a person whose body lies within their district. It is irrelevant whether the cause of death arose within a coroner's district or not. If the deceased is now lying within that district then the coroner has a duty to hold an inquest. This would apply even to deaths occurring outside England and Wales. An inquest may be held with or without a jury at the discretion of the coroner. There are cases, however, which must be heard before a jury. They are:

- death in a prison or in such place and circumstances as to require an inquest under any other Act;
- death in police custody or resulting from an injury caused by a police officer in the execution of their duty;
- death caused by accident, poisoning or disease, notice of which is required to be given under any Act to a government department or to a health and safety at work inspector; or
- death which has occurred in circumstances which if continuing or recurring may be detrimental to the health or safety of the public.

A coroner may summon a jury before an inquest proceeds or at any stage during any inquest which has begun without a jury.

10.2.3 **The coroner's officer**

The coroner's officer works under the direction of the coroner and liaises with bereaved families, police, doctors and funeral directors. The role of the coroner's officer has historically been performed by a serving or retired police officer. Whilst the role has now largely been civilianized, an understanding of their responsibilities is useful. A busy coroner's district may have more than one coroner's officer. The coroner's officer will frequently visit the scene or place where the body lies and, as the coroner's representative, cannot be denied access to the body. For obvious reasons anyone seeking access to the deceased should properly and formally prove their identity before access is granted.

The main tasks of the coroner's officer are as follows:

- to receive reports of sudden and unnatural deaths and to initiate and carry out inquiry into that death and the identification of the deceased;
- to liaise with relatives, witnesses, doctors, pathologists in order to obtain statements, reports and other documentation on behalf of the coroner;

- to establish if a death certificate can be issued and to arrange and attend post mortems;
- to inform relatives of the cause of death and to arrange for the release of the body to the undertaker;
- to arrange, if required, the inquest and to ensure that interested parties attend by summons or otherwise.

In many cases, the coroner's officer is the public face of the coroner and the impression they make is of vital importance to the way that the service of the coroner and his court are perceived. The coroner's officers are of invaluable assistance to police officers appearing at inquests or having any dealings with the coroner himself. They will play a prominent role during the actual sitting of the inquest, often acting as usher and supporting and advising relatives and civilian witnesses.

10.3 The Function of the Court

10.3.1 A court of inquiry

As a court of enquiry, the coroner's court is unlike any other court in the English legal system. It does not seek to apportion blame or establish criminality. It is fact and not fault finding. Proceedings are neither accusatorial nor adversarial. It is a court of inquiry, conducted on behalf of the Crown and seeks to answer the three questions enshrined in r 36 of the Coroners Rules 1984 which states:

> R. 36. MATTERS TO BE ASCERTAINED AT INQUEST
>
> (a) who the deceased was;
> (b) how, when and where the deceased came by his death;
> (c) the particulars for the time being required by the Registration Acts to be registered concerning the death.

This Rule continues to explain that neither the coroner nor the jury shall express any opinion on any other matters.

In many cases the answers to these questions are straightforward but in a minority of cases the questions present considerable difficulty. The issue of how the deceased came by their death is frequently the most difficult to answer.

10.3.2 Preliminaries

Once the coroner has made the decision to hold an inquest then s 8(1) of the 1988 Act states that it should be held as soon as practicable. The Coroners Rules, rr 16 and 17 further stipulate that every inquest should be opened, adjourned and closed in a formal manner and should be held in public. The coroner has the discretion to exclude the public from an inquest or part of an inquest if he considers that it would be in the interest of national security to do so. Applications by interested parties to have the public excluded are rare.

The date of a coroner's inquest will be set in the same way as a hearing at the magistrates' or Crown court. A decision is made by the coroner as to which witnesses he wishes to hear evidence from and they will be notified of the date, hour and place of the inquest. Rule 19 places an obligation on the coroner to inform certain classes of people. They are, most significantly, the spouse, near relative or representative of the deceased, the chief officer of police (if appropriate) and any other person who, in the opinion of the coroner is a properly interested person. Police officers will be warned to attend an inquest in exactly the same way that they are warned to attend other courts and in accordance with local policy. Witnesses within the coroner's district may be notified to attend informally or by the issue of a summons. The attendance of witnesses from beyond the district may have to be secured by means of a Crown Office subpoena. There are procedures to secure the attendance of serving prisoners in a manner similar to other 'production' procedures. The warning of witnesses is not a matter for the police and will be the responsibility of the coroner and his officer.

Public funding is not usually available to fund legal representation at an inquest. Legal advice may be available, subject to a means test, to those who require advice regarding proceedings in the coroner's court.

10.3.3 **Contempt**

The coroner has the power to punish those whom he finds to be in contempt of the court. The refusal, for example, by a witness to take the oath, affirm, or answer any questions may amount to contempt although the principle against self-incrimination is preserved by Rule 22. The coroner's power to punish is restricted to the imposition of a maximum of one month's imprisonment.

There are specific powers to deal with jurors and witnesses. The coroner can authorize the issue of an arrest warrant for the non-attendance of any properly notified witness or juror. The warrant is issued for contempt of summons and will not be backed for bail (see **6.5.8** above for an explanation of this term). It is addressed to 'the coroners officer and all the constables and other Her Majesty's officers for the peace' and should be taken from the court, lodged at a police station and circulated in the same way as warrants issued at the Crown Court and magistrates' court.

The offences of perjury and perverting the course of justice can be committed in relation to inquests.

10.3.4 **Disclosure and admissible documents**

As there are no parties to proceedings at the coroner's court there is no duty of disclosure in relation to any of the evidence in the possession of the coroner. There is, however, a rule governing the admissibility of documents at inquest. Rule 37 determines that the coroner may admit documentary evidence relevant to the inquest from any living person, which is likely to be undisputed. He must first announce at the beginning of the enquiry that the evidence will be admitted and name the maker or author of the document. An interested party may object to such an admission. Such evidence may include police officer's statements. If it becomes apparent during the course of the inquest that a document is relevant to that inquest then the coroner can admit it if the maker or author of it is not present and its content is unlikely to be disputed. The coroner may admit documentary evidence made by a deceased person if it is relevant to the inquest. Evidence admitted under r 37 will be read aloud unless the coroner directs otherwise. It has become customary for coroners not to read aloud suicide notes or psychiatric reports admitted under r 37.

10.4 **Incomplete Proceedings**

10.4.1 **Opening and adjourning the inquest**

Having decided that an inquest should be held there are certain circumstances in which the coroner will formally open the inquest and then, having been satisfied on certain points, will adjourn proceedings *sine die*, that is, not to a specific date but indefinitely.

The circumstances in which the coroner shall adjourn the inquest are specified in ss 16(1) and 16(2) of the 1988 Act and require that he has been appropriately informed by the magistrates' court that somebody has been charged with an offence under: s 1 or 3A of the Road Traffic Act 1988 (death caused by dangerous driving or drunken careless driving); s 2(1) of the Suicide Act 1961 (aiding, abetting counselling or procuring the suicide of the deceased) or s 5 of the Domestic Violence Crime and Victims Act 2004 (causing or allowing the death of a child or vulnerable adult). Alternatively, the coroner may be informed by the DPP that somebody has been charged with an offence committed in circumstances connected with the death of the deceased (but which is not one of the above) and the DPP requests the adjournment.

In such circumstances the inquest will be formally opened with or without a jury and the majority of witnesses and interested parties will not be summoned to attend. The inquest is usually opened simply to obtain evidence of identity and cause of death. The coroner's officer, and the senior police-investigating officer will be present. The coroner will open proceedings and all evidence is given on oath. Evidence of identification and cause of death may be given by the police officer or the coroner's officer. Identification evidence may include fingerprint, medical or other documentary evidence where more formal 'next of kin' identification has not taken place. Either officer can give evidence of cause of death and it is not necessary for a pathologist or other forensic or medical expert to attend the initial hearing. The senior police investigating officer will be required to give an outline of the events surrounding the death of the deceased.

The opening of an inquest in any circumstances allows the coroner to order the release of the body of the deceased for burial unless any interested party, usually the legal representative of any defendant, requires a second post mortem.

10.4.2 **Requesting an adjournment**

This is regulated by s 16(1) of the 1988 Act and would generally apply to those cases where the disclosure of the death is quickly followed by the arrest and charge of a suspected person. There are many cases where a death is discovered or disclosed and no person brought before the courts in connection with it. Those entitled to make a request for an adjournment can be investigated by a competent authority. The authorities making the request are the Chief Officer of Police, the DPP and the Lord Chancellor. All are now considered further.

The chief officer of police

The chief officer of police may seek an adjournment on the grounds that a person may be charged with one of the offences specified in s 16(1). In practice the senior investigating officer represents the chief officer. In seeking such an adjournment the senior investigating officer will follow the same procedure as in compulsory adjournment and will provide evidence, on oath, of identification and cause of death. An outline of the circumstances surrounding the death is given and the request is made for proceedings to be adjourned. The coroner may ask directly whether an adjournment is sought and the reasons for it. This is a statement of the obvious which the officer must nevertheless be prepared to answer. The adjournment must be for at least 28 days or longer and should be to a fixed date.

The coroner is obliged to adjourn proceedings having received the request but the proceedings should not be taken lightly or for granted. Authoritative presentation of the facts and the request are of paramount importance. The opening of the inquest should be held in public and may attract particular public and media interest. The press may record the account given by the senior police-investigating officer. In giving the brief facts of the case the officer should not mention the name of any person or persons wanted in connection with the death or suspected of committing an offence in connection with it. Such statements could be damagingly prejudicial to any future trial. Additionally, the officer may have to withhold certain details relating to the death such as the specifics of a particular wound or the weapon used if revelation of such facts could jeopardize the investigation itself. What is revealed at a coroner's inquest must always be for public consumption unless contrary to the interests of national security.

The Director of Public Prosecutions

An adjournment may be requested by the DPP under r 27 of the Coroners Rules on the grounds that a person may be charged with an offence committed in circumstances connected with the death of the deceased which is not an offence specified by s 16(1) of the 1988 Act. Proceedings are again adjourned for at least 28 days. In practice the functions of the DPP are undertaken by the chief Crown prosecutors of the CPS or their delegated representatives.

The Lord Chancellor

The Lord Chancellor may, by s 17A of the 1988 Act, seek an adjournment when a public inquiry conducted or chaired by a judge is being, or is to be, held into events surrounding the death of the deceased and he considers that the cause of that death is likely to be adequately investigated by the inquiry. Public inquiry into major disasters, for example, train crashes, and multiple deaths are the most obvious examples of when such adjournment would be sought.

Notwithstanding the circumstances in which the coroner must and shall adjourn proceedings, any inquest may be adjourned where the coroner considers that this is the correct and proper course of action to take. Adjournment may be necessary, for example, when there is delay in receipt of a post mortem report or where there is another gap in the evidence. An adjournment may also be required when the coroner himself considers from evidence heard that a person may be charged with an offence specified in s 16(1) of the 1988 Act and that the adjournment is necessary to prevent proceedings becoming accusatory. If the coroner adjourns for this reason he must do so for at least 14 days and send the evidence to the DPP or CPS.

Any adjournment is made in a formal manner and in cases where a jury has been called the coroner has power to require witnesses and jurors to enter into oral undertakings to attend at a later date. This undertaking, called a recognizance, may mean the forfeiture of a sum of money to the Crown in the event of non-attendance.

10.4.3 Resumption

The coroner is not compelled to resume an inquiry which has been adjourned. If the facts surrounding the death of any person have been comprehensively aired at a trial, hearing or other public inquiry then further inquiry and the attendant trauma may be deemed unnecessary and undesirable. Indeed, a coroner may only resume an inquest, adjourned at the Lord Chancellor's request if, in his opinion, there is exceptional reason for doing so. If such an inquest is resumed the findings of the enquiry can be admitted under r 37A.

10.4.4 Protracted and complex investigations

Whatever the reason for the adjournment the coroner will not fix a date for the resumption until the results of any criminal proceedings in the magistrates' or Crown court are formally made known to him. The police investigation into a death may be complicated and protracted. The coroner will not fix a date for the resumption of an inquest into such a death until such time as he is informed by the senior police-investigating officer that the enquiries are frustrated or exhausted and no charges are likely to be brought against any person. The coroner may periodically wish to hear from the officer in charge of a protracted enquiry and will adjourn the case accordingly.

The senior police-investigating officer must always be prepared to attend an interim hearing and satisfy the inquisition of the coroner by answering questions about the nature of the enquiries that have been carried out and those that are proposed. The coroner will often adjourn such cases *sine die* (indefinitely). Whilst it is not desirable for the police to dictate the length or timing of adjournments, the coroner may occasionally be prepared to accede to their wishes. If a date for resumption is fixed the coroner must give reasonable notice of the date and time to all witnesses, jurors and other interested parties.

If an adjournment is not requested by either the police or the CPS then the coroner will proceed to hold an inquest regardless. If any suspect for a murder remains untraced or is already dead, then the inquest will also proceed. In these circumstances it remains the duty of both the coroner and the police not to reveal the identity of the suspected person.

10.5 The Coroner's Inquest

10.5.1 Opening

The court must be opened formally but the particular manner of doing so has not been prescribed. Most coroners now preside over their courts in suit and tie although the practice of wearing wigs and gowns has not completely died out. Barristers will not normally wear their formal attire.

The coroner or their officer might open proceedings at an inquest without a jury in the following way:

> Oyez Oyez Oyez. All manner of persons who have anything to do at this Court before the Queen's Coroner for this county touching the death of [name], draw near and give your attendance, and if anyone can give evidence, on behalf of our Sovereign Lady the Queen, when, how, and by what means [name] came to his death, let him come forth, and he shall be heard.

In difficult cases the coroner may choose to sit with his deputy or assistant deputy and in technically complex matters they may sit with a suitably qualified and competent assessor. The assessor may be allowed to ask questions of witnesses. The deputy or assistant will not play an active part although the coroner may consult with them. The coroner must take notes of the evidence given at an inquest. Proceedings are usually tape-recorded and a stenographer is not present. Witnesses are called to the stand and will give evidence on oath or affirmation, quoting this from a prepared card. Police witnesses should identify themselves and their working address in the normal way and will address the coroner as 'Sir' or 'Madam'. In cases involving juries, the coroner will open proceedings by addressing the jury as to the function of the coroner's court and the duties of the coroner. They will draw their attention, in particular, to the questions which the inquest seeks to answer (see above at **10.3.1**) He will explain the inquisitory nature of the proceedings and the unique position the coroner's court holds within the English legal system.

10.5.2 **Order of witnesses**

The order in which the witnesses are called is at the discretion of the coroner but it is usual for the first witness to give evidence of the identification of the deceased. This witness will frequently be a member of the deceased's family but can be a police officer or even the coroner's officer. It is then usual for the order of the witnesses to follow the same chronological order as the actual occurrence of events being inquired into. In the more serious cases being investigated by the police, the senior police-investigating officer may follow the identification of the deceased with an outline of the case. This is similar to the way in which counsel for the prosecution will open a Crown Court trial. Civilian or independent witnesses will follow. Police evidence will normally be called after the independent witnesses. Medical or pathological evidence will be called last.

It must be stressed that no two inquests are the same and that there are no hard and fast rules relating to the order of appearance of witnesses even though inquest proceedings are regulated by s 11 of the Coroners Act 1988. The peculiarities of a case may reverse the order described above, with the exception of the identification evidence. The logic of the chronological sequence is generally accepted as the most convenient. Thus, in a case of suspected suicide, the next of kin may provide evidence of identification. Family and friends may provide evidence of the deceased's movements, lifestyle and state of mind. A police officer may provide evidence of how and where he found the deceased and produce exhibits such as medication and a suicide note. The pathologist will finally give evidence of the cause of death.

Witnesses can usually sit in court until they are called to give evidence. If there is likely to be a conflict of evidence or there is to be evidence from a group of several witnesses, such as police officers, then the coroner has the power to exclude those witnesses from the court. The police officer should always seek the advice of the coroner's officer in such situations.

It is the jury's privilege to recall at any time throughout the inquest, any witness whom they wish to re-examine. A witness can be released only by the coroner after they have given evidence and been examined or they are not required to give evidence. Any witness who has been released may leave the court.

10.5.3 Examination by the coroner and others

Coroner's Rules, rr 20(1), 21 and 22 govern the examination and questioning of witnesses in the coroner's court. Rule 20(1) describes the right of any properly interested person to question a witness at an inquest either in person or by a legal representative. Rule 21 states that, unless a coroner determines otherwise, a witness at an inquest shall be examined first by the coroner and, if the witness is represented, lastly by his own representative. Rule 22 guards against the self-incrimination of a witness and states that no witness at an inquest shall be obliged to answer any question tending to incriminate them. The same rule allows the coroner to inform a witness that they do not have to answer such a question.

Witnesses are first examined by the coroner who will usually have their statement in front of them. The coroner will avoid asking leading questions about contentious matters but may direct the witness's attention to a particular subject. The witness will give their name, address and occupation. In cases where retaliation is feared, these details may be written down and passed to the coroner.

Any interested party or their legal representative may then examine the witness. If there is more than one party intending to examine the witness then the coroner will decide on the order of questioning. The party questioning should stand when doing so. In allowing such examination the coroner must safeguard the inquisitorial process and protect the witness. The coroner must ensure that all questioning is directed towards establishing the matters which the inquest seeks to determine and as defined by r 26. A legal representative is entitled to suggest that a witness may be mistaken and to probe their evidence provided the line of questioning is relevant and fair.

If the coroner allows a police officer to examine a witness then a barrister or a solicitor should represent that officer. It is not usual for the police to be represented unless an attack on their professional competence is anticipated.

10.5.4 Giving evidence

The most common mistake made by police officers giving evidence at the coroner's court is to misunderstand the inquisitorial nature of the proceedings. The coroner will, more often than not, be favourably disposed towards the officer who may be the only professional witness giving evidence before him. In recalling what took place the officer will be providing invaluable assistance to the court and its function. Those present, especially relatives of the deceased may well find the officer's evidence upsetting. The officer who reports an incident is frequently the most important witness at an inquest and puts matters on a formal footing.

Officers may refresh their memories from notes and statements in exactly the same way as they do at magistrates' and Crown court. The officer who asks to do so will be questioned by the coroner as to how and when such notes were recorded before being allowed to refer to them. Officers may formally produce any exhibits which they have gathered and must remember to bring with them anything which has not already been handed to the coroner's officer but which will be referred to by them. Exhibits will be handed to the coroner or his officer for inspection by them or any other interested party. Whatever the exhibit number or reference given to an exhibit by the police prior to proceedings, once it is produced, it will be given another number which will be preceded by the letter 'c'.

The coroner's court is not bound by the strict laws of evidence. The Civil Evidence Act 1995 abolished the rule against the admissibility of hearsay evidence in civil proceedings and this applies to the coroner's court. Accordingly, hearsay evidence is admissible. The coroner will wish to hear everything that may tend to reveal the truth of how, when and where the deceased came by their death. Thus, in recording everything that may have been said or reported at the scene of a fatal accident, suicide or suspicious death, a police officer is gathering evidence which may be given at an inquest. The admissibility of hearsay evidence does not dispense with the need for the 'best' available evidence to be given if it is available!

In many cases in which a number of police officers are involved, the coroner will only wish to hear the evidence of one or two of these officers unless the conduct and competence of the police officers themselves is called into question. It is the practice of most coroners to keep police officers at their court until the end of the inquest. The coroner can release any witness whose evidence has been heard.

For further guidance on giving evidence readers should refer to **Chapter 13**.

10.5.5 **Summing up, verdict and closure**

Whilst no one is permitted to address the coroner or jury as to the evidence given at an inquest, any interested party may make legal submissions to the coroner with regard to any summing up in a jury case. The jury in such cases may retire while the submissions are made. In summing up the coroner must ask the jury to take account of all the evidence before them. The coroner will direct that they cannot make recommendations or 'qualify' any verdict with remarks of their own. The coroner will describe the verdicts which can be returned. If the evidence points strongly to a particular conclusion then the coroner must direct the jury towards the corresponding verdict. If there is no jury there is no need for a summing up. In these cases reference may be made to the evidence given. In all cases the verdict will be delivered publicly.

The maximum number of jurors in the coroner's court is 11. A majority verdict of nine to two is acceptable from the outset although the coroner will express the desire that they should reach a unanimous verdict. If a jury cannot reach a verdict they will be discharged, another summoned, and the inquest will be started again.

The formal record of an inquest is called the inquisition. It contains the reasons for the holding of the inquest and the verdict. It is signed by the coroner alone or by the coroner and those members of the jury who agree with the verdict.

There are 10 common verdicts which are reached by an inquest. Some of the phrases have passed into common usage and, whilst frequently misunderstood, have emotive and sometimes controversial meaning for many who hear them. They are:

- Industrial disease
- Want of attention at birth
- Dependence on drugs/non-dependent abuse of drugs
- Suicide
- Accident/misadventure
- Execution of sentence of death
- Lawful killing
- Unlawful killing
- Open verdict
- Self-neglect or lack of care

Of the above verdicts some are more common than others, for instance, misadventure, unlawful killing and open. The former indicates that an action was deliberately taken by the deceased or another which in itself was lawful but unpredictable consequences have resulted in the death of the deceased. Unlawful killing, as is obvious, confirms that the deceased was the victim of homicide (including murder, manslaughter or infanticide). Where an 'open' verdict has been returned the inquest has been unable to clearly establish the cause of death. Regardless of the verdict returned it remains a matter for the investigative and prosecution authorities to investigate and institute, where appropriate, criminal proceedings.

The decision to re-open or to initiate a criminal investigation following a verdict, for example, of 'unlawful killing' will be made by the CPS or the DPP. A transcript of proceedings will be obtained and examined before such a decision is made. It is important to note that neither the record of inquest proceedings, the inquisition, nor any other record of evidence heard at an inquest is admissible evidence of the facts stated therein. If any notes of evidence are to be used at a later trial then the coroner must produce them although this would normally be the subject of agreement between the prosecution and defence.

Whilst police officers have a duty to support witnesses and bereaved relatives they must always be mindful that an inquest is not conducted on behalf of the family and that they may have to manage the disappointment and distress that an unwelcome or unexpected verdict may cause. Officers designated specifically to liaise with the families of murder victims should contact the coroner's officer in order that they be notified of any relevant dates and, most importantly, of any difficulties relating to the release of the body for burial.

There is no particular form of closure for the coroner's inquest and the coroners officer may simply call 'silence' and ask for those present to rise as the coroner leaves the bench. The following is an example of a more formal closure:

> Oyez oyez oyez. All manner of persons who have had anything to do at this court before the Queen's Coroner for this County touching the death of [name], having discharged your duty may depart hence and take your ease.

10.6 **Exhumation**

Section 23 of the Coroners Act 1988 enables a coroner to issue a warrant for a body to be exhumed for the purposes of holding an inquest or inquiry, or in furtherance of any criminal investigation or proceedings. Before a warrant is granted it must be proved that there is a necessity to examine the body for the purpose of criminal proceedings. If there are no proceedings pending or contemplated and an inquest has been held and completed then the coroner ceases to have jurisdiction and cannot order an exhumation. Exhumation does not apply to those bodies that have been cremated even though it is clearly possible to recover the ashes of the deceased.

A warrant to exhume should be applied for by the senior police-investigating officer or their deputy and the application follows much the same procedure as application for any other warrant by police. The coroner must first be satisfied that the police have 'reasonable evidence' which justifies the application. Consultation between the senior police-investigating officer and the coroner's officer will ease the process of the application. The required documentation may vary from one force area to another. The warrant will be addressed to the person in charge of the burial ground or cemetery.

A coroner may be willing to open and adjourn an inquest on the day of an exhumation and, subject to the issues which may be raised by any legal representatives, may also be willing to issue a certificate allowing reburial at the time of adjourning the inquest. An exhumation is an unusual occurrence and most police officers will never attend one and even less will ever apply for a warrant. Though rare, preparation for the application and exhumation must be as thorough as possible. The forensic, religious and family issues are complex. A body lying in a family or multiple graves with other bodies interred above it cannot be exhumed until any bodies which physically prevent its removal have also been exhumed. Each body requires a separate warrant. The order of the coroner may override the wishes of the family in respect of exhumations but in dealing with families the coroner, the police and the coroners officer should always bear in mind the provisions of Article Nine of the Human Rights Act 1998 which defines the citizen's right to manifest their religion or beliefs.

Most exhumations will take place during the hours of darkness to ensure privacy and the coroner may wish to be present. Once the body has been identified and the necessary examination made then it can be reburied by order of the coroner.

10.7 **Treasure**

The concept of 'Treasure Trove' has been abolished by the Treasure Act 1996. The coroner has a duty to inquire into any treasure reported to them as found in their district. Treasure is defined by s 1 of the Treasure Act 1996 and constitutes any ancient objects containing a substantial proportion of gold and silver or any other property of value. The coroner must be notified of any finding of treasure if the finder has reasonable grounds for believing that the object is treasure as defined. A coroner's inquest will decide whether the object is treasure and consequently, ownership.

10.8 **Conclusion**

The coroner's court is not to be feared. Its unique position within the English legal system has been established for hundreds of years but only in recent years has it become the focus of a great deal of media attention. At the time of writing the Home Office has initiated a fundamental review of the coroners system in England, Wales and Northern Ireland and reform would seem to be inevitable.

In the wake of the 'Dr Shipman' case in East Manchester there have been calls for all deaths to be reported to the coroner's office for investigation and for cases of doubt to be referred to the coroner. In this way an unnatural pattern of deaths, such as that caused by Shipman, would be brought to the attention of the authorities at an earlier stage. There is also a great debate about whether and how a death should be regarded as 'natural' simply because the illness has been diagnosed and a death certificate issued. Should the death of a hospital patient during treatment or the death of a long retired factory worker from asbestosis be regarded as natural? Are these matters perhaps which ought to be settled by inquest?

Blame will always be apportioned in the wake of controversial cases and demands will be made for criminal investigation or public enquiry. This is not the intention of the coroner's inquisition and police officers also must not react personally or unprofessionally to what may be seen or claimed by others to be an unsatisfactory verdict. The coroner's court does not accuse but simply seeks to explain and clarify in the most objective way possible. Whatever reform is mooted, an inquisitorial as opposed to adversarial nature of the court should not necessarily be regarded as a bad thing. It may not be unreasonable to suggest that the coroner's inquest, when it eventually takes place, reveals the truth and establishes the facts more fairly, more thoroughly and with more dignity than many other court proceedings.

Coroner's Court Procedure

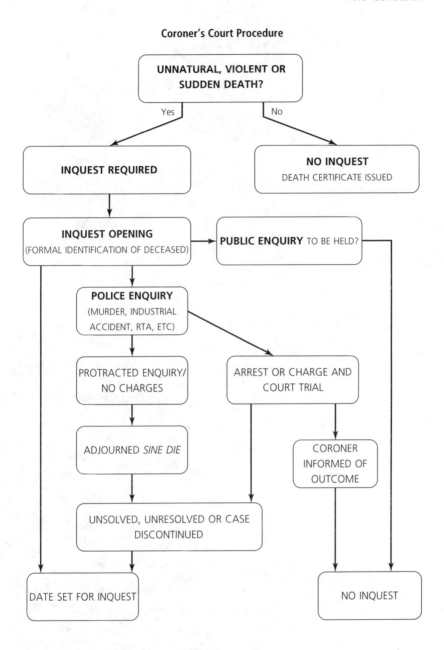

Please refer to sections 10.4.1 to 10.4.4 for useful explanation when considering this diagram.

Preparing for Court

11.1 **Police Officer as Witness or the Officer in the Case**

The vast majority of officers required to attend court do so to give evidence about their involvement in the investigation of an offence. There are generally three categories of 'involvement'. They are:

- as witness to an event or aspect of the investigation;
- as officer in the case (OIC); or
- As witness *and* OIC.

11.1.1 **Witness**

The police officer as a witness to an incident or as part of an investigation will have made a written statement that has been served on the defence. The statement will frequently have been based on an original note or will be an 'original' statement made at the time of, or shortly after the events recorded therein. It may have been made by reference to some other original source document such as a custody record, scene log or crime report.

This officer should first ensure that they know what court they are required to attend, where and at what time. It is always helpful to arrive early. They should acknowledge the court warning they have been served with and perhaps take steps to contact the OIC. They should try to obtain a copy of their statement if they do not already have one and confirm that any original notes or other exhibits will be available at the court for them to refer to.

It may be that they are familiar with the court that they are going to. In this case they will know how to get there and where the best place to park is. Officers will frequently be called to give evidence, particularly at Crown Court, or at a court that they have never previously been to. If this is the case then they will have to consider what has previously been taken for granted. Going to the wrong court or driving around for 30 minutes looking for a parking space are not the best ways to prepare for giving evidence.

Officers can and do get called suddenly to court with little more than a moment's notice. This can be a worrying and nerve-wracking experience. It may be that an officer is called to give evidence when a trial is half way through. That officer may not initially recall the name of the defendant nor what role they played in the investigation. It may be that the officer has not even been required to make a statement in the course of the investigation. In either event the officer should find out as soon as possible what the case concerns and their involvement in it. Having arrived at court the officer should make contact at the first opportunity with the prosecutor dealing with the case, or where this is not possible, perhaps because the trial has already started, make sure that they report their arrival to the court usher (see **3.2.5**) and then wait in the room provided for witnesses to be called. They should not discuss the case in any way with a witness who has already given evidence! This is quite improper and may well result in the case being stopped resulting in a re-trial or matters being discontinued because of possible prejudice to the defendant. Any enquiries by the defendants' representatives should be referred to the prosecutor.

An officer who has not previously made a statement about the case will not normally be allowed to give evidence until they have done so. There is no reason why statements cannot be taken during the course of a trial but this will, where necessary, be a matter dealt with and requested by the prosecutor. Once any statement is made it must be copied and served on the defence and the court. There is no requirement for the statement to be typed. Such late service of evidence must be agreed with the defence or ordered by the court. Having been given the opportunity to make a statement or to refresh their memory from existing exhibits or documents, the officer should now have sufficient grasp of why they have been called and what evidence they may have to put before the court. They may now try to relax and prepare themselves for giving that evidence (see **13.2.5** below).

11.1.2 **Officer in the case (OIC)**

The officer in the case will usually be responsible for the preparation of the case file that has been forwarded to the Crown Prosecution Service (CPS) and be the first port of call if additional work is required to ensure the case file is complete before the matter can proceed. They should know what type of file is required and make sure it is completed in time. Where assistance is required, the officer should ask senior colleagues or consult the 'manual of guidance' (see below) or available CPS staff.

11.1.3 **The Manual of Guidance for the preparation and submission of files (MG)**

The police officer will soon learn that there appears to be a specific form for everything. Case file preparation is a very good example of this and in an effort to ensure standardization and conformity throughout the police service a 'Manual of Guidance for the Preparation, Processing and Submission of Files' has been produced (referred to by police officers as the 'Manual of Guidance'). The most recent version of this 'manual' (renamed the Prosecution Team Manual of Guidance) is usually available at police stations or may be viewed via the web at <http://police.homeoffice.gov.uk/news-and-publications/publication/operational-policing/prosecution-manual-section3>. It contains examples of all of the relevant forms along with comprehensive guidance on their completion. Each form has the prefix of MG and this is most frequently followed by a number. They are commonly referred to as 'MG forms'. Currently the numerical range is from MG1 through to MG20 (see below). Thankfully, not every MG form is required for every case file.

11.1.4 **Building a case file**

The 'Manual of Guidance' is currently divided up into four sections. Section one gives definitive guidance on how to build the required case file and prescribes what forms must be included and for which cases. Section two deals with pre-charge consultation between investigators and duty prosecutors; section three includes forms and guidance notes and section four concerns prosecution team supervision and case management. All police officers must know what file to complete, its contents and any time-limits that apply.

11.1.5 **Decision to charge**

Inappropriate charging by police has led to many cases being ultimately discontinued by the CPS. The Criminal Justice Act 2003 removes this responsibility from the police in all but the most straightforward cases. Section 2 of the MG at para 2.1.6 explains that the decision to charge in most indictable only, either-way and summary only cases is now made by the Crown Prosecution Service (CPS) representative 'resident' at many police stations (so-called 'Duty Prosecutors').

In order to inform the CPS about their decision to charge, the police must send one of two pre-charge reports, the 'pre-charge expedited report' which is sent in straightforward cases where a guilty plea is anticipated in the magistrates' court or a 'pre-charge evidential report', which is sent in cases which are likely to be contested or heard in the Crown Court.

Whenever a decision has been made to charge a suspect then one of three different types of case file must be submitted to the CPS. They are the 'expedited' file, the 'evidential' file and the 'full' file. Each file has a slightly different structure increasing in requirements, culminating with the 'full' file.

Content of Expedited and Evidential Charging Decision Reports and Case Files

STRAIGHTFORWARD AND 'GUILTY PLEA' CASES		CONTESTED OR CROWN COURT CASES		
Pre-charge Expedited Report For charging decision – to custody officer or Duty Prosecutor	**Post-charge Expedited File** For EFH court hearing	**Pre-charge Evidential Report** For charging decision – to custody officer or Duty Prosecutor	**Post-charge Evidential File** For EAH court hearing	**Upgrade to Full File** For Crown Court or contested cases
MG 3 – Report to Crown Prosecutor (for offences where CPS decide charge) MG 11(s)* – Key witness statement(s) or Index (if visually recorded) (if witnessed by police, use MG11 of one officer) MG 15 – SDN or verbal summary of admissions. (SDN can be written on officer's MG11) Phoenix print (suspect pre-cons, cautions, etc.)	MG 1 – File front sheet MG 4 – Charge sheet MG 5 – Case file summary (unless the statements cover all elements of the case) MG 6 – Case file information (if there is information for the investigator to record) MG10 – Witness non-availability (PYO only) MG 11(s)* Key witness statement(s) or Index (if visually recorded) SDN – may be written on MG15, MG6 or MG11 of officer Phoenix print (suspect pre-cons, cautions, etc.) **Where applicable, include the following:** MG 2 – Initial witness assessment MG 3 – Report to Crown Prosecutor (for offences where CPS decide charge) MG 3A – Further report to Crown Prosecutor MG 4A – Conditional bail form MG 4B – Request to vary police conditional bail MG 4C – Surety/Security MG 7 – Remand application MG 8 – Breach of bail conditions MG 11 – Other witness statements already taken MG 13 – Application for order on conviction MG 18 – Offences taken into consideration (TIC) MG 19 – Compensation form (plus supporting documents) Copy of documentary exhibits/photos Police racist incident form/crime report (in racist incident cases)	MG 3 – Report to Crown Prosecutor (suggest charges) MG 5 – Case summary (unless the statements cover all elements of the case) MG 6 – Case file information MG 11(s) – Key witness statement(s) or Index (if visually recorded). If witnessed by police, use MG11 of one officer, summarise evidence of others MG12 – Exhibits list MG15 – Interview record: SDN / ROTI / ROVI (SDN can be on MG5, officer's MG11 or MG15) Crime report and incident log Any unused material which might undermine the case (disclosure schedules are not required at this stage) Copies of Key documentary exhibits Phoenix print (suspect pre-cons, cautions, etc.)	MG 1 – File front sheet MG 3 – Report to Crown Prosecutor MG 4 – Charge sheet MG 5 – Case file summary (unless MG11(s) cover all elements of case) MG 6 – Case file information (if there is information for the investigator to record) MG 10 – Witness non-availability MG 11(s) – Key witness statement(s) or Index (if visually recorded) MG 12 – Exhibits list Copies of Key exhibits/photos MG 15 – Interview record - SDN / ROTI / ROVI (SDN can be on MG5, officer's MG11 or MG15) Phoenix print (suspect pre-cons, cautions, etc.) **Where they are applicable, include the following:** MG 2 – Initial witness assessment MG 3A – Further report to Crown Prosecutor MG 4A/B/C – Bail/surety/security MG 7 – Remand application MG 11 – Other witness statements already taken MG 13 – Application for order on conviction MG 18 – Offences TIC MG 19 – Compensation form plus supporting documents Police racist incident form/crime report (in racist incident cases)	MG 6C – Schedule of Non-sensitive unused material MG 6D – Schedule of sensitive material MG 6E – Disclosure officer's report MG 9 – Witness list MG 11 – All other statements Custody record **Where applicable, include the following:** MG 2 – Initial witness assessment MG 6B –police officer's disciplinary record Phoenix print (witness pre-cons, cautions, etc. see the JOPI)

Further Upgrading?
Not required if the case is disposed of at the first court appearance.
If a 'not-guilty' plea is entered or the defendant elects Crown Court, prepare a Full File.

Once a charging decision has been made, the 'Pre-charge Expedited Report' becomes the 'Post-charge Expedited File' for court.

Once a charging decision has been made, the 'Pre-charge Evidential Report' becomes the 'Post-charge Evidential File' for court.

Further Upgrading?
Where it is clear that the case will be heard in the Crown Court, or a not-guilty plea is likely, a Full File should be prepared and submitted with the MG3.

*Include details of pre-cons for witnesses who have provided 'Key' MG11s if case involves a remand in custody

Crown Copyright—http://www.cjsonline.gov.uk/framework/ccmf/annex/to.html

147

11.1.6 **MG forms**

Section three of the Manual of Guidance sets out each of the MG forms in chronological order. There is a description and annotated example of each form to assist completion. A complete list of MG forms can be found in section three of the MG and include:

- **MG1** File front sheet
- **MG2** Initial witness assessment
- **MG3** Report to Crown Prosecutor
- **MG4** Charge sheet
- **MG5** Case summary (see below)
- **MG6** Case file information (C/D & E below)
- **MG7** Remand application (bail or custody)
- **MG8** Breach of bail conditions
- **MG9** Witness list
- **MG10** Witness non-availability (see below)
- **MG11** Witness statements
- **MG12** Exhibit list
- **MG13** Application for order on conviction (for example, an ASBO—see **6.5.2**)
- **MG15** Record of taped interview (ROTI), video (ROVI) or short descriptive note (SDN)
- **MG18** Offences taken into consideration (TICs—see below)
- **MG19** Compensation form
- **MG20** Further evidence information

These forms are the basis of all prosecution and advice files submitted to the CPS. It would be wrong to suggest that one MG form is more important than another but the significance of four of the MG forms are worthy of further discussion.

Form MG5 (Case Summary) is a précis drafted by the police and often quoted by the prosecutor to the court. A well-prepared MG5 that precisely, accurately and concisely provides the facts relating to the offence is much appreciated by every prosecutor, especially when it has been typed. Where the prosecutor has to struggle to read this document because it is virtually illegible, this does not inspire confidence in the court or in members of the public sitting in the public gallery.

As is discussed in **3.1.8**, the law governing the disclosure of prosecution evidence relating to *unused* material (material that does not form part of the prosecution case) is regulated by the Criminal Procedures and Investigations Act 1996 which applies to all cases where the defendant is charged with an indictable only or either-way offence and any summary offence in respect of which he intends to plead not guilty. Additional reference should be obtained from the Attorney General's Guidelines on Disclosure 2000 and the Joint Operational

Instructions. The entire process may seem complex but it is not and police officers very quickly come to terms with what is required.

Form MG6 is one of a series of five forms including, MG6C, MG6D and MG6E specifically designed to deal with the disclosure of sensitive and non-sensitive unused material. It is impossible to exaggerate the importance of the accurate completion of these forms. Comprehensive guidance for their completion is to be found in pp 85 to 109 of the 'Manual of Guidance'. In practice MG6C forms are pink in colour to easily distinguish them from their counterparts. The prosecutor will rely upon the honesty and accuracy of those who compile these forms.

11.1.7 Initial prosecution disclosure

Section 3(1)(a) of the Criminal Procedure and Investigations Act 1996 (CPIA) describes the duty of the prosecutor to disclose any material which 'has not previously been disclosed to the accused and which might reasonably be considered capable of undermining the case for the prosecution against the accused or of assisting the case for the accused'. The Crown Prosecution Service must disclose any such material or declare in writing that no such material exists (s 3(1)(b)).

'Any material' does not apply only to statements or other real or documentary evidence. It includes such things as crime reports, 'first descriptions' and any other material gathered in the course of the police investigation. Examples of material included within s 3(1)(a) of the CPIA 1996 and clearly capable of undermining the prosecution case, etc would include where a witness has provided the police with a description that the suspect was blonde but the person arrested and charged had black hair. The process of formally declaring the existence of such material or declaring that no such material exists is referred to as 'primary prosecution disclosure'. The duty to disclose any such material is a continuing one (s 7A of the CPIA 1996). This means that the position must be kept under constant review to ensure fairness.

The significance of form MG10 (witness availability) may only be appreciated when it is too late. It is a confidential form completed to assist the prosecutor when dates are being proposed in court for the listing of subsequent hearings and trial dates. Whoever completes this form, usually the officer in the case, must do so accurately. Their colleagues will be unhappy if they are on holiday (annual leave) or on a rest day and are then warned to attend court. Obviously, the same applies to civilian witnesses.

Form MG18 is for use where there are offences to be taken into consideration (often referred to as TICs). These are offences with which the defendant has not been charged but wishes the court to consider when determining sentence. They should be detailed on form MG18 and must be signed and acknowledged by the defendant. The offender is not convicted of these offences but where they have been taken into consideration the offender will not be charged with them in the future. The attraction to the offender is that it allows them to make a fresh start.

Prosecution Files

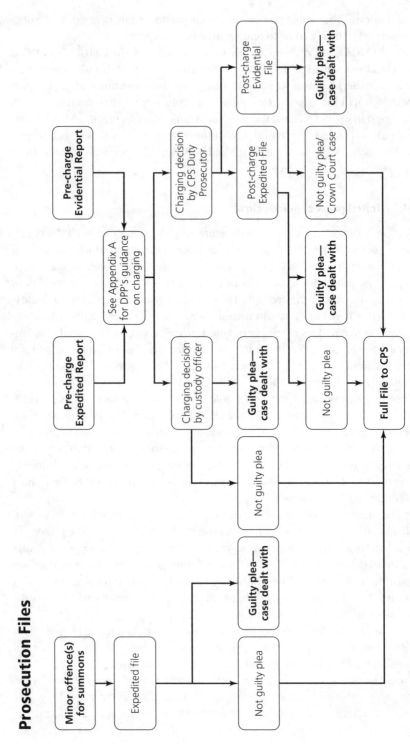

Crown Copyright—http://www.cjsonline.gov.uk/framework/ccmf/annex/to.html

11.1.8 **Liaising with the CPS**

This process begins pre-charge with the submission to the CPS of form MG3 and a pre-charge report requesting charging advice. If the case is to be contested then it will be allocated to a specific section within the CPS, which will deal with all the cases in a particular court. The case will have been given a unique reference number (URN) by the police at an early stage and it will retain this number throughout its life in the prosecution system. The URN incorporates specific digits and letters identifying the police force and station of origin, a numerical and year identifier.

Most police stations have a unit which deals with prosecutions and liaises daily with the CPS. This unit may be called different things depending on which area it is in. Their role is to remove a great deal of the burden of preparing cases for court from the individual officer. They will co-ordinate and dispatch witness warnings based upon the information they are supplied with by the officer in the case (OIC). They may photocopy files and create the bundles of statements and indices that will be submitted to the CPS. They will carry out a great deal of invaluable work and whilst these departments and their staff are always very busy they are always willing to assist officers with case file enquiries.

Where necessary the CPS will document requests for clarification of further action, usually in the form of a dated memo or letter to the 'Officer in the Case' (OIC). Many of these memos will be straightforward and self-explanatory. If clarification is required, then the OIC should contact the CPS as soon as possible by telephone or, if time allows, in writing quoting the URN. If the URN is not available, most prosecutors will recall the case from the defendant's name. It is preferable to speak to the prosecutor who wrote the memo but they may well be in court prosecuting as many are for at least three days per week. Where this is the case the lawyer may have left the file with another prosecutor or member of staff who will be pleased to assist. Prompt response to a memo or letter is essential to progress the case and establish a good working relationship with the prosecutor or team responsible for the prosecution. Further evidence or information about a case must be sent to the CPS accompanied by a duly completed form MG20.

It is good practice, certainly in more serious and complex matters, to arrange a 'conference' with the CPS prosecutor in charge of the case. It is likely that the CPS will welcome this initiative if it comes from an officer. The sooner this takes place the better. It would be normal for the police officer to travel to the CPS offices but it is not uncommon for a prosecutor to come to a police station. This may be more convenient if there is a great deal of material to view for disclosure purposes, or if there are video or computer disk recordings which form part of the prosecution case.

Where the CPS have instructed a barrister for a Crown Court case it is likely that the barrister will send any requests they may have to the CPS who will in turn forward them to the police. It may be that the CPS will send a copy of the letter received from the barrister to the police. Conferences with a barrister will usually be arranged by the CPS but could take place at the barrister's chambers, the CPS offices or even a police station. Arranging a conference is a positive and constructive step to take. Matters that may have appeared complex and even unnecessary in a CPS letter can be more easily explained and put into their proper context at such a meeting.

In complex and serious cases it is advisable for the OIC to write a detailed report to accompany a full file. This report will be in addition to the MG5 which would have accompanied the 'evidential' file. It will be a great deal more detailed than the MG5 as the officer will have had the benefit of seeing the case develop over a period of weeks. The benefits of writing a report are twofold. First, it will give the CPS and the barrister a valuable overview of the case. They will still have to read key statements but a well written, comprehensive and concise report will make the process of reviewing the case that much more efficient. Secondly, the very process of writing a report will help the OIC to understand every aspect and detail of their own case. In order to write it they will have to read every statement and document and be familiar with every available evidential exhibit and interview. This type of report should be numerically paragraphed in order that the CPS lawyers can refer to parts in it in future correspondence. CPS lawyers will welcome any suggestions made by an officer which will help the jury or the court to understand more clearly the evidence put before them. This could include the use of visual aids or any other method of conveying evidence to the court.

11.1.9 Witness liaison

The Criminal Justice and Police Act 2001 defines a witness as follows:

> A person who provides, or is able to provide, information or documentation which might be used in evidence in proceedings, or might:
> - confirm other evidence which will or might be admitted in those proceedings;
> - be referred to in the course of evidence given by another witness in those proceedings; or
> - be the basis for any cross-examination during those proceedings.

Many cases fail because witnesses do not attend court as required. Whilst significant advances have been made in making giving evidence a less intimidating experience, the OIC has to ensure that the witnesses will actually attend. They will be assisted by 'witness liaison'. This duty extends beyond simply recording dates to avoid and then warning the witness of the time and place at which they should attend. In difficult cases, particularly of a violent or sexual nature, officers should formally liaise with the witnesses in the weeks and months leading up to the trial and ensure that they have contact with the witness service. An initial willingness on the part of a witness to give evidence can quickly evaporate into fear and anxiety and a desire not to give evidence. In addition, witnesses will often change their addresses and telephone numbers and do not always remember to notify the police. They should also ensure that the witnesses are physically able to get to court and consider whether it is appropriate and necessary for them to be offered transport. The OIC must therefore be proactive in ensuring that these crucially important details are periodically updated.

The officer should also ensure in conjunction with the CPS that all necessary preparations have been made in respect of any 'special measures' required such as screens for witnesses. The MG2 form has been designed to ensure that this is not overlooked by the OIC.

It is good practice to formalize the witness liaison process by keeping a record of all contacts that the police have with witnesses in the same way that they now do with victims and their families. This record would be a transparent account of all these dealings and would naturally be a 'sensitive' document for disclosure purposes. Later accusations that officers offered inducements to, or 'coached' victims could thereby be systematically countered and rebutted. It may be that the OIC is able to liaise comfortably and effectively with all of the witnesses but it may be sensible where there are too many witnesses to delegate this task amongst colleagues.

11.1.10 The OIC: final preparations

Before leaving home or their station all witnesses, especially police officers should consider the following questions:

- Do I have the correct date and time of the hearing?
- Do I know where the court is?
- Are the witnesses required for that day warned and able to attend?
- Do I have the correct papers and necessary exhibits?
- Will there be sufficient officers in attendance to deal with all eventualities?
- Is my dress appropriate?

If the answer to any of these questions is 'no' then the witness must pause and reconsider their position. Certain difficulties can be remedied at the court but others cannot. They must leave plenty of time to get to the court and meet with the CPS and witnesses before the trial begins.

11.2 Preparing for an Application

When preparing for an application it is essential to know exactly what a court is being asked to order and on what grounds. To put it bluntly, officers should ask themselves 'what do I want and why?' It is also necessary to know the law that governs the application which may involve reference to the relevant Act and section for the application.

It goes without saying that any application to the court should be made on the correct form. To avoid delay and embarrassment, officers should arm themselves with an appropriate number of copies of each form. Preparations to make an application for a warrant at both magistrates' and Crown court are different but must be no less rigorous and are described elsewhere in other chapters of this work.

11.3 **Preparation: General**

Complacency is the enemy of sound preparation for going to court. Nothing can be taken for granted and an officer, particularly an OIC, must never assume that 'somebody else' will have taken care of something. Whatever advance notice or warning the police officer receives this must serve as the trigger to ensure that everything necessary for the progression of the case has been done. The size and complexity of the case will inevitably dictate what is required and often it is impossible to prepare for every eventuality. The efforts of the police officer will be appreciated by prosecutors, the court and perhaps, most importantly, the victim. The reward for the officer is that they will be able to attend court confident that they will be a credit to their profession.

Trial Procedure

12.1 **Introduction**

Whether it takes place in the Crown Court or in the magistrates' court, the fundamental parts of a criminal trial are the same, and the sequence of events is very similar. The principles that govern which witnesses must attend the trial, how they give their evidence, and the questions they may be asked are common to all trials. There is one obvious distinguishing feature of Crown Court trial which affects its procedure, and that is, of course, the need to accommodate the jury.

The order of events in a trial will be familiar to officers. Since the Crown bring the case, the prosecution present their evidence first. Normally this will include live witnesses (oral evidence) as well as evidence that is read. After the prosecution has presented its case, it is the turn of the defence who may or may not call the defendant and other witnesses. Finally, after all of the evidence, the trial concludes with closing speeches, although here the procedure differs according to whether the trial is in the magistrates' court or the Crown Court.

In the past, cases in the magistrates' court were prosecuted by the Crown Prosecution Service and defended by solicitors whereas trials in the Crown Court were prosecuted and defended by barristers. However, the distinction is no longer so clear. It is common for junior barristers to act in the magistrates' court and for solicitors with higher court advocacy qualifications to appear in the Crown Court. For the sake of convenience and simplicity this chapter will refer to prosecuting counsel and defence counsel, even though the advocate may hold different qualifications.

12.2 **The Prosecution Opening**

The trial begins with the prosecution counsel providing an outline of the case against the defendant(s). The opening speech sets the scene and will give the jury or the magistrates a flavour and an understanding of the case they are about to hear. The nature of the charges against the accused will normally be explained (although this may be omitted in the magistrates' court in the case of very common charges such as excess speed) and there will be an outline of the evidence upon which the prosecution rely. Prosecuting counsel will summarize what witnesses will be called and why and how their evidence will prove, beyond reasonable doubt, the guilt of the defendant. Prosecuting counsel will not refer to any evidence that the defence claim should be excluded from the trial (see **12.8** for legal submissions and the trial within the trial).

During the opening and throughout the case, the duty of prosecuting counsel is to outline the facts upon which the Crown intends to rely. Their task is to present the case moderately and fairly but firmly. As such, over-emotive language will not feature in the opening.

12.3 **The Case for the Prosecution**

Having opened the case, the prosecutor will proceed to call evidence to support the allegations against the defendant. The evidence will be presented in a way that will make it most easily understood which, in most cases, will be in chronological order. In the vast majority of cases this will involve the calling of relatively few live witnesses.

Before a witness for the prosecution can be called, their evidence must be disclosed to the defence before trial in the form of statements and exhibits. Witnesses will not be allowed to give evidence if their statement has not first been seen by the defence.

12.3.1 **Live and read evidence**

The basic rule is that all witnesses must attend court unless their evidence can be agreed by both parties. Evidence that is 'agreed' is non-contentious and where this is the case there is usually nothing to gain from requiring the witness to give their evidence in person to the court. It follows that if any of the material facts in a witness's evidence are contentious (that is, not agreed), they must attend trial and the defence advocate must put to that witness the defendant's case (what the defendant says happened) so far as it is within their knowledge. On the other hand, if there is nothing controversial in the statement, the defence will almost invariably 'agree it' (although not obliged to do so) and the prosecution counsel will simply read the statement to the court. Several types of statements, such as those concerning forensic examinations and the continuity of exhibits (effectively, the audit trail for the exhibit) are very often capable of agreement and will normally be read by the prosecuting counsel. Such agreed facts and statements may be reduced further into a written summary or series of 'admissions' which will be read by prosecuting counsel and provided to the jury or magistrates. The purpose of this is to quickly but systematically put evidence before the court which forms a part of the evidential chain but which is not controversial or contested.

It goes without saying that the witnesses who are called to give live evidence will normally be the most significant. They will include the witnesses whose evidence the defence challenge. However, it is not unusual for witnesses to be required even though there is no dispute with their evidence. This will occur when the defence seek evidence that is not included in a witness statement; questions along these lines are said to be 'outside the statement'. This is frequently the position with respect to the officer in the case who may be asked about records held by the police or other aspects of the investigation even though there is no challenge to the evidence they give for the prosecution.

The officer's attendance may be requested by the prosecution or the defence. In many cases their presence will be of considerable assistance in the smooth running of the trial and in larger trials the attendance of a dedicated exhibits officer is often invaluable. An experience common to many officers is that they are required to attend court but are not required to give evidence. It should not be assumed that is as a result of incompetence or inefficiency on anyone's part. The most common reason for this is the last minute change of plea by the defendant, which given human nature, is unlikely to stop happening.

Unnecessary attendance of officers may arise from a failure by the defence to indicate that the officer's presence is not required. This, of course, represents an avoidable and undesirable drain on police resources. In the Crown Court defence counsel is under a duty to obtain sufficient instructions to decide which prosecution witnesses should be cross-examined. Defence counsel must ensure, so far as is possible, that no other witnesses should be required to attend court at the request of the defendant. Perhaps the presence of the judge's critical eye over the proceedings is also associated with the fact that such occurrences are far less frequent in the Crown Court.

It is possible for a further statement to be taken from a witness at the court during the trial itself. If this does happen, it will be with the knowledge of the defence and prosecution counsel and copies of it must be made and served upon the defence and given to the court and the judge.

12.4 **Examination in Chief**

When a prosecution witness is called to give evidence, the first stage is that the prosecution advocate will take the witness through their evidence contained in their statement. This is called examination in chief. The purpose is to put the witness's version of events, their story, before the court. In so doing the prosecutor seeks to draw out or 'adduce' testimony which supports the facts which the prosecution wish to establish and rely upon to prove the case beyond reasonable doubt.

The starting point is the witness's statement. The prosecutor will have a copy in front of them and will be familiar with its contents. The questions will be simple and open, allowing the witness to give their version of events in response to questions such as what, why, how, where and when. Leading questions may be asked on matters that are not disputed by the defence, for example the date and place of the incident. The prosecutor will deal only with matters contained in the statement and previously disclosed to the defence and is not entitled to spring surprises by eliciting new material.

During the course of witnesses' evidence exhibits may be referred to and produced. The term exhibit is used to indicate an item shown to the court as evidence such as a till receipt in the case of an allegation of shoplifting, (see **12.1.11** below). Whatever the reference number given to an exhibit by the person producing it, the court will allocate a separate sequential number which will thereafter be used when referring to it.

Occasionally the magistrates or the judge will also ask questions of the witness during examination in chief to clarify specific points. When it is completed, the witness will be asked to remain in the witness box and will be cross-examined (questioned) by the defence advocate.

12.5 **Cross-examination**

Cross-examination of a witness is the most dramatic and tense part of the trial procedure and the part most frequently shown on television. The difficulties which witnesses, and police officers in particular, experience during cross-examination and examination in chief are considered in depth in **Chapter 13** below. For the moment, it is enough to consider the purpose of cross-examination by the defence, which is twofold:

- to challenge the evidence in chief insofar as it conflicts with the defence case;
- to elicit facts favourable to the defence case that did not emerge or were insufficiently emphasized during examination in chief.

The object is to put before the court evidence which supports the position of the cross-examining party. Leading questions (those that suggest or include the answer) may be put as well as any questions designed to test the knowledge or memory or the existence of any bias or prejudice. Questions may be asked to highlight evidence of any statements previously made by the witness which are not consistent with their evidence in chief.

Defence counsel can, within reason, ask any question provided it is relevant and unlikely to prompt an inadmissible answer. Whilst the prosecution counsel may raise an objection to specific questions or lines of questioning, the court will be the sole arbiter of what may be asked. The Code of Conduct of the Bar provides guidelines and restrictions on the type of questioning allowed (as does the Guide to the Professional Conduct for solicitors). The Code provides that '[counsel] must not make statements or ask questions which are merely scandalous, or intended or calculated only to vilify, insult or annoy the witness or some other person'. Furthermore, '[counsel] must not suggest that a victim, witness or other person is guilty of a crime...' unless such an allegation is relevant or well founded.

12.6 **Re-examination**

Following cross-examination, the prosecutor may wish to re-examine the witness. Just as with examination in chief, leading questions are not permitted. The purpose of re-examining a witness is to undo some of the damage that has been done in cross-examination by clarifying aspects of the evidence raised in cross-examination or emphasizing some positive aspect of the witness's evidence that was not apparent during examination in chief. However, re-examination must be confined to matters raised during cross-examination. It cannot be used as an excuse to repeat evidence that has already been given or to introduce evidence that was forgotten in examination in chief.

12.7 **Practicalities**

It is good practice and quite proper for a police officer present as both witness and officer in the case to assist the CPS by furnishing witnesses with a copy of their statement so that they may refresh their memory before giving evidence. An advantage the prosecution enjoys over the defence is that prosecution witnesses are likely to have recorded their recollection of an incident shortly after the incident occurred. Accordingly, the opportunity for witnesses to refresh their memory in this way should not be overlooked.

Having read through the statement, when the time comes for them to give evidence witnesses will be led into the court by an usher who will direct them to the witness box. The usher will then ask them if they wish to swear a religious oath (depending on their faith) or affirm. They will swear to tell the truth by holding up their holy book and using an appropriate form of words. The oath given on the bible is as follows:

'I swear by Almighty God that the evidence I shall give will be the truth, the whole truth and nothing but the truth.'

The words of the affirmation are:

'I do solemnly and sincerely and truly declare and affirm that the evidence I shall give will be the truth, the whole truth and nothing but the truth.'

Having affirmed or taken the oath the witness will be asked to confirm their name and allowed to choose whether to stand or sit. Police officers will normally stand. They will then wait for the prosecutor to address them.

If there is more than one defendant then there is often more than one defence advocate and the prosecution witnesses will be cross-examined by each in turn. Having completed their evidence, the witness will normally be thanked by the judge and, in the ordinary course of events, released. A witness who has been released by the judge is free to leave the court building but may stay if they wish to do so.

12.8 **Legal Submissions and the Trial Within a Trial**

If the defence, having read the statements upon which the Crown seek to rely, consider that some of the evidence to be adduced is either inadmissible or unacceptably prejudicial to the defendant then they may ask for it to be excluded.

Defence counsel will inform prosecution counsel in advance what evidence it is that they are objecting to and that they intend to ask for its exclusion. In the Crown Court, the judge must resolve the issue in the absence of the jury whereas in the magistrates' court, it will be a decision for the bench to make. Sometimes the matter is most conveniently dealt with before any witnesses are called. In the Crown Court, words to the effect of 'a point of law has arisen, Your Honour, that need not concern the jury' will be used. Once the jury has left the court, defence counsel will raise their objections or 'make their submissions'. Prosecuting counsel will respond, the judge will make a ruling and the jury will be recalled and the trial will continue. The evidence, the whole or part of it, will either be in or out (that is, ruled admissible or inadmissible). As indicated, this process of argument may take place at any stage during the prosecution case.

If the issue is not the evidence itself but the manner in which it has been obtained then there will be a '*voir dire*'. The '*voir dire*', or 'trial within a trial' as it is commonly known, is not a rare occurrence. The most common example is the admissibility of confession evidence obtained by the police. If there is to be a '*voir dire*' it will normally take place at the point in the evidence when that evidence was to be adduced. The jury will be sent out and the officer who gives the relevant evidence will be called into court. The officer will enter the witness box and swear the following oath or other slight variation:

'I swear by Almighty God that I will answer truthfully any questions which the court may ask of me.'

Their evidence will then be presented as normal and the officer will be cross-examined. If the evidence of other officers is required, they too will be called and cross-examined. The defendant may then be called to give evidence and is liable to cross-examination by the prosecution. Having heard the evidence the judge will then make a ruling. If the way in which the evidence was obtained is deemed to have been unfair or improper then it may be excluded by virtue of s 76 (if it is a confession) or s 78 (in respect of any type of evidence) of the Police and Criminal Evidence Act 1984 (referred to as PACE). Rulings made at a trial where, for whatever reason, the jury is discharged should remain in force for any subsequent trial.

Evidence that is objected to by the defence will not be referred to in the opening speech. If it is ruled to be inadmissible then the jury will never hear of it and neither party nor the judge will refer to it in any way. If the evidence is allowed then the jury will be recalled and the evidence will take its logical place in the prosecution case.

The '*voir dire*' is not limited to confession evidence. Other matters which regularly arise relate to identification issues, in particular the conduct of identification parades, group and video identifications and confrontations with witnesses. If a '*voir dire*' is required then the issue to be discussed will usually go to the heart of the prosecution case. The resolution of the trial within a trial in the favour of the prosecution can and should never be taken for granted and prosecuting counsel will need to consider what action to take if the contested evidence is ruled inadmissible. It may be that the case can no longer continue. Where this is the case the defendant must be acquitted.

12.9 **Exhibits**

Exhibits will be produced before the court at the most relevant times during the evidence. The person who produces the exhibit in their statement need not be the person who physically produces it in the court. A knife, for example, used as a weapon and exhibited by a police officer may be referred to by another witness who can identify it. If this is the most appropriate moment in the trial to produce the item then it will be so produced and given a court reference number. It scarcely needs to be said that an exhibit like any other evidence cannot be adduced unless a statement referring to it is first served upon the defence. The exhibit will be given a unique reference number and will thereafter be referred to during the trial by that number. Exhibits referred to during proceedings become the responsibility of the court itself and will be looked after and secured by the court usher. Most Crown Courts will have facilities to store exhibits for the duration of a trial.

12.10 **No Case to Answer**

Notwithstanding the rigours of the Code for Crown Prosecutors, cases may still proceed where there are shortcomings in the evidence and at the close of the prosecution case the judge or the defence counsel may feel that the prosecution have not adduced evidence sufficient to demonstrate that there is a case for the defendant to answer (referred to as a prima facie case). It may be that there is insufficient evidence on an element of an offence, for example 'intention to permanently deprive' in a case of theft. If this is the case then the defence will make a submission of 'no case to answer'. If the defence overlook such a submission, then the judge may invite them to do so. Such a submission of 'no case to answer' is often referred to as a 'Galbraith' submission after a case of the same name that formulated the procedure.

In the Crown Court, the jury will retire so that both parties and the judge can discuss the matter fully and freely. This is to avoid the possibility of the jury's verdict being influenced by the ruling. In the magistrates' court, the matter will simply be heard by the bench.

If there is more than one count on the indictment, then defence counsel may make their submission in relation to any or all of the counts and prosecuting counsel will be invited to reply. The judge will listen to the arguments and make a decision. The jury is then brought back in to court. If the judge agrees that there is no case to answer in relation to the indictment then this will be explained to the jury. The judge will then ask the jury to appoint a foreman and will direct the clerk of the court to take from that foreman a verdict of not guilty to the indictment and all the counts on it.

If the judge finds that there is no case to answer in relation to some of the counts on the indictment but not others then the jury will be directed at the end of the trial to return verdicts of not guilty in respect of these counts. The remaining counts, for which there is a case to answer, will continue to be heard and the defence will begin their case

12.11 **The Defence Case**

Defence counsel will only make an opening speech where they are to call witnesses in addition to the defendant. If the defendant only is to be called then there can be no opening speech. Witnesses called by the defence to give evidence as to the defendant's good character, referred to as 'character witnesses', do not constitute witnesses for the purposes of an opening speech.

The accused cannot be forced to give evidence but will usually do so. If the accused does elect to give evidence they will do so from the witness box and before any other witnesses are called to give evidence. Witnesses cannot be compelled to answer questions that may incriminate them. This is not so with the accused for obvious reasons. The rules governing what can and cannot be revealed to the jury about a defendant's previous convictions have recently been changed (see **13.4.5** below). This naturally has an impact on the circumstances when the defence may wish to attack or cast doubt on the good character of a prosecution witness as doing so may lead to the defendant's convictions being revealed to the jury. These matters are discussed in **Chapter 13, 'Giving Evidence'**.

If the defendant does give evidence, it is important that the officer in the case is in court to hear it. Occasionally, the prosecution advocate will ask the officer in the case if there are any specific matters that they should raise during cross-examination. There may also be matters that arise during the defendant's evidence 'in chief' or cross-examination which the officer may wish to discuss with the prosecution barrister and which invite further questioning and exploration. The prosecution barrister is not infallible and neither will the good prosecution barrister believe they are. It can be a frustrating experience for the police officer to sit at the side of the court saying to themselves, 'Why doesn't he (or she) ask this?' The same officer who remains silent or does not sit in court for the cross-examination will invariably be the one who criticizes the barrister the most. The officer should speak to the barrister before the defence case opens and be in court for the cross-examination.

During cross examination, officers should allow counsel considerable latitude as there are many different styles of cross-examination which are equally effective. However, if there is a burning issue which has not been addressed, an officer should take the opportunity to speak to counsel if there is a natural break in proceedings. Alternatively, an officer might be able to pass a note at a discreet and opportune moment to counsel, their junior or the CPS. Prosecuting counsel will not thank the police officer at the close of the case for pointing out questions that they believe should have been asked.

Counsel for the defence is under no obligation to call any evidence whatsoever and may not do so for a number of quite proper tactical reasons. However, in general, the decision of the defendant not to give evidence may result in an inference being drawn by the jury or magistrates as to why. Obviously a defendant who chooses not to give evidence cannot be subjected to cross-examination. Their credibility as a witness cannot be tested. Accordingly, the strategy is normally adopted only where the defendant is likely to be a poor witness. When the defence has called the evidence they wish to, then the trial will proceed to counsels' closing speeches.

12.12 Closing Speeches

In the Crown Court counsel for the prosecution will make the first of the closing speeches. In the magistrates' court, the prosecution have no right to make a closing speech. In closing, the barrister will remind the jury of the salient points of the prosecution case and draw their attention to any contradictions in the defence case. Police officers are often disappointed by what they perceive to be a lack of vigour and conviction in the closing speech of the prosecuting barrister. However, prosecution counsel is not permitted to employ emotive language to secure a conviction. Their duty is not to secure a conviction at all costs. Instead, their role is to be coolly objective about the evidence that the jury have just heard. It is often said that such an approach is more likely to persuade a jury.

The last word belongs to the counsel for the defence. This is the part of the trial where the defendant wants to see their barrister earn their money and it is invariably more impassioned and imploring than the closure of the prosecution. The very best defence closing speeches can and do persuade juries in the face of overwhelming evidence. Notwithstanding the scrupulous objectivity and fairness of the judge's summing up, it is often the defence counsel's words which ring longest and loudest in the jury's ears.

Giving Evidence

13.1 **Myths**

No other part of a police officer's duty is surrounded by as much myth and anecdote as the giving of evidence at court. The tales of cruel humiliation by or titanic verbal triumphs over the finest QCs in the land are passed from one generation of officers to the next. The police service has entered an era where an officer's evidence is likely to be tested to the full. If it ever was, the witness box is no longer a place to take lightly or a stage to demonstrate the quality of wit. It is ironic that whilst the evidence of police officers is now more likely than ever to be true, the public's, the jury's and the magistrates' perception of the police has changed. The result is that officers' evidence is more likely than ever to be disbelieved.

One of the most damaging myths surrounding the giving of evidence at court is that 'you've either got it or you haven't'. That is, an officer is either blessed with the eloquence and cunning to outwit defence lawyers and convince juries, or is not. In fact, giving evidence well is largely down to training and preparation. Nevertheless, most officers believe that they are good at giving evidence. The reality, however, is that some officers are good witnesses whilst others are not.

One reason is that there is no assessment of court performance with the exception, perhaps, of one or two probationary appearances. An officer's contemporaries, often the sternest critics, will rarely watch their colleges in court even where they are allowed to, and an officer will never see themselves giving evidence. The prosecution barrister will frequently praise an officer but is unlikely to criticize a bad performance. The CPS rarely, if ever, comment upon the way in which an individual officer presents their evidence. Yet to tell a detective officer that they are a poor witness is to cut to the core of their self-esteem.

13.1.1 **Towards improvement**

Just as a police officer can improve their performance in the interview room and in promotional interviews so they can improve their performance in the witness box. There are three principles which must inform improvement. They are:

Recognition that improvement is required

So much of what is accepted as good practice when giving evidence is 'received wisdom' perpetuated by so-called experienced officers. The officer will tell you exactly how to handle an aggressive cross-examination and how to 'stonewall' any number of pertinent questions that the jury need to hear answered. They will describe the tone of moral indignation that you must adopt when accused of being evasive or even untruthful and, most important of all, they will tell you exactly how to 'get the defendant down'. A realization that this advice is anecdotal and may be deeply flawed is an essential first step.

Preparation

An appreciation of the value of intelligent preparation is essential. A cliché commonly heard in connection with police work is 'poor preparation leads to poor performance'. It applies to giving evidence as much as to any other part of an officer's duties.

Understanding the police officer's role

A misunderstanding of the role of the police officer as a witness is a major cause of poor performance. The officer is there to give an account of their part in a sequence of events which has led to their presence at the court, not to act as prosecutor or engage in a personal duel with defence counsel. See **13.3** below.

13.2 **Preparation**

13.2.1 **When to start**

As we have seen in the previous chapter, preparation for court starts when an investigation begins. From the moment evidence is gathered, the police officer should be aware that their actions may have to be accounted for in a court. Whenever a document will be referred to in court, it should, where circumstances allow, be meticulously compiled. It should be comprehensive, accurate and legible. Over long periods of time police officers are involved in dozens if not hundreds of incidents and what may seem obvious and unworthy of note at the time may be crucial but long-forgotten in several months or years. The fact that police officers deal with a great number of similar incidents is one of the principal reasons for keeping notes.

13.2.2 **Original notes**

The vast majority of police officers who give evidence will refer to a notebook. Notes come in many forms and include arrest notebooks, pocketbooks, exhibit books, observation logs, identification procedure notes, breath test procedure booklets or even miscellaneous scraps of paper which were all that were available to the officer at the time.

An officer may wish to complete a s 9 (MG11, see **11.1.6**) statement instead of notes. This is permissible but may lead to inconvenience at a later stage when the original statement is not so readily available having been filed in a box with many other original statements. The Metropolitan Police now use an 'evidence and action book' (book 124A) which has the s 9 declaration incorporated and is effectively both notebook and admissible statement.

The importance of timely, diligent and thorough note taking cannot be over-emphasized. Ideally, the time the note was made should be recorded and to this end automatic timing devices have been introduced by police forces. If they are available they should be used. If such a device is not used it does not render the note inadmissible but does open a potentially productive angle of attack for the defence. If the notes were made in collaboration with other witnesses then that fact should also be recorded.

The officer who does not follow these simple guidelines and who has difficulty reading their own writing will regret it when they refer to their note under pressure in the witness box.

13.2.3 **The officer's statement**

The s 9 statement (MG11) is the bedrock of any prosecution case. It should be thorough and accurate as it will be served on the defence and represents the evidence that the officer will give. A detailed statement is an advantage in many ways. First, a comprehensive account recorded near to the time will assist recollection in the future. Secondly, generally speaking, the more detailed the account, the more credible it will be. Thirdly, from the point of view of the defence, if an officer's statement indicates a good recollection of events, it suggests that officer's evidence will be more difficult to challenge.

If an officer wishes to avoid being called unnecessarily then it is a good idea to make the statement purely factual. For example, it is unlikely that a defendant would agree he was 'difficult' when approached by officers. However, if that evidence was not important, the statement might say merely that the defendant was asked to move on but did not do so. In this way, the prospects of the statement being agreed and accepted by the defence would increase and reduce the possibility of the officer being called to give evidence.

Evidence from an original note, with the exception of the note that is produced itself (referred to as an exhibit), will be transferred into the s 9 statement which is served on the defence. In the ordinary course of events, the defence lawyer will also have a copy of the original note and the statement will invariably be checked against it. There may be additional evidence in the statement which is not in the note, but if so officers should consider the reason for this.

Where there is no administrative facility for the proof reading of a statement typed by someone else the officer must do it himself. It can be a boring and laborious task and it is one that is best shared with a colleague. The officer familiar with his own handwriting should read the statement and their colleague should check the typed copy. A discrepancy between a hand-written statement and the typed copy used by the court may well be focussed upon either by the defence or the judge. At the very least it will appear unprofessional and even worse, possibly suspicious, potentially damaging the credibility of the evidence. More damagingly, if the discrepancy is significant it may give rise to confusion about the meaning of the statement itself, not just for the defence, but for the magistrates or jury as well.

13.2.4 **The witness's statement**

With the exception of statements provided by professional witnesses such as forensic scientists, forensic medical examiners, pathologists and police officers themselves, all other statements will be taken (that is, written at the dictation of the witness) from witnesses by police officers or employees of the police service (so-called 'statement takers', often retired police officers). Being mindful that the witness need not attend court where a statement will suffice, the officer should be diligent in the taking of statements. While this might seem to be stating the obvious, the quality of statements taken and served suggests it is not universally understood.

The words written by the officer at the dictation of a witness *must* be those used by the witness regardless of more suitable alternatives. If a statement is an accurate transcription of what a witness is saying in their own words, it will often have the 'ring of truth' about it and will enhance its standing in the eyes of the lawyers. A statement that is obviously constructed will have the opposite effect.

When taking statements from witnesses, the 'officer' should not paraphrase the way that witness speaks. Many witnesses intimidated by the procedure in which they are involved or due to time constraints may be inclined to skim read their statement, if they read it at all, and may blindly and unthinkingly sign it. Subsequently when that witness is presented with their statement at court on the morning of the trial they may be confused by it or, more seriously, may even disagree with its content and wish to change it. Police training such as the PEACE interviewing model, 'cognitive' approach to interviewing and more recently the 'Achieving Best Evidence (ABE)' programme have addressed the issues surrounding the credibility of witness statements.

Both prosecution and defence will base their examination of the witness on their statement. It will quickly become obvious if the vocabulary and style of the statement is not that of the witness before them.

With the best intentions, an inexperienced officer is often tempted to paraphrase what a witness says. To do so could be fatal for the case. It is only human for witnesses to be vague in their recollection of events. The police officer will occasionally meet a witness whose powers of recollection are exceptional. However, the vast majority of witnesses will be uncertain about aspects of their statement. The officer must learn to accept the weaknesses and uncertainty of the witness they are dealing with and must accurately record what they say. The legitimate 'jogging' of a person's memory is totally acceptable, suggestion and speculation is not.

The interviews of 'significant' or crucial witnesses are increasingly tape-recorded. Whether an officer actually takes the statement in the course of the tape-recorded interview itself, or whether they take it at a later stage having referred to the recording, they must ensure that the statement corresponds to what was said in the interview. Again paraphrasing and deviation are unacceptable. The tapes will often be transcribed and copies of the transcripts and the tapes served upon the defence. They will be checked before the trial and discrepancies highlighted. This also applies to the preparation notes that an officer makes before and during the taking of a statement. Whether such notes are exhibited or served as 'unused material' is a matter for local policy but they will be scrutinized by the defence and compared with the statement.

13.2.5 **Psychological preparation**

The aim of the adversarial system is to ensure that the defendant has a fair trial. Whilst the lawyer must comply with the requirements of their professional organizations (the Code of Conduct for barristers and the Guide to Professional Conduct for solicitors) they are obliged to 'at all times promote and protect fearlessly and by all proper means his lay client's best interests'. The officer must consider what they would expect from their defence lawyer defending them in a similar situation. They would not, it is suggested, wish their barrister to make allowances for a fearful or inexperienced witness.

The officer should not enter the witness box with a 'game plan' but should be open minded. Whilst officers should not allow themselves to be pressurized into agreeing with suggestions, an officer's standing in the eyes of the court will be considerably enhanced if they are prepared to make concessions where appropriate. The officer is not expected to know or have seen everything.

It is unnecessary for any witness to anticipate specific lines of questioning depending on the nature of the case and the defence being advanced. The 'defence statement', however, is an unreliable indicator of what to expect. The officer will not know in advance (and does not need to know) what particular details of the prosecution case the defence will seek to test and should not be surprised if asked about issues that he had not anticipated. It is dangerous to expect only one particular line of questioning during cross-examination and the officer should expect the unexpected.

The mental preparation that the officer makes should be reflected in the advice that they give to the lay witnesses. All witnesses will have their evidence challenged during trial (referred to as cross-examination). This is quite proper and must not be taken as a personal attack upon the witness. Lay witnesses may be offered a degree more protection by the judge than the officer is but, normally speaking, they are there for their evidence to be tested otherwise they would not have been called (see 12.3.1 for an explanation of why witnesses may be called even if there is no challenge to their evidence). Crucially a witness may not be aware of all of the evidence in the case and they must be warned to be patient with questions that appear irrelevant or unnecessarily personal.

13.2.6 **Familiarization**

Officers should not be embarrassed by the fact that they are unfamiliar with a court or have not been into a courtroom for some time. When officers arrive at the courtroom where they are to give evidence they should introduce themselves to the usher (see **3.2.5**) for that particular court. It is that usher who will call them into the court and lead them to the witness box. Most courts will open at or before 10am for the morning session and 2pm for the afternoon session and the officer should go into the court beforehand to familiarize themselves with its layout. They should note the position of the witness box and the relative positions of the bench and, in the Crown Court, the jury box. The witness box will have a folding seat in it.

The officer must decide whether they wish to swear an oath or affirm. Obviously, the purpose of this declaration is to confirm to the court that the witness will tell the truth. The appropriate wording is printed on a card for the witness to repeat whilst holding the relevant text (for example, bible, Koran, etc) in their right hand. Those who do not believe in a 'god', affirm. Indecision in making the choice will convey the wrong impression to the court. Every aspect of this process of familiarization should also be offered and explained to the lay witnesses.

13.2.7 **Waiting**

Once a case starts the officer who is to give 'contested' evidence will not be allowed to sit in the court. They must wait elsewhere, usually in a witness room, until they are called to court. Waiting to give evidence can be a difficult and lonely experience. Even the most seasoned officer will often experience a degree of tension. Like the officer who has never lost a case, the officer who tells you that they do not get nervous at court cannot have been often nor had their evidence tested to any great extent.

The nervous police officer will require self-discipline to use the time before entering the courtroom properly. The temptation to sit chatting in the police room or reading the paper is enormous. There may be time to do these things but only when they are confident that their preparation is complete. If there is to be a delay before they are called and if they have not already done so the officer would be well advised to use the time profitably by answering the following questions:

- Do I wish to refresh my memory from my notes or original statement?
- Do I produce any exhibits? If so where are they?
- Do I know the words of the basic 'caution?' (This is the name given to a specific collection of words repeated to a suspect to advise them of certain fundamental rights as per COP C, para 10.1—reproduced below.)
- Am I familiar with the relevant legislation and provisions of PACE and the Codes of Practice (COP)?
- Is my appearance correct?

- How do I address the court?
- Are my mobile phone and pager turned off?

The answers to these questions are central to establishing a firm platform from which the officer can confidently give their evidence. They might be addressed as follows:

- 'Yes, I do wish to refresh my memory from my notes or original statement.'
  If the officer wishes, as is advisable, to do this before as well as during their evidence, they must make sure that they have the notes with them and that they are not in the courtroom with the case papers. They should take the notes into the court with them and be prepared to explain when, where and who they were made with. If the notes were not made at the time or as soon after the incident referred to as possible, the officer should be able to explain why. Copies of a lost or misplaced original note may be allowed (admitted) but not without argument and objection. The officer should use the time available to read and understand their notes.
- 'Yes, I may have to produce an exhibit.'
  The officer must know where the exhibit is and ensure that it is brought to court in the first place. Far too many officers make assumptions about what exhibits will be required for examination by the court or the defence. Quite simply, if there are items exhibited in the prosecution case then they must be available at court. Best evidence requires that the actual item be produced but if it is not practical, say for reasons of its size or condition (for example, a car) then a photograph will usually suffice. It is best to take a 'kitchen sink' approach to exhibits and have them all available for a trial. The more serious cases will have a dedicated exhibits officer who will carry the burden of exhibit security.
- 'Yes, I do know the words to the caution.'
  Officers are often asked to repeat the words of the basic caution by both prosecution and defence. Failure on the part of an officer to recite it correctly will damage their credibility at a stroke. The correct form of words is given in Code C of the Codes of Practice (COP) - C 10.5 and is as follows:

  > You do not have to say anything. But it may harm your defence if you do not mention when questioned something which you later rely on in Court. Anything you do say may be given in evidence.

- 'Yes, I am familiar with the relevant legislation and provisions of the Codes of Practice.'
  The police officer is not expected to be an expert on the law nor familiar with the detail of case law. They are, however, expected to have a working knowledge of the elements required to prove the offence for which the defendant is on trial. If they have made an arrest they must know the power under which they have made it and on what grounds they made it. The level of expectation with regard to knowledge of the law will vary depending on the status

and position of the officer giving evidence. For example, the knowledge of an officer employed on traffic duty will obviously be different to that of an officer dealing with public sector corruption. What is non-negotiable is a knowledge of PACE and the Codes of Practice as both are of universal application to criminal offences. The defence, not to mention the judge will show no mercy to the officer who does not know these provisions. It is particularly important that an officer with statutory responsibilities under PACE is familiar with them.

- 'Yes, my appearance is what is expected of me.'

First impressions are vitally important. Members of the jury will consciously and subconsciously make assessments of the appearance of every witness who gives evidence to the court. Their first impression of that witness may influence the importance (weight) given to their evidence. The critical eye cast over the police officer will be doubly acute and their appearance may be thought to reflect their approach to their role.

Where an officer is called suddenly and without any advance notice to give evidence at court then that court must take them as they find them. It may be obvious to the jury because of what has gone before that the person was so called but that officer should make short polite explanation and excuse to the judge or magistrate for their appearance at the earliest possible opportunity.

- 'Yes, I know how to address the court.'

This question should not be difficult to answer especially in the magistrates' court where it is singular, 'Your Worship' or plural, 'Your Worships' or 'Sir' or 'Madam'. Most Crown Court judges are addressed as 'Your Honour'. If at the Old Bailey it will be 'My Lord'. If there is any doubt then ask the court usher at the earliest opportunity.

- 'Yes, I've turned off my phone and pager.'

If the officer manages to do nothing else before entering the courtroom they must at least do this. Even lawyers will occasionally fall foul. However much it may brighten the jury's day, nothing is calculated to enrage the judge more.

13.2.8 Final preparations

An officer preparing to give evidence at court may be disturbed by an almost infinite number of unwelcome distractions. If the summons into court is felt to be imminent then under no circumstances should the officer leave the vicinity of the courtroom. They should certainly not choose that moment to go to the bathroom or take refreshments. If they are required to go elsewhere in the building or asked to quickly do some photocopying they should decline and explain why. They may have to ask another officer, member of the court staff or CPS to take care of the matter for them. Not to appear in court directly after the usher calls is impolite and unprofessional.

The court will not be favourably disposed to the officer who keeps them waiting. If the delay is of a significant duration then the court may order an adjournment and the officer will start their evidence only after being admonished. Perhaps the most important reason why the officer should not allow themselves to be distracted is that they may then enter the court in a state of disorientation, their concentration and calm broken. One cannot imagine a politician being asked to photocopy several bundles of paper immediately before getting to their feet in a packed House of Commons. Why then should a police officer do so at a crucial point in criminal proceedings?

13.3 **The Officer's Role**

13.3.1 **Requirements and expectations**

The process of examination, re-examination and cross-examination has been explained in **Chapter 12, 'Trial Procedure'**. A brief description of the practicalities of entering the witness box and giving evidence has also been given above. The police officer, however, needs to be informed in greater detail about these practicalities and must also understand the true nature of their role and the context in which they give their evidence. They therefore require further explanation here.

All references are made to Crown Court procedure for the sake of simplicity. The issues and practicalities explored, however, apply equally to the magistrates' court notwithstanding the different mood and expectation that the presence of a jury creates.

13.3.2 **Evidence gatherer and not prosecutor**

The most common mistake made by police officers giving evidence at court is to misunderstand their role. They are not the prosecutor and they have no power to decide the guilt or otherwise of the defendant on trial. This fundamental misunderstanding of their role is the main reason for mistakes made by officers. They try so hard to convict the defendant that they do not do themselves or their actions justice. Officers should remember that it is not their responsibility to present the case against the defendant: that is the job of prosecuting counsel.

The officer's role is simply to give their evidence to the court and to answer questions properly put to them. A police officer is not expected to be a legal expert or accomplished orator but is expected to be a thorough evidence gatherer with a keen eye for detail. They will provide one piece of a jigsaw that the jury will then consider along with other evidence to determine the guilt or innocence of the defendant.

Going hand in hand with this misunderstanding is the tendency for officers to take the attacks and cross-examination of defence counsel too personally. This problem can be most acute in the magistrates' court where officers will time and again encounter solicitors whom they have met frequently at the police station. It should be borne in mind that the officer who avoids becoming emotionally involved when giving evidence is most likely to impress the jury.

13.4 **Prosecution Witness**

The processes of examination and cross-examination have previously been described (see **12.4–12.6** above) and this section deals with the witnesses and in particular the police officer's response to them. Creating a good first impression is the best place to start.

13.4.1 **A good start**

When the waiting is over the courtroom door will open and the usher will appear and call the officer's name. There is no denying that a police officer is a different type of witness to the lay witness whom they may follow. It is pointless trying to pretend otherwise. The jury's expectations of the police officer will be different and a display of over-familiarity with the proceedings may be perceived by them to be disinterest, that this is 'just another case'. This is a very bad first impression to give to the jury. The officer should appear confident but involved and respectful.

Having familiarized themselves with the court, the officer can, without hesitation, walk slowly and purposefully to the witness box. The entrance to most witness boxes is raised and a step has to be negotiated. Once in the box the officer should face the judge and wait for the usher. At the Crown Court there will be a microphone attached to the front of the witness box. The officer may wish to adjust the microphone position if it so suits them. The usher will ask if the officer wishes to swear or affirm. Again without hesitation they should make their choice. The usher will give them a card and a Bible (if this is appropriate). Whatever text is chosen, be it a Koran, Bible or other, it should be raised in the right hand and the card held in the left hand. The words of the oath or affirmation printed on the card should be read clearly and deliberately. The officer should always read from the card. A flamboyant attempt to reel off the oath without using the card may badly and comically backfire. In addition, it will merely remind the jury that the officer is a professional witness and may serve to further raise the jury's expectations of how well they can be expected to give their evidence. It would be polite to thank the usher as the card and holy book (if used) are handed back. The officer will notice that the prosecution counsel will already be on their feet.

At this stage the court will need to know the identity of the officer and their rank, number and station. They will have heard their name mentioned by prosecution counsel and called by the usher but they will need to hear it again from the officer himself. In order to maintain their respect for the court, it is better for the officer to wait until prosecution counsel asks for these details. Although the practice in the magistrates' court is to provide these details before being asked, it is suggested that the same approach should be adopted, and the officer should wait to be asked. If the prosecution counsel or lawyer, used to the more assured approach of most police officers, does not ask the judge may do so. Failing that, the officer should simply volunteer the information. Most judges will look directly at the officer as a sign that they have their attention even if they say nothing. The officer should state their full name, rank and the station or department to which they are currently attached. These words will be addressed to the judge and the jury and should be concluded with the appropriate mode of address for the court, namely, 'My Lord', 'Your Honour' ('Sir/Madam', or 'Your Worships').

13.4.2 Memory-refreshing documents

Police officers are no more likely than lay witnesses to possess superhuman powers of recollection. A trial is not a contest to see who has the best memory. A considerable amount of time may have passed between the disputed events and the trial itself. This passage of time may be months or years. The law allows witnesses to refresh their memories from the statement which they made to the police before they are called to give their evidence.

Lay witnesses who have made a statement to the police should be furnished with a copy of it before they enter the witness box. They should read it and refresh their memory from their statement. The witness may be allowed to refer to it in the witness box and will also be able to produce contemporaneous notes such as the registration number of a car written on a cigarette packet.

Police officers are trained to make an original note in order that they may refer to that note whilst giving evidence to provide the best possible account of what happened. It is perfectly lawful and reasonable for an officer to have made this note in collaboration with another or other officers and to ask to refer to it when giving evidence. However, once the document has been used to refresh the officer's memory, whether before or during their evidence-in–chief, the defence can inspect it. The officer, however, should not read from the notes unless asked to do so. Simply reading from the notes may also suggest to the jury that the officer does not have a reliable recollection of the incident.

13.4.3 Giving evidence

It would be impossible to compile a definitive guide to giving evidence. There can be no exhaustive list of dos and don'ts and no group of police officers will ever agree unanimously about any single recommendation. The best that can be done is to gather together a number of points that broadly represent what could be described as good practice.

When giving evidence an officer *should*:

- speak clearly and deliberately
- make use of the microphone if it is available
- sit down if this is more comfortable
- ask for a drink of water (if required)
- address answers to the judge and jury as the fate of the case rests in their hands
- maintain eye contact with both judge and all the jury members in the same way they would during a briefing or interview
- use their notes if they have to but not bury their head in them or read long chunks of them verbatim unless asked to do so
- always be polite
- be themselves and do not try to use words or phrases that they would not ordinarily use
- speak plainly and truthfully
- if they make a mistake try to put it behind them and move onto the next question
- ask the barrister to repeat a question if they did not hear it
- ask the barrister to explain a question if they did not understand it
- ask the barrister to slow down if necessary

When giving evidence officers *should not*:

- expand on an answer without being specifically asked
- try to answer or predict the next question
- become impatient
- allow the barrister to talk over them or shout them down
- be sarcastic or patronizing
- venture an opinion unless directly asked about a matter where they may have an informed opinion or area of expertise
- use police jargon for example, PNC, 'producer', or slang unless this is a direct quote
- try to learn their notes or evidence by heart
- be contemptuous of or amused by a particular line of questioning
- obviously differentiate between the defence and prosecution barristers by the way in which they respond to them
- be drawn into an argument with the defence barrister

After examination and cross-examination has taken place counsel for the prosecution may wish to re-examine the witness. This is a comparatively rare process used to clarify matters raised during cross-examination. The decision to re-examine should not be interpreted by the officer as a good or a bad sign.

Once re-examination has taken place and counsel do not wish to ask any further questions the officer must remain where they are and look to the judge to see if they have any further questions. If the judge has no questions they will say so. The judge will often thank an officer for their evidence and indicate that they are released, which is to say that they will not be required to give any further evidence. At this stage the officer should thank the judge and leave the witness box with as much dignity as they can muster. It may be that they are to leave the court or it may be that they wish to stay in the court and listen to proceedings. Officers may benefit from taking a moment to compose themselves outside the courtroom before returning to watch the proceedings if they wish.

13.4.4 'I put it to you, officer...'

These are the words which frequently precede an assertion that the officer is mistaken, wrong or untruthful in what they say. It is the moment when the defence barrister will suggest the particular version of events that supports their client's case. The law requires that before a particular submission can be made on behalf of a defendant, the matter must be put to the relevant witness. These words so often instil unnecessary fear and trepidation into the officer giving evidence. This should not be so. They are an opportunity for the officer to affirm what they have said. The experienced officer may have taught officers to view this as a statement and not a question and therefore not to answer it. This is wrong: to the jury it is an assertion which requires a response.

Barristers very rarely attack the truthfulness of what an officer is saying as this could lead to evidence of their client's previous convictions (if any) being revealed to the jury. The barrister may 'put it to' the officer that something did not happen but the officer should be firm in their response. If an officer is accused of lying they should respond in the same way they would to any other assertion by taking the opportunity to state that what is being suggested is not the case. An outburst of bluster and indignation, an appeal to the judge or prosecuting counsel for help, is not the way to deal with this. Officers may take same comfort from the fact that over-aggressive cross-examination, even of police officers, is often counter-productive.

Police officers can be questioned about any previous improper conduct on their part although this is also likely to lead to any convictions of the defendant being revealed to the jury. This would certainly include any criminal offences they may have been convicted of (rare) or any proven disciplinary matters (not as rare, these should be declared on form MG6B—see **11.1.6**). This questioning would obviously be carried out, and not unreasonably so, in order to discredit their evidence in some fashion. An officer cannot be questioned about matters which have not been dealt with or complaints which have not been adjudicated on by the Police Complaints Authority (PCA).

13.4.5 **Evidence of bad character**

The provisions of Part Two of the Criminal Justice Act 2003 (CJA 2003) came into effect in December 2004. In general, evidence of a defendant's previous convictions and other misconduct will normally be admissible in criminal trials provided it is relevant. This reverses the previous position, where evidence of a defendant's bad character was generally not admissible in criminal proceedings. This is a major change and the provisions allow into court evidence that may be prejudicial to a defendant and so are subject to strict control.

Section 101(1) of the Act provides:

In criminal proceedings evidence of the defendant's bad character is admissible if, but only if–

(a) all parties to the proceedings agree to the evidence being admissible,

(b) the evidence is adduced by the defendant himself or is given in answer to a question asked by the defendant in cross-examination and intended to elicit it,

(c) it is important explanatory evidence,

(d) it is relevant to an important matter in issue between the defendant and the prosecution,

(e) it has substantial probative value in relation to an important matter in issue between the defendant and a co-defendant,

(f) it is evidence to correct a false impression given by the defendant, or

(g) the defendant has made an attack on another person's character.

The most important provision is (d) which is likely to feature in a large number of cases. This is because the CJA 2003 provides that matters in issue include:

• whether the defendant has a propensity to commit offences of the kind with which he is charged; and

• whether the defendant has a propensity to be untruthful.

A propensity to commit offences of the kind with which the defendant is charged can be proved by previous convictions for an offence of the same description or category as the one with which they are charged. An offence of the same description is defined as one which would be written in the same terms in a charge on the indictment. For example, offences of violence might well be admissible as offences of the same description where the accused was charged with causing grevious bodily harm. Categories of offence are defined by order of the Secretary of State. So far, only two categories of offence have been prescribed by the Secretary of State which are theft and sexual offences committed against persons under the age of 16. So, for example, if a person was charged with indecent assault on a female aged under 16 and had previously been convicted of the same offence on a different victim, the offences would fall within the same category and would automatically be admitted unless it was unjust to do so.

A propensity to be untruthful might be demonstrated by convictions for perjury or deception offences. However, a conviction for theft would not normally
qualify because although it is dishonest, the propensity to steal is not the same
as a propensity to tell lies. However, evidence that a defendant has been convicted of an offence having denied it and given evidence on oath might well be
admissible under this section.

Although clarification of the law has been welcomed, the provisions have
been the subject of considerable criticism. For example the Law Commission
had previously considered a provision that made the propensity to be untruthful a matter in issue in all cases and concluded that:

> Where the defendant simply denies the truth of some or all of the prosec-
> ution's evidence in relation to the offence charged, and makes no attempt
> to attack anyone else's credibility, we think it virtually inconceivable that
> evidence of the defendant's general untruthfulness could ever have sufficient
> probative value to outweigh the risk of prejudice.

There is a more restrictive regime in relation to evidence of bad character of
persons other than the defendant. Section 100(1) of the Act affords protection
to witnesses other than the defendant (including police officers). It states:

(1) In criminal proceedings evidence of the bad character of a person other
than the defendant is admissible if, and only if—
 (a) it is important explanatory evidence,
 (b) it has substantial probative value in relation to a matter which—
  (i) is a matter in issue in the proceedings, and
  (ii) is of substantial importance in the context of the case as a whole,
  or
 (c) all parties to the proceedings agree to the evidence being admissible

It is not difficult to understand why the legislation has been criticized. An obvious point is that the rules appear to make it more difficult to adduce evidence of
bad character from prosecution witnesses than it is from the defendant. There is
also concern that to reveal evidence of bad character generates a risk that a jury
will convict a person because of their history rather than on the basis of the
evidence against them. Since around 70 per cent of defendants have criminal
convictions, it is argued that this will undermine the presumption of innocence
which lies at the heart of the legal system.

13.4.6 Evidence of interviews

Officers are frequently required to give evidence of an interview they have conducted with a defendant. Virtually all interviews are now recorded on audio tape
and presented to the court in the form of a 'transcript' which is exhibited by the
interviewing officer. The tapes themselves are very rarely played. If the tape is
played then the interviewing officer's statement may be read before the tape is

switched on. A poor interview will sound that much worse when heard and not read. This can also be a tiresome experience for the jury as it may contain long silences punctuated with coughing or the rustling of paper.

The court will usually rely on the transcript of the interview and the interviewing officer will be called into the court to give evidence that the interview took place. There will then follow a 'call and response' form of evidence where the prosecution barrister will normally assume the role of the defendant and the officer themselves. The jury will have copies of the transcript before them and will follow proceedings.

This type of evidence can become repetitive and even tiresome for the jury, the barrister and the officer. It is very important that the officer maintains their concentration and, whilst dramatic excellence is not required, an officer should try to inject some life and meaning into the reading. Interviews may be of considerable length and the jury will be bored by a monotonous recitation of what is already before them.

Written interview transcripts are commonly edited before they are given in evidence. Words, sentences or whole passages may be deleted for a variety of reasons. When this is done it is normally by mutual agreement between the defence and the prosecution. If agreement cannot be reached then the judge will rule on the matter. It is generally the responsibility of the CPS to ensure that this is done accurately and that sufficient copies are supplied to the court although officers may be asked to assist.

13.4.7 **Video evidence**

Use of evidence from CCTV systems is now commonplace in courts. It has been accepted that the officer in the case or an officer involved in the case may be treated as an expert on a particular sequence on a video recording. An example might be a public disorder incident where the officer is required to give some form of commentary on the action in order to clarify what is taking place for the benefit of the whole court. In such a case the officer will usually also be required to control the video equipment by manual or remote means. It is important that officers familiarize themselves with the equipment and ensure that the tape is ready. Delay whilst the tape is wound will exasperate everyone in the courtroom and reflect badly on the officer's competence and efficiency.

13.4.8 **Antecedents**

The presentation of a convicted person's antecedents (previous convictions) to the court is no longer the responsibility of the OIC. The prosecution barrister will carry out this task. There are very rare occasions when the barrister may call the OIC but this will have been discussed in advance and will not be sprung upon an unsuspecting officer at the last minute.

The preparation of antecedents is normally the responsibility of the appropriate criminal justice support unit at the station. The staff who have prepared the details may not, however, be there at the court to answer for their accuracy. It is the responsibility of the OIC to ensure that there is sufficient detail, where required by the prosecuting barrister, about previous convictions for the judge to be able to properly consider them. The types of questions that will be asked are obvious. If the defendant is convicted again for an offence for which he has a previous conviction then the details of that conviction must be available. It is not a question of merely knowing the date place and sentence but also the date, venue and circumstances of the offence. By convention, the person's last three convictions are treated as of particular importance.

If the defence objects to the details of a particular conviction then the OIC must be in a position to verify those particulars. Unfortunately this is much easier said than done. The only way that a conviction can be ultimately proved is by calling an officer who was present at the conviction and can identify the convicted person. This is, of course, totally impractical. Convictions should be served on the defence at the earliest stage possible in order that any disagreement can be considered. The recording of previous convictions on the Police National Computer has proved on occasions to be inacurate. Where the defence persists with their objections, particularly where it is likely to have a significant impact on the sentence, the prosecution may seek an adjournment.

13.4.9 **Perjury**

Section 1(1) of the Perjury Act 1911 states:

> If any person, lawfully sworn as a witness or an interpreter in a judicial proceeding willfully makes a statement material in that proceeding, which he knows to be false or does not believe to be true, he shall be guilty of perjury...

This would apply to all proceedings in any court where the witness takes the oath or affirms and includes criminal and civil proceedings. Proceedings would include all warrant and order applications. Whether the false statement is material to the proceedings or not will be a question for a jury to decide. The maximum penalty for perjury is seven years' imprisonment.

13.4.10 **Attempting to pervert the course of justice**

It is an offence at common law to do an act tending and intended to pervert the course of public justice. Deliberate destruction of statements, documents or exhibits required for court purposes would be an attempt to pervert the course of justice. It is an indictable offence. This encompasses a great many ways in which justice can be perverted and often overlaps with the more specific offences of perjury and witness and jury intimidation. An example would include a false claim by a defendant that someone else was driving their car when it was caught exceeding the speed limit by a speed camera.

13.5 **The Officer in the Case (OIC)**

The ways in which the OIC can prepare their case for court have been discussed in the previous chapter. The unique demands of the role during the course of proceedings at court are considered below.

13.5.1 **A demanding role**

The officer in the case (OIC) obviously has a number of responsibilities which go beyond their own preparation to give evidence. Many OICs, as we have seen, will not actually be giving evidence about a specific incident but will have co-coordinated the preparation of the case and overseen the gathering of the evidence. They may be required, however, at any stage of the trial to give evidence about the conduct of the investigation. In very serious cases where a Senior Investigating Officer (SIO) is involved, evidence about the conduct of the investigation is likely to be given by that officer. The presence of the OIC will be required by the CPS quite simply because they will have the most intimate knowledge of the case and their assistance will be invaluable to the prosecuting barrister. The designated CPS caseworker will in all probability not be present throughout the trial itself.

For the OIC the start of a trial can be particularly fraught. However many pre-trial discussions and conferences they may have had with the CPS and prosecution counsel, there will always be matters to attend to on the morning of a trial. The best advice that can be given is to arrive at the court as early as possible and to seek out the CPS officer with responsibility for the court where the case is to be heard and, if necessary, the prosecuting barrister. It is not uncommon for there to have been a change of prosecuting barrister since the case was last discussed and the newly instructed prosecutor may ask for additional details or amendments.

The officer in the case will frequently either not be giving evidence at all or may simply be giving evidence of interview or charge. These are not generally matters which will be contested and the interests of the trial will be much better served by the OIC's presence in the court itself for as much of the trial proceedings as are realistic. Most prosecuting counsel will feel reassured and supported by their presence.

The CPS, over-stretched as they are, cannot be relied upon to have help readily available but will allow their facilities to be used. The moment before a trial begins is not the time to debate whose responsibility a particular task is and if there are last minute requirements they must be attended to. Most courts now have facilities for the playing of audio and videotapes and it is no longer the tiresome issue that it was for police officers. Providing they have been properly notified, it is the responsibility of the court to ensure that these facilities are available.

Officers will occasionally be asked to deputize for another officer at court because the original OIC is for whatever reason unavailable. If this happens the 'new' OIC will be expected to have a sound working knowledge of the case. The temptation to tell anyone who is prepared to listen that 'it is not my job' will be great but must be resisted. It is neither helpful nor professional. It may be particularly damaging to the morale of prosecution witnesses or victims and their families.

The officer with overall responsibility for a case must be pro-active not only in the preparation of the case for court but ensuring that it runs as smoothly as possible at court. One of their primary responsibilities is to ensure that the lay witnesses in the case are aware of their role.

13.5.2 **Police and witnesses**

An understanding of their own role in giving evidence at court allows the police officer to understand and empathize with the predicament of lay witnesses. There can be no more disheartening experience for the nervous witness than to realize that the person to whom they look for guidance is in a worse state than they are. The officer who can neither describe to the witness what they can expect nor suggest ways of dealing with it should expect nothing but poor performance from that witness.

Volunteers from the witness service undertake to prepare witnesses for giving attendance at court but the scope and breadth of this help is necessarily limited by the knowledge of their members. The officer in the case should not take anything for granted with regard to the witnesses in their case and should not assume that someone else will have assisted them. Provisions at court for witnesses are constantly criticized. It is a wider problem than the hard-pressed officer in the case can hope to address. The worst an officer can do, however, is to compound the problem by failing to spend an adequate amount of time with the witnesses in their case.

13.5.3 **The civil courts**

Police officers are being increasingly called to give evidence in the civil courts. Civil litigation, perhaps in expectation of financial reward (referred to as damages), is often seen as a more desirable option than the criminal justice system. Officers will be aware that the standard of proof required in the civil court is 'on the balance of probabilities' that is to say, more likely than not, which under normal circumstances is a lower standard than required for criminal proceedings. Nevertheless, the approach to giving evidence recommended here is as appropriate to the civil court as it is to the criminal court.

Civil actions are sometimes taken out against Chief Officers of Police following acquittal of the defendant. This underlines the need for improvement in the quality of evidence given in the first instance. A common type of case will involve an attempt by a claimant to prove that their arrest and therefore subsequent detention was unlawful. The action will almost invariably be brought against the Chief Constable or the Commissioner who will be held responsible for the officers under their control. An action against a particular officer, can be brought but this is rare. Whether the defence of that action is funded by the Chief Constable or the Police Federation (professional body representing officers below the rank of Superintendent) will depend on the circumstances of the case. Put simply, the better the quality of the evidence given in the criminal court the smaller the possibility that the officer will have to convince the civil court.

13.6 **Summary**

The police officer is well advised to remember that the courtroom is not their natural habitat. It is a foreign environment where the judge and the barristers rule. However experienced an officer may be, they have spent a small fraction of time in the courtroom by comparison with the most junior of defence counsel. It is all the more important therefore that the police officer make the most of the relatively short but disproportionately important time that they do spend there.

Far too many police officers see their time in the witness box as a personal duel between themselves and the defence barrister. Nothing could be more damaging. It may be that the barrister to whom they take an instant dislike has also been the victim of crime. They may dislike their client more than the officer does. However, the barrister must protect and promote the interests of their client at all times. If their client's case requires an attempt to discredit the evidence of the police officer, the barrister is obliged to use all their abilities to weaken the officer's evidence.

The witness box is the proverbial 'sharp end' of an officer's duty. It is the place where the officer's skill, humanity and professionalism are most publicly and meaningfully tested. It is the place where poor preparation will have immediate, embarrassing and sometimes catastrophic results. More than anywhere the witness box is where the officer's ability as an evidence gatherer is truly put to the test. It is a place, however, where the officer need not feel isolated or incompetent. It is a place to be respected but not feared.

Complacency, arrogance and lack of preparation are the greatest enemies that a police officer can have before they enter the witness box. Nothing must ever be taken for granted and their own and the service's reputation is at stake. It is often said that the defence is less likely to win the case than the prosecution is to lose it.

Conclusion

14.1 **Change and Reform**

The end of the last decade saw a number of significant changes to the criminal justice system brought about by legislation in response to the changing attitudes and expectations of society. The pace of change has accelerated in the 21st century. In recent years the Criminal Justice Act 2003, the Sexual Offences Act 2003, the Courts Act 2003 and the Anti-Social Behaviour Act 2003 have been introduced with enormous effect. Yet the pace of legislation continues unabated with (at the time of writing) the Drugs Act 2005, and the Domestic Violence, Crime and Victims Act 2004 still to enter into force. In the pipeline are plans to strengthen the law relating to terrorism and immigration. Already, today's police officer is expected to be familiar with more offences and more remedies than any of their predecessors.

In the criminal courts a particularly important change was made by the introduction of the Criminal Procedure Rules which came into force on 4 April 2005. The rules are intended to promote a culture change in the court's management of criminal cases. They introduce new powers and responsibilities for courts to manage cases actively and to reduce the number of ineffective hearings and consequent delay and cost.

The Criminal Procedure Rules recognize that making use of technology is part of active case management. It is a theme which is constantly emphasized by all agencies involved in the system. The Auld Report of 2001 identified the need for much greater use of information technology within the criminal justice system and recommended the introduction of single electronic case files managed by a Case Management Agency. This has not yet come to pass but the police, the courts and the CPS are progressing towards such a solution and a number of pilot schemes have been run, notably in the Warwickshire Constabulary. The immense financial, administrative and training implications may explain why progress has been slower than expected.

Another area in need of the reform is the relationship between the police and the CPS. The review of the CPS carried out by Sir Ian Glidewell in 1998 identified that neither the police nor the CPS have overall responsibility for the preparation of a file and recommended the establishment of single integrated case file management units. The introduction of the most recent Manual of Guidance (see **11.1.2**), the foreword of which is written jointly by the President of the Association of Chief Police Officers (ACPO) and the Director of Public Prosecutions, is a firm step in the right direction, as is the presence of a Crown prosecutor in many police stations to advise the police as to what charges should be brought against a suspect.

14.2 **No Witness, No Justice**

It goes without saying that witnesses are fundamental to the criminal justice process. Despite considerable improvements in recent years, witnesses complain of inadequate notice, being kept waiting for excessive periods of time, and the financial cost of their attendance. Both adults and children can find the process of attending court extremely intimidating.

In the years 2002 to 2003 15% of all 'cracked' and ineffective trials were due to problems with witnesses. There are considerable implications in inconvenience and cost for every trial that ends this way. Victims, families, witnesses and police are likely to suffer avoidable stress as a result.

These concerns led to the 'No witness, no justice' Government initiative commissioned by the Prime Minister and Attorney General in March 2003 to improve victim and witness care before, during and after court proceedings. Partners in the programme are the Association of Chief Police Officers (ACPO), the CPS, the Criminal Justice Group (a Home Office body which is responsible for the development of criminal law and policy) and the Prime Minister's Office of Public Services Reform. The objective is to provide the necessary support and information to improve the experience of those who attend court.

The 'No witness, no justice' programme creates witness care officers. Having had their individual needs assessed by an interviewing police officer, the witness or victim is allocated a suitable witness care officer from the point of charge through to the conclusion of a case. If a witness or victim experiences particular difficulties, action can be taken in advance of a trial. The witness will know exactly who to contact for information and assistance.

The need for reform in the way witnesses are cared for is beyond reasonable argument. The police have made great advances in their care of victims and families of crime but simply do not have the resources to deal adequately with all of the witnesses from whom they take statements. The aims of the 'No witness, no justice' programme are admirable. It is encouraging that the programme is now supported by the 'Victims Charter' which explains exactly what support (and from whom) a victim can expect. This Charter may be viewed at www.homeoffice.gov.uk/justice/victims/charter/index.html.

Notwithstanding the admirable intentions of the legislation contained in the Youth Justice and Criminal Evidence Act 1999 and the Government's 'No witness, no justice' programme, the poor treatment of witnesses and victims by the courts continues to blight the public and the police officer's perception of the justice system. The 1999 Act requires the prosecution to convince the judge or magistrate that a witness is genuinely intimidated and in need of the measures available. There should be a presumption that a witness to a serious offence who does not have any particular allegiance to either the defendant or the prosecution will feel intimidated by the consequences of giving evidence. It is the police officer who must explain to the vulnerable and intimidated witness why they will not be shielded from the defendant and their friends in the public gallery.

It is society who will pay the price when a victim or witness refuses to attend court.

14.3 **Closing Speech**

For all the difficulties that the police officer may encounter when going to court, it can and should be a positive and rewarding event. Tackling the experience head-on with confidence grounded in a thorough understanding of the criminal justice process is the way forward. Timidity, arrogance or ignorance merely support the defence.

Some of what is advocated here as good practice may be seen as plain common sense. There will be many who may honestly claim, 'well I knew that and do that already'. There will be others who dismiss any suggestion that they might not know best. I have watched many police officers give evidence and am well placed to say that there is, with few exceptions, room for improvement.

No officer can enter the witness box and, in an instant, put into practice all that they have read and been told. Like the golfer who tries to concentrate too hard on every aspect of their swing, the officer who strains for the perfect performance for the prosecution risks missing their target entirely. Good performance at court is not an innate skill, nor a fine art. It depends on experience, the exercise of sound judgement, and common sense. With knowledge of the strange and sometimes hostile environment of the courtroom, these attributes can be developed and refined.

Going to court will never be simple but neither should officers make it more difficult than it need be. Police officers may never relish the experience, but they can learn to be more confident, more professional and more effective for the brief but important time that they are there. This will include constantly updating their skills base and keeping up to date with new legislation and procedural requirements, the most recent examples in 2006 including a new 'Code of Practice' and the sweeping changes made by the Serious Organised Crime and Police Act 2005.

Appendix 1
Sample Search Warrants and Forms

FORM 1(Front)

Application for warrant to enter and search premises under section 8 Police and Criminal Evidence Act 1984
(Section 15 of the Police and Criminal Evidence Act 1984)

*delete/complete as applicable

(Specify name of court ....) **Magistrates' Court (Code**...............)

Application is today made before me the undersigned by *(specify name of applicant)*:

....

for the issue of [*a *specific premises* warrant] [*an *all premises* warrant] under section 8 Police and Criminal Evidence Act 1984

The applicant says [*on oath] [*affirms] that there are reasonable grounds for believing:

(a) that an *indictable* offence, namely *(specify Act & section)*

.... has been committed;

(b) that there is on

[*the *one set of premises* situated at *(specify premises)*; ....

....;]

[*the *sets of premises* described in the Schedule attached;]

material that is likely to be relevant evidence and be of substantial value to the investigation of the offence and does not consist of or include items subject to legal privilege, excluded material or special procedure material, namely *(identify, so far as is practicable, the material sought)*

....

....

....

....

....;

(c) *delete whichever of (i) to (iv) is NOT applicable:

*(i)   that it is not practicable to communicate with any person entitled to grant entry to the premises;

*(ii)   that it is practicable to communicate with a person entitled to grant entry to the premises but it is not practicable to communicate with any person entitled to grant access to the evidence;

*(iii)   that entry to the premises will not be granted unless a warrant is produced;

*(iv)   that the purpose of a search may be frustrated or seriously prejudiced unless a constable arriving at the premises can secure immediate entry to them; *AND*

(d) that to achieve the purpose for which the warrant is being applied it is necessary that the warrant authorises entry to and search of *each* set of premises;

[*on ONE occasion only.]

*subject to any second and subsequent entry being authorised in writing by an inspector or above,

[*on NOT MORE THAN *(enter words & number)* .... occasions.]

[*on an UNLIMITED number of occasions.]

(e) [*that persons be authorised to accompany the officer executing the warrant.]

FURTHER INFORMATION:

1.   **All applications;** explain why it is believed the material sought will be found on the premises to be searched.
2.   If applicable, describe any person(s) to be authorised to accompany the officer executing the warrant.
3.   If the application is for an "*all premises*" warrant; explain;
     (a)   Why it is believed necessary to search premises occupied or controlled by the person in question that are not specified in the Schedule; and
     (b)   Why it is not reasonably practicable to specify in the Schedule ALL the premises the person occupies or controls and which might need to be searched.
4.   If authority to enter and search the premises on more than one occasion is needed, explain why, and how many, further entries are needed to achieve the purpose for which the warrant is to be issued.

....

....

....

....

....

....

....

(continue over if necessary)

Date: .... Signature of Applicant ....

This application [*with Schedule] was taken and sworn/affirmed before me

District Judge (Magistrates' Court)
Justice of the Peace.

FORM 1(Rear)

FURTHER INFORMATION *(continued)*:

1. **All applications;** explain why it is believed the material sought will be found on the premises to be searched.
2. If applicable, describe any person(s) to be authorised to accompany the officer executing the warrant.
3. If the application is for an "*all premises*" warrant; explain;
   (a)   Why it is believed necessary to search premises occupied or controlled by the person in question that are not specified in the Schedule; and
   (b)   Why it is not reasonably practicable to specify in the Schedule ALL the premises the person occupies or controls and which might need to be searched.
4. If authority to enter and search the premises on more than one occasion is needed, explain why, and how many, further entries are needed to achieve the purpose for which the warrant is to be issued.

....

....

....

....

....

....

....

....

....

....

....

....

....

....

....

....

....

....

....

....

....

....

....

....

Date: .... Signature of Applicant ....

This application [*with Schedule] was taken and sworn/affirmed before me

District Judge (Magistrates' Court)
Justice of the Peace.

Application approved by (name and rank) ....
(Inspector or if urgent, next most senior officer, see Code B 3.4)

Signature: .... Date: ....

FORM 2(Front)

Schedule to search warrant/application under section 8 Police and Criminal Evidence Act 1984
Premises to which entry and search is authorised

*delete/complete as applicable

(Specify name of court ....) **Magistrates' Court (Code...............)**

Date: ....

The premises authorised to be entered and searched under the warrant to which this schedule is attached are:

[*The following specified premises

(1) ....

(2) ....

(3) ....

(4) ....

(5) ....

(6) ....

(7) ....

(8) ....

(9) ....

(10) ....]

and/or

[*Premises occupied or controlled by (name) ....]
which it is not reasonably practicable to specify in the application. <u>A District Judge/Justice of the Peace may not issue an "all premises" warrant to enter and search premises occupied or controlled by the above named person **unless** he/she is satisfied that because of the particulars of the offence referred to in the application, there are reasonable grounds for believing that it is necessary to search premises occupied or controlled by that person which are not specified above in order to find the material sought and that it is not reasonably practicable to specify ALL the premises the person occupies or controls and which might need to be searched.</u> Entry to such premises also requires prior authority in writing from an inspector or above.]

Date: ....

District Judge (Magistrates' Court)
Justice of the Peace

The officer in charge of the search (Code B2.10) is to complete this table; [(1)] s.16(3A) PACE   [(2)]s.16 (3B) PACE
(a) in the case of an **all premises warrant**, BEFORE entry to any premises which are **not specified** that warrant; and/or
(b) in the case of **a warrant authorising multiple entries**, BEFORE entry to any premises for the **second or any** subsequent time.

An inspector or above has given written authority to enter the premises below under the warrant to which this Schedule is attached:

No	Premises (Specify premises to which the authority relates)	Reason for authority (enter Yes or No)		Officer in charge of the search (Signature/rank/station/date)
		[(1)]To enter premises not specified in an all premises warrant.	[(2)]To enter premises on a 2nd or any subsequent time.	
1				
2				
3				
4				

(continued over *Yes/No)

THIS SCHEDULE TO BE RETURNED WITH THE WARRANT TO THE APPROPRIATE PERSON IN ACCORDANCE WITH SECTION **16(10)** PACE

FORM 2(Rear)

The officer in charge of the search (Code B2.10) is to complete this table; [1] s.16(3A) PACE [2]s.16 (3B) PACE

(a) in the case of an **all premises warrant**, BEFORE entry to any premises which are **not specified** that warrant; and/or

(b) in the case of **a warrant authorising multiple entries**, BEFORE entry to any premises for the **second or any** subsequent time.

An inspector or above has given written authority to enter the premises below under the warrant to which this Schedule is attached:

No	Premises (Specify premises to which the authority relates)	Reason for authority (enter Yes or No)		Officer in charge of the search (Signature/rank/station/date)
		[1]To enter premises not specified in an all premises warrant.	[2]To enter premises on a 2nd or any subsequent time.	
5				
6				
7				
8				
9				
10				
11				
12				
13				
14				
15				

THIS SCHEDULE TO BE RETURNED WITH THE WARRANT TO THE APPROPRIATE PERSON IN ACCORDANCE WITH SECTION **16(10) PACE**

FORM 3(Front)

Warrant to enter and search premises for evidence of an indictable offence
(Section 15 of the Police and Criminal Evidence Act 1984)

delete/complete as applicable

(Specify name of court ....*) Magistrates' Court (Code*...............*)*

Date: ....

On this day an application supported by an information was made by *(specify name of applicant)*:

.... for the issue of

warrant under section 8 of the Police and Criminal Evidence Act 1984 to enter:

[*the *one set of premises* situated at (specify premises);* ....

....]

[*The *sets of premises* described in the Schedule attached]

and search for *(identify so far as is practicable the material sought):*

Authority is hereby given for any constable, [*accompanied by such other person or persons as are necessary for the purposes of the search], to enter the said premises on the number of occasions specified below within *three months* from the date of issue of this warrant and on *each such occasion* to search for the material in respect of which the application is made.

Number of occasions that each set of premises may be entered and searched under this warrant is:

[*on ONE occasion only.]

*subject to any second and subsequent entry being authorised in writing by an inspector or above,

[*on NOT MORE THAN *(enter words & number)* .... occasions.]

[*on an UNLIMITED number of occasions.]

District Judge (Magistrates' Court)
Justice of the Peace.

COPIES TO BE MADE:

(a) For a warrant which specifies only one set of premises and does NOT authorise multiple entries (no Schedule) – TWO copies.

(b) For *any other warrant to which a Schedule of the premises to which entry is authorised* – as many copies as are required. An occupier is not entitled to be given details of, or any information about, other premises to which the warrant authorises entry. Whenever premises are entered under a warrant to which a Schedule is attached, the copy that is given to the occupier or left on the premises should be endorsed by the officer in charge of the search to specify the premises entered on *that* occasion.

SEE OVER FOR ENDORSEMENT TO BE MADE AFTER EACH ENTRY & SEARCH UNDER THIS WARRANT

THIS WARRANT AND ITS SCHEDULE (IF APPLICABLE) TO BE RETURNED TO THE APPROPRIATE PERSON – SEE SECTION 16(10) PACE

FORM 3(Rear)

ONE ENDORSEMENT TO BE COMPLETED FOR **EACH** ENTRY AND SEARCH BY A CONSTABLE EXECUTING THE WARRANT
(Use continuation sheet(s) if necessary)

delete/complete as applicable

Entry No. 1	Date/Time of Entry: .... Authorised by inspector [*Yes] [*Not applicable]
	Premises entered & searched on this occasion (specify): ....
	....
	*1. The following material sought was found (list)
	*2. The following articles other than article sought were seized (list):
	*3. No material was found or seized.
	4. *Copy warrant specifying the premises entered on this occasion handed to occupier. *Copy warrant specifying the premises entered on this occasion left on premises (specify where left)
	....
	*Delete/complete as appropriate Signature(s) of constable(s) executing warrant on this occasion:

Entry No. 2	Date/Time of Entry: .... Authorised by inspector [*Yes] [*Not applicable]
	Premises entered & searched on this occasion (specify): ....
	....
	*1. The following material sought was found (list)
	*2. The following articles other than article sought were seized (list):
	*3. No material was found or seized.
	4. *Copy of warrant showing the premises entered on this occasion handed to occupier *Copy of warrant showing the premises entered on this occasion left on premises (specify where left)
	....
	*Delete/complete as appropriate Signature(s) of constable(s) executing warrant on this occasion:

Continuation endorsement sheet?   Yes ☐ No. ☐   ☑ Tick one box

Endorsement sheet 1 of (total) ___

FORM 4(Front)

Warrant to enter and search premises for evidence of an indictable offence (Section 15 of the Police and Criminal Evidence Act 1984) **COPY FOR OCCUPIER OF THE PREMISES ENTERED**

*delete/complete as applicable

(Specify name of court ....*) **Magistrates' Court (Code**...............**)**

Date: ....

On this day an application supported by an information was made by *(specify name of applicant)*:

.... for the issue of

warrant under section 8 of the Police and Criminal Evidence Act 1984 to enter:

[*the *one set of premises* situated at (specify premises); ....

....]

[*The *sets of premises* described in the Schedule attached]

and search for *(identify so far as is practicable the material sought):*

Authority is hereby given for any constable, [*accompanied by such other person or persons as are necessary for the purposes of the search,] to enter the said premises on the number of occasions specified below within *three months* from the date of issue of this warrant and on *each such occasion* to search for the material in respect of which the application is made.

Number of occasions that each set of premises may be entered and searched under this warrant is:

[*on ONE occasion only.]

*subject to any second and subsequent entry being authorised in writing by an inspector or above,

[*on NOT MORE THAN *(enter words & number)* .... occasions.]

[*on an UNLIMITED number of occasions.]

District Judge (Magistrates' Court)
Justice of the Peace.

TO BE COMPLETED BY THE OFFICER IN CHARGE OF THE SEARCH IF THE PREMISES ENTERED ARE NOT SPECIFIED ABOVE:

For the information of the occupier, the premises entered on this occasion are:

(Premises: ....

You are not entitled to be given details of, or any information about, other premises to which the warrant authorises entry.

Signed ....Date: ....Time: ....
        Officer in charge of the search:

COPY FOR OCCUPIER OF THE PREMISES ENTERED

For police purposes   FORM 5(Front)   For police purposes

For police purposes

Record of authority given by inspector or above to execute search warrant issued under section 8 Police and Criminal Evidence Act 1984
(See Section [1]16(3A) and [2](3B) Police and Criminal Evidence Act 1984 and Code B 6.3A and 6.3B)

Insert Police force references as required

The written authority of an inspector or above not involved in the investigation is required:
  *(a) in the case of an **all premises warrant**, [1]BEFORE entry to any premises which are **not specified** that warrant; and/or*
  *(b) in the case of a **warrant authorising multiple entries**, [2]BEFORE entry to any premises for the **second or any subsequent time.***

Each signed authorisation below applies to the search warrant issued under section 8 of the Police and Criminal Evidence Act 1984 on (date) .... at

[Specify name of court. ....] Magistrates' Court (Code ....) on application made by *(specify name of applicant)* ....

No.	Premises (Specify premises to which authority relates)	Authority is given as follows to enter: (complete **A** and/or **B** as applicable)		Authorising officer (Signature/rank/station/date)
		[1]**A** Premises not specified in all premises warrant: State reason it was not reasonably practicable to specify these premises when the application for the warrant and why entry now necessary	[2]**B** Premises for a 2nd or subsequent time: State number of previous entries why a further entry is necessary to achieve the purpose for which the warrant is issued.	
1				
2				
3				
4				
5				

*(continued over ***Yes/No)***

199

For police purposes   FORM 5 (Rear)   For police purposes

No.	Premises (Specify premises to which authority relates)	Authority is given as follows to enter (complete **A** and/or **B** as applicable)		Authorising officer (Signature/rank/station/date)
		[1]**A**: Premises not specified in all premises warrant: State reason it was not reasonably practicable to specify these premises when the application for the warrant and why entry now necessary	[2]**B** Premises for a 2nd or subsequent time: State number of previous entries why a further entry is necessary to achieve the purpose for which the warrant is issued.	
6				
7				
8				
9				
10				

Appendix 2
Useful References

The research for this book has been carried out exclusively during my day-to-day work as a police officer working on the Metropolitan Police Specialist Crime Directorate. The following websites, however, have been particularly useful in ensuring that it is as legally correct and current as possible.

www.opsi.gov.uk/legislation

www.cps.gov.uk

www.cjsonline.gov.uk

www.dca.gov.uk (Dept. of Constitutional Affairs)

www.homeoffice.gov.uk

www.legalservices.gov.uk

www.lawsociety.org.uk

www.barcouncil.org.uk

www.cabinetoffice.gov.uk (No witness, no justice)

www.victimsupport.org.uk

www.criminal-courts-review.org.uk

Glossary

Adduce call or to put forward in evidence

Adjourn suspend or delay the hearing of a case until another time (on the same or on a different day)

Admission (of evidence) acceptance by the court of the evidence into proceedings—the court may not allow all evidence to be used in the proceedings

Advance information information about the case against an accused, normally handed over in the magistrates' court before he or she enters a plea; also referred to as advance disclosure

Advocate a person who presents another's case in court; barrister or solicitor

Affidavit a sworn statement of evidence

Affirm to make a formal declaration to give true evidence without taking a religious oath

Anti-Social Behaviour Orders an order that forbids a person from doing certain activities designed to protect the community from anti-social behaviour

Appellant a person or party who appeals

Arraignment the formal process of putting charges to the defendant in court and asking them whether they plead guilty or not guilty

Arrest warrant a court order to arrest a person

Bail release of a person from custody subject to a duty to surrender at an appointed time and place; it may be conditional or unconditional, granted by the police or by a court

Basis of Plea the defendant's account of how they committed a crime; this may differ from the prosecution version of how the offence was committed

Bar council the professional body for barristers

Bill of indictment a written accusation of a crime against one or more persons

Bind over an agreement with the court to be of 'good behaviour', failing which the person may forfeit a sum of money set by the court

Clerk of the Court a Crown Court judge's assistant; *see also* Justices' Clerk

Code for Crown Prosecutors structured guidance governing decision to prosecute; the basis of the evidential and public interest tests

Committal for sentence the procedure whereby a person convicted in a magistrates' court is sent to the Crown Court for sentencing when the magistrates consider their sentencing powers insufficient

Committal proceedings preliminary hearing in a magistrates' court before a case is sent to be tried or sentenced in the Crown Court

Community sentence a sentence in the community which may involve restriction of liberty, reparation and/or programmes to rehabilitate the offender

Conditional discharge an order which does not impose any immediate punishment on a person convicted of an offence, providing they do not commit further offences in a specified period

COP Codes of Practice issued under PACE, latest consolidated edition effective from 1 January 2006

Costs the expenses of a court case, including the fees of the solicitors and barristers and the court

Counsel a barrister

Criminal Defence Service body that operates the public funding scheme

Cross examination questioning of a witness by a party who did not call the witness

Disclosure provision of material in the possession of the prosecution to the defence which may assist the defendant

Duty solicitor the solicitor who is on duty to provide assistance at the magistrates' court or to attend the police station, free of charge

Early Administrative Hearing a preliminary hearing in the magistrates' court for cases that are unlikely to be disposed of at First Hearing by way of a guilty plea

Early First Hearing a preliminary hearing in the magistrates' court for cases that are likely to be disposed of at First Hearing by a guilty plea

Either-way offence an offence which may be tried either in the magistrates' court or in the Crown Court

Evidence in chief evidence given by a witness for the party who called them

Evidential test the first test that must be satisfied in the decision to prosecute; *see also* Code for Crown Prosecutors

Ex parte a hearing where only one party may attend and argue their case

Exhibit an object (eg a weapon, drug, document, etc) presented as evidence in court

Hearsay evidence from a witness of what another person stated (verbally or in writing) on a prior occasion.

In chambers 1. in the judge's chambers; or 2. in private (the courtroom may still be used to hear the case)

In open court in a courtroom which is open to the public

Indictable offence an offence that may be tried in either the Crown Court or magistrates' court

Indictable only offence an offence which can be tried only in the Crown Court

Indictment a formal document at the heart of proceedings in the Crown Court which contains the charges against a defendant

Information a formal document which informs the magistrates of the allegation of an offence for which a summons or warrant is required

Inter partes a hearing where both parties attend and argue their case

Justice of the peace a lay magistrate or a District Judge (magistrates' courts)

Justices' clerk legal adviser to the magistrates who also has various powers and duties in a magistrates' court such as making a record of proceedings

Law society the professional body for solicitors

Live link video equipment that allows a witness to give evidence from outside the court room in which a case is being heard

Manual of Guidance comprehensive guidance for the police on the preparation of case files that includes forms MG1- 20 (renamed the Prosecution Team Manual of Guidance)

Newton Hearing a hearing to decide whether the defendant should be sentenced on the basis of the Crown's version of events or in accordance with their basis of plea—evidence will be required to prove the Crown's case

Officer in the Case The officer with overall responsibility for a case investigation

PACE Police and Criminal Evidence Act 1984

Party a person or organization involved in a case, either as prosecutor or defendant

Plea and Case Management Hearing (PCMH) an important hearing in the Crown Court where the defendant enters their plea and orders are made to manage the case to trial or sentence

Preparatory hearing a hearing which is part of a trial and is sometimes used in complex cases to decide issues without requiring the jury to attend

Prima facie case a prosecution case which is strong enough to require the defendant to answer it

Public interest immunity privilege from disclosure on the grounds that it is in the public interest to maintain confidentiality of the material

Public interest test the second test that must be satisfied in the decision to prosecute; *see also* Code for Crown Prosecutors

Remand to send a person away until the next hearing of the case, the remand may be on bail or in custody

Representation order an order authorizing public funding (representation paid for by the state) for a defendant

Sending for trial procedure whereby indictable offences are transferred to the Crown Court without the need for a committal hearing in the magistrates' court

SOCAP Serious Organised Crime and Police Act 2005

Special measures measures to provide protection to witnesses (eg a screen separating witness from the accused) intended to improve the quality of their evidence

Stay a stop of proceedings by order of the court

Summary offence an offence which can be tried only in a magistrates' court

Supervision order a type of sentence placing a young offender under the supervision of a local officer

Surety a person who guarantees that a defendant will attend court

Witness a person who gives evidence, orally or by written statement in court

Witness summons a document served on a witness requiring them to attend court

Youth court magistrates' courts with jurisdiction over matters relating to young persons

Index